UNDERSTANDING
READING

FRANK
SMITH

UNDERSTANDING
READING
—— A Psycholinguistic Analysis
of Reading and Learning To Read

HOLT, RINEHART AND WINSTON, INC.

New York   Chicago   San Francisco   Atlanta
Dallas   Montreal   Toronto   London   Sydney

Copyright © 1971 by Holt, Rinehart and Winston, Inc.
All Rights Reserved
Library of Congress Catalog Card Number: 79–136457
ISBN 03–084849–0
Printed in the United States of America
    6 038 9876

To George A. Miller

Preface

This book attempts to shed light on some of the fundamental aspects of the complex human skill of reading—linguistic, psychological, and physiological—and on what is involved in learning to read.

This is not a book about reading instruction. There is no comparison of instructional methods nor is there any effort to promote one method at the expense of another. The current instructional methods are probably not much inferior to the methods we shall develop as we learn more about learning to read. So many instructional methods have been tried, and so many succeed (in some instances at least), that further permutations in the game of instructional roulette are unlikely to produce any great gain, either by chance or design. What will make a difference is an understanding of the reading process.

Part of the process of enlightenment is to demonstrate that fluent reading is more complex than is frequently believed, and learning to read is far more involved. Fortunately, a child can overcome instructional deficiencies and seek for himself the information that will help him to acquire reading skills—if given the chance—far better than he is usually given credit for.

The process of reading is not very well understood. Researchers do not yet know enough about the developed skills of the fluent reader, the end product of the instructional process, let alone the process of acquiring these skills. But researchers are beginning to realize that reading will not be completely understood until there is an understanding of all the perceptual, cognitive, linguistic, and motivational aspects not just of reading, but of living and learning in general. Dramatic advances are being made in the study of all these areas, but all too often the results of these advances are not available to those assisting a child who is learning to read—especially, the reading teacher. The first stage of enlightenment is to show that many questions remain unanswered—that there is no justification for dogmatism about reading or learning to read. The second stage of enlightenment is to dissect the reading process as analytically as possible, to examine all the parts and requirements of this complex process, and to give at least an idea of what is involved.

That is the precise purpose of this book—to provide an idea of what must be involved in reading and learning to read. The aim is not to propagandize, but to offer insights. One insight that this book will attempt to give is that the child is not as helpless in face of the task of learning to read as we sometimes think. A feeling for what the child can do, and what he needs, can be a most important insight that can develop from a clearer understanding of what reading involves.

My reluctance to be dogmatic about instructional methodology is based on more than academic puritanism. It is an open question whether classroom "experts" who make uninformed pronouncements on linguistics and psychology cause more damage than linguists and psychological theorists who make categorical assertions about how reading should be taught, especially if these assertions are given a false authority by a reputation that is irrelevant to the classroom.

The reading process and reading instruction are two quite independent domains of inquiry. Workers in each area should influence each other, perhaps much more than they do, but only by sharing information and stimulating hypotheses; they cannot pass judgment on each other's methods. A theory is useful as a summary and framework for what is known, and as a source of new ideas; a theory is tested by data acquired under rigorously controlled laboratory conditions. Instructional techniques, on the other hand, are of value only if they are proved to be effective in the classroom by the achievement of instructional and other educational objectives. Nothing in this book should be interpreted as a direct condemnation or justification of the teacher's approach, although I hope the teacher will find a better understanding of why some methods may be successful, and how they might be improved.

An understanding of reading requires some acquaintance with research in a variety of disciplinary fields; that is why more than half of this book is devoted to such topics as language, communication, learning theory, the acquisition of speech, and the physiology of the eye and brain. These topics are discussed in an attempt to make them understood, which means that there is an assumption that the reader of this book has neither the experience nor the time to undertake deep or specialized study in these areas. After stressing that reading is more complicated than we generally allow, and that our ignorance of it is more profound than we usually admit, I owe it to my own readers not to make the issue more confusing by blinding them with reflected scholarship or losing them in fields of footnotes. At the risk of offending the specialist, all these diverse subject areas have been covered only to the extent that they are relevant to the topic of reading. For those who wish to pursue any topic further, some introductory sources are listed at the end of each chapter.

This book is designed to serve either as a text for a basic course in the reading process, or for individual reading by anyone wanting to learn more about the subject matter—including parents. The book is particularly addressed to reading teachers and other educators interested in the accomplishment of reading, and to college students requiring an introduction to reading as an example of the higher cognitive skills of man.

A word about my credentials: I do not claim to be a teacher of children, which is another reason why I would not presume to assert that a particular instructional method is superior to any other. My area of research and interest is the intricate and fascinating and beautiful human quality—"skill" is really too cold a word—of language. I had a ten-year career as a writer and editor before my growing curiosity about the intellectual processes that underlay both my own literary activity and its effect on readers led me to the centers of research, first as an inquiring visitor, then as a student, and finally as a researcher. And my interest in language focused into an interest in reading, not because I was primarily concerned with instruction—I was not—but because the eye can tell us so much about language. The mere fact that the eye can move, so that researchers may see and measure where it stops to pick up information, makes it far more communicative an organ than the mute and static ear. Not even the keenest observer can say what the ear is doing unless he is equipped with the most sensitive of complicated instruments.

Even with instrumentation, the knowledge acquired by researchers of auditory processes comes from within the recesses of the head, not from its surface. The very immobility of the human ear means that it contributes practically nothing to the process of listening. If the evolutionary process dictates that superfluous organs shall wither away, then the human ear may be destined to disappear from the face of the earth. The main hope for survival of the ear is as part of the visual system; without it, how could we keep our spectacles on?

I began by using reading as a way to study language, and ended by using language as one of the ways in which to understand reading. This transition from a general to a specific interest in reading occurred over several years and at a variety of locations: the Center for Cognitive Studies at Harvard, the United States Office of Education's Project Literacy at Cornell, and its Southwest Regional Laboratory for Educational Research and Development near Los Angeles, and presently at The Ontario Institute for Studies in Education at Toronto.

The content of this book reflects both my experience and interests. In particular, the book could not have been written had I not been influenced —some might say indoctrinated—by the heady psycholinguistic atmosphere of Cambridge, Massachusetts, in the 1960s. To Noam Chomsky, George A. Miller, Jerome S. Bruner, and other linguists and psychologists at Harvard University and the Massachusetts Institute of Technology I acknowledge an intellectual debt, although I must hasten to free them from any responsibility for the use I have made of their scholarship. I have delved selectively and arbitrarily into their theory and data, added my own interpretations, and integrated it all into a model of reading that goes beyond what any one of them individually might care to say. But as I have said, this book is written to stimulate the layman rather than to satisfy the scholar.

On second thought, George Miller ought not be surprised at this product of his influence. In his tradition-breaking presidential address to the American Psychological Association in 1969, Miller suggested that the commitment of psychologists to promote human welfare might best be met by "giving psychology away" to the general public. He cited reading as a particular example of an area in which psychology could be used to give people skills to satisfy their urge to feel more effective. I would be particularly pleased if this book could be regarded as a first fruit of Miller's vision.

Miller and Bruner are two among many friends—mentors, colleagues, and students—who have contributed personally to this book, either directly or through their influence on my thinking. Others who should be mentioned are Thomas G. R. Bower, Peter Carey, Bruce Cronnell, Eleanor J. Gibson, Deborah Lott Holmes, Paul Kolers, Harry Levin, Gillian Marwick, David Olson, John Ross, and Rose-Marie Weber. Mary-Theresa Smith provided essential encouragement, tolerance, and constructive criticism. And without Connie Tyler's exceptional skill in detecting significant differences in the visual uncertainty of my drafts, the entire mission could have aborted on the writing pad.

Toronto, Canada   F. S.
October 1970

Contents

Contents

UNDERSTANDING
READING

1

Understanding Reading

Reading is a specialized and complex skill involving a number of more general skills that have to be understood in any serious analysis of the subject. The common assertion, for example, that reading requires special skills of visual discrimination—such as the ability to discriminate between two letters—is an oversimplification that completely misses the main point of one aspect of reading. The main point about the visual aspect of reading is not that a child requires a special kind or degree of acuity to discriminate between two letters; probably any child who can distinguish between two faces at six feet has the ability to do that. The child's problem is to discover the critical differences between the two letters, which is not so much a matter of knowing how to look as knowing what to look for. As we shall see, such knowledge is not taught, it is discovered by the child for himself by means of perceptual and cognitive skills common to many aspects of visual perception.

The processes of visual perception, therefore, are one of the general areas that must be basically understood before the more specific question of reading can be approached. Aspects of these topics are relevant not only for understanding the skill of a mature reader, but also for comprehension of the prior knowledge and learning strategies that a child brings to the task of learning to read. Because of the preliminary diversions, a detailed analysis of reading will not begin until Chapter 7. Whenever possible, however, some indication will be given of the relevance of a particular topic to the question of reading.

The preliminary chapters are by no means intended to be comprehensive or balanced presentations of the topics covered; this is not a book about linguistics or learning or information theory. Instead, I shall give a minimal background of fact and theory to outline for the reader as much of a topic as appears essential for an understanding of reading. A few references will be given at the end of these chapters to put the interested reader on the trail of more complete information. The following brief sketches of the content and relevance of the general chapters in the first part of the book may be helpful.

Chapter 2, "Communication and Information." This chapter makes the point that reading is a communication process in which the reader plays an active role. It introduces the notion that all aspects of reading, from the identification of individual letters or words to the comprehension of entire passages, involve the reduction of uncertainty, and can therefore be regarded within the powerful conceptual framework of information theory, an outline of which is provided.

Chapter 3, "Language and Reading." Reading is a language activity, and recent developments in the understanding of all aspects of language—particularly the "transformational" or "generative" view of grammar—provide a framework for constructing a model of reading. This chapter also shows how many of our everyday assumptions about the nature of language may be misconceived.

Chapter 4, "The Acquisition of Language." Many of the skills employed by a child in learning about speech are also relevant to the task of learning to read. An understanding of the rapid manner in which speech is learned also provides an insight to the remarkable cognitive capacity displayed by a child in his first years of life.

Chapter 5, "Learning (1): Habits." The "habit-formation" approach to learning of B. F. Skinner which is here expounded is not compatible with the "cognitive" approach underlying most of this book. But the Skinnerian view is significant and influential, particularly, in my opinion, in the area of motivation. It should not be ignored in any consideration of the conditions under which reading is learned and practiced.

Chapter 6, "Learning (2): Knowledge." Here is an alternative point of view to Skinner's; this approach is concerned with the manner in which the individual acquires, organizes, and employs his accumulated knowledge of the world. This chapter is preparation for developing the portrayal of a reader as an active seeker of information from his visual environment. It provides an introduction to contemporary views of thought, learning, and memory to complement the earlier discussion of language.

Chapters 7 and 8. These two chapters explore the intimate relationship between the eye and the brain. They illustrate the manner in which the eye picks up information at the command of the brain, and the way in which the brain interprets and elaborates this visual information. Once again, the picture that develops is quite different from our everyday conception of the process of vision. A major thesis of this book is that the brain—our prior knowledge of the world—contributes more information to reading than the visual symbols on the printed page. These two chapters bring us to the threshold of our subject matter, the cognitive processes of reading.

But it seems inappropriate to wait until halfway through a book before the subject that is its title is discussed. It will be less demanding, perhaps, on the tolerance of the reader if a rough outline of the discussion of reading is presented first. Here, then, is an advance notice of how reading will be analyzed from Chapter 9 on. Only the barest bones of an outline are presented, with no superfluous justification or even explanation. The preview is rather concentrated, and the remainder of this chapter can perfectly well be skipped by the reader who prefers to start a story at the beginning rather than at the end.

Analyzing the Reading Process

A number of distinctions are made in this book that are not always clearly observed in discussions of reading. The first distinction is between *learning to read* and proficient reading, or *fluent reading* as it will be termed. The beginning reader has to acquire special skills that will be of very little use to him once he develops reading fluency.

I shall occasionally observe that life seems particularly hard for the beginning reader—so many necessary things are difficult for him at the outset that will be easier when his reading skills develop. For example, the mere fact that a child cannot read very fast puts a heavy burden on memory and attentional systems that are both inexperienced and overloaded with all kinds of instructions and rules. By the time the novice has built up enough speed to take some of the strain off his memory, many of the earlier rules have become unnecessary or overlearned and automatic, and the memory load is reduced in any case.

The second major distinction is between *word identification* and *reading for comprehension;* this is, of course, a distinction frequently mentioned in the reading literature, but rarely maintained. However, it will be argued that reading to identify words and reading to obtain information are processes with similar aspects but quite different outcomes, and that it is possible to read for comprehension without actually identifying individual words. To clarify this distinction, the term "word identification" rather than "reading" will be used when comprehension is not in question.

Two processes of word identification will themselves be distinguished, *immediate* and *mediated* word identification. The possibility that the skilled reader normally identifies a word by discriminating all or some of its component letters and putting together the sound of the word by some knowledge of spelling or phonic rules will be examined and rejected. I shall argue that this type of word identification, to be termed *mediated word identification,* usually occurs only when the reader encounters a word that he has not previously seen in print. The identification is "mediated" because instead of the reader's going directly from the ink marks on the page to the identification of the word, some additional nonvisual processes of word synthesis intervene. It is, of course, the unfortunate beginning reader who has to do most of the mediated word identification in reading. The ability to go directly from the ink marks to the identification will be termed *immediate word identification.* The term "immediate" does not imply that the identification is instantaneous, but that it is direct and as fast as any nonlinguistic act of recognition can be, for example the identification of a tree or ship or face or any other object that cannot possibly be mediated by reading off the name in any alphabetic sense. One either knows or does not know the name for most objects; but because written words are constructed from letters, there is an alternative to immediate identification in the form of some mediating method of working out what the name must be from the identification and integration of word parts.

The raw material of reading, whether for immediate word identification or for identification of the letters or groups of letters from which the name of the word can be determined, will be termed *distinctive features.* Features are elements of the visual aspect of words, the inkmarks on paper. I shall refer to these collections of inkmarks, to the visual stimuli of reading, as the *visual configuration,* or the *visual array.* This terminology will permit me to distinguish, where necessary, between the word (or letter) that is represented by the inkmarks on paper, and the inkmarks themselves. Normally, we use the words "word" and "letter" to refer both to the inkmarks on the paper and to the word or letter that the marks represent; this is a frequent source of confusion. It is not always apparent that when we say "He can't read that word" and "He doesn't know that word" the term "word" is being used in two quite different senses.

Features, then, are elements of the visual configurations of letters or words; obviously, any feature of a letter could also be a feature of a word. Features may be common to more than one visual configuration, whether letter or word. For example, *b*, *d*, and *h* share one or more common features that *p*, *n*, and *v* do not. I shall explain in due course why I am reluctant to say exactly what these features are, although they are clearly related to such obvious aspects of letters as the ascenders of *b*, *d*, and *h*, the curved strokes of *c*, *o*, and *s*, and possibly the symmetry of *w*, *o*, and *v*. Features are distinctive (to a reader) when their discrimination permits a reduction in the number of alternative letters or words that a visual configuration might be. Any one distinctive feature conveys some information about the letter or word to which it belongs, although perhaps not enough information to permit its unqualified identification. The discrimination of an ascender, for example, indicates that a letter is not *a* or *c* or *e*, among others, and that a word is not *is, any, impressionism* or many other alternatives, but will not distinguish among letters or words that do include ascenders. However, the more distinctive features that are discriminated, the more alternatives are eliminated. We shall see that just five distinctive features are (theoretically) sufficient to distinguish all the letters of the alphabet, and that discrimination of barely a dozen or so features may permit identification of a word from among scores of thousands of alternatives, provided the reader has acquired some knowledge about which sets of features are critical for particular words. Once again, this is an aspect of reading that clearly favors the experienced reader over the beginner.

The actual identification of a word, whether immediate or mediated, will be conceptualized as a process of categorization. A category, from the point of view of letter or word identification, may be considered as a unique cognitive grouping to which particular visual configurations can be allocated, together with a name. The name of the category is the "name" of the letter or word, the letter or word as it would be spoken.[1] All configurations allocated to the category "b", or the category "chair", for example, are given the name "b" or "chair". Each category is specified cognitively (in the mind of the reader) by descriptions that determine which configurations may be allocated to that category. These descriptions will be called *feature lists,* because in effect they list the features that a configuration has to have in order to be allocated to a particular category. The combination of features in the visual configuration *h* permits the allocation of that configuration to the category "h"[2] because those features are compatible with a feature list that is associated with that category and that specifies the required features of configurations that shall be allocated to the category. The visual configurations *h* and *H* are also allocated to the cate-

---

[1] Superscripted numbers refer to notes at the end of each chapter.

gory "h" because their features are compatible with alternative feature lists for the same category. Immediate word identification occurs only when the reader has a feature list that will permit allocation of a configuration to a named word category. Absence of an appropriate feature list (because the reader has not had the opportunity to construct one during his earlier reading experience) prevents immediate identification of a word since identification of the word must be mediated through discovery of the name by some other procedure, such as "sounding out" the word by the application of phonic rules to its component letters.

The two alternative methods of word identification may be represented by diagrams. In Figure 1(a), identification proceeds directly from discrimination of the features in a visual array to allocation of the array to a category that has a name; such identification is essentially no different from examining a visual stimulus and allocating it (on the basis of distinctive features) to a class that has the name "tree" or "Dalmatian dog" or "steamroller". In Figure 1(b) the reader has to learn a category name by some mediating process (which may be phonic, but could be simply asking someone who can read the word immediately) in order to allocate the array to a category. Once the array—category—name relations have been established, as in Figure 1(b), the reader can construct a feature list for the named category so that in the future similar configurations may be allocated to the category immediately.

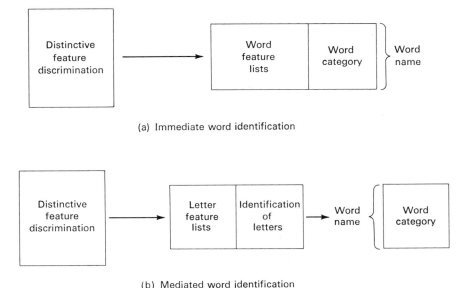

(a) Immediate word identification

(b) Mediated word identification

Figure   1   Immediate and Mediated Word Identification

In short, I shall propose that the elements that are distinctive features of the visual configurations of letters may also (in particular combinations) be the distinctive features of words, and that the same process of immediate identification may be used for whole words as for individual letters. In other words, the immediate identification of words can bypass the identification of letters, as indicated in Figure 2.

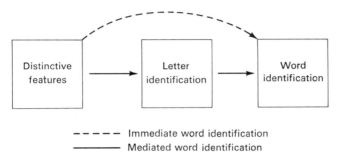

----- Immediate word identification
——————— Mediated word identification

Figure 2 Immediate and Mediated Word Identification

The entire question of reading for comprehension is too complicated to discuss at this point. In fact, there are so many unknowns involved that it is only possible to consider comprehension obliquely, even after discussion of relevant other areas. However, I shall hypothesize that there are two ways of reading for comprehension just as there are two ways of identifying words: *mediated comprehension* requires the prior identification of words, while *immediate comprehension* can be accomplished by going directly from the visual features to the meaning. Once again, only the fluent reader can take the immediate shortcut; the beginner must do everything the hard way. The possible extent of immediate comprehension depends, as does immediate word recognition, upon a number of factors including the knowledge a reader has built up during his reading experience of the way words and letters (and therefore distinctive features) occur together in the language. As an example, it is obvious—to an experienced reader of English—that if the first letter of a word is *t,* the next letter will almost certainly be *h, r, w,* or a vowel. If the first word of a sentence is "we", a verb is very likely to follow. This kind of prior knowledge, which reduces the alternative number of possibilities that a letter or word can be, is termed *redundancy*.

It may be in order to clarify the use of expressions like "prior knowledge" or "using rules" or "reducing alternatives" that will appear frequently in the coming pages, together with terms like "seeking information" and "establishing lists", all of which may imply processes and knowledge of which most of us are unaware. But it can be easily demonstrated that it is not necessary to have conscious access to knowledge that we use or to processes that we employ. There are many regularities in our spoken language that we are not aware of until they are pointed out to us; several examples of these will be given. We shall also see that the actual rules that a child acquires in mastering both spoken and written language must be quite different from the rules that the teacher tries to teach him. Because the way in which human beings actually store and use knowledge is not accessible to consciousness, we often mislead ourselves into thinking that we can teach the actual rules though at best we can only point to regularities in which the unknown rules appear to be exemplified. Perhaps the most obvious indication that we have skills that we cannot explain is provided by linguists, who still cannot adequately construct a set of rules—a "grammar"—for distinguishing reliably between grammatical and ungrammatical English sentences, although nobody would suggest that the linguists cannot themselves recognize an ungrammatical sentence when they meet one.

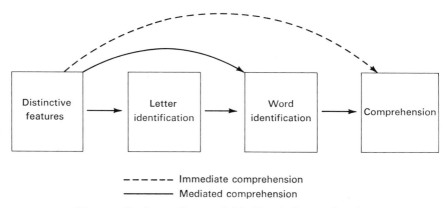

Figure   3   Immediate and Mediated Comprehension

One skill that the fluent reader is typically unaware of is the use of redundancy, or alternative sources of information. Most of us would say that we are never aware of the relative frequency of various combinations of letters in the words that we read, but we shall see that we do possess and use this type of knowledge. Another source of information that skilled readers use has nothing to do with visible properties of words, but is related to their frequency in a particular context and their relation to other words. One might think that for any given reader, a particular word would be just as easy or difficult to read in whatever circumstances it occurred (provided such factors as type size and lighting are unchanged, of course).

But this is not the case; ease in identifying a word depends very much on the words around it and on our prior knowledge. A skilled reader will in fact be defined as one who makes the maximum use of redundancy in both identification and comprehension.

The picture that will be drawn of the skilled reader is perhaps not very close to the popular stereotype of reading. I shall propose that the ability to put letters together to form words has very little to do with the actual process of reading (as opposed to learning to read) and that even the ability to identify words loses its importance when one "reads for meaning". I shall propose that the actual marks on a printed page are relatively less important than the knowledge of language that a skilled reader has before he even opens the book. And the description of the visual process will imply that the information that passes from the brain to the eye is more important in reading than the information that passes from the eye to the brain. A beginning reader will be depicted as being constantly seduced to do the right thing for the wrong reason, discouraged from making the "mistakes" from which he will learn, and deprived of information when he needs it most.

But this introductory discussion has begun to run too far ahead of itself. It is too early to be contentious or provocative. Enough has been said to show that the book really is concerned with reading, even if this is not apparent from the titles of many of the chapters.

References

At the end of each chapter I shall list one or two books that will be of interest to readers who wish to pursue topics in that chapter further. Citations indicated in the text by superscripted numbers will be set out in the Notes at the foot of each References section. The sources of these citations will usually be too technical for anyone but the specialist; these sources are mentioned primarily more to acknowledge credit for the origin of my information or inspiration.

I am aware of no book (at the time of writing) that deals with all the material covered in *Understanding Reading,* and few books treat any of the topic areas in the manner that I have handled them. Unfortunately, most well-informed books that treat the topics that I cover are usually written for the specialist, although I shall try to recommend the exceptions. Some references are of relevance to more than one of my chapters, and a few of these are listed below.

There are two collections of papers with an approach that is frequently similar to that of this volume. In general, they reflect the growing "psycholinguistic" tendency to emphasize the linguistic over the visual aspects of reading:

K. S. GOODMAN (ed.), *The Psycholinguistic Nature of the Reading Process* (Detroit: Wayne State University Press, 1968).

H. LEVIN and JOANNA WILLIAMS (eds.), *Basic Studies in Reading* (New York: Harper & Row, Publishers, 1970).

For a scholarly, original and literate representation of the individual as an active, thinking, planning, information-processing, decision-making human being, an older but very influential book must be recommended (although it is not on the topic of reading at all):

G. A. MILLER, E. GALANTER, and K. H. PRIBRAM, *Plans and the Structure of Behavior* (New York: Holt, Rinehart and Winston, Inc., 1960).

A little more complex, but "introductory" in their fields, are two more specialized books whose approach is generally congruent with my own; their content is indicated by their titles, with both tending to emphasize visual processes:

ELEANOR J. GIBSON, *Principles of Perceptual Learning and Development* (New York: Appleton-Century-Crofts, 1969).

U. NEISSER, *Cognitive Psychology* (New York: Appleton-Century-Crofts, 1967).

An introductory psychology text is an essential starting point for anyone beginning to discover more about the topics of *Understanding Reading.* There are large numbers of such texts on the market, with varying areas of strength (no introductory text can please any one person all the time), and none that I have encountered has anything useful to say about reading. I like the following because it gives a fair—though necessarily sketchy—outline from more than one point of view of such central topics as learning, visual perception, language, and individual differences:

W. N. DEMBER and J. J. JENKINS, *General Psychology: Modeling Behavior and Experience* (Englewood Cliffs, N.J.: Prentice Hall, Inc., 1970).

The better introductory texts, like all the books cited in this section, are particularly useful as sources for more specialized references in the experimental or theoretical literature.

There are also two (among many) volumes of readings that I have found useful on a number of aspects of language and thought:

J. P. DE CECCO (ed.). *The Psychology of Language, Thought and Instruction* (New York: Holt, Rinehart and Winston, Inc., 1967).

R. C. OLDFIELD and J. C. MARSHALL (eds.), *Language: Selected Readings* (Baltimore: Penguin Books, Inc., 1968).

The former is an exception in that it has a section on reading, which is not, as it happens, the reason that I recommend it.

I am not currently aware of any book on reading that has anything like the scope of the present volume—with one brilliant exception. This exception was published in 1908 and was such a milestone that it was republished 60 years later—not as a monument but as a book whose time had come:

E. B. HUEY, *The Psychology and Pedagogy of Reading* (Cambridge, Mass.: M.I.T. Press, 1968).

Other books on reading and reading instruction should be examined not for what they say that might elaborate on points made in this volume, but for what they say that is different.

Notes

1. In visual perception generally, many categories exist without having names. Objects do not have to have distinctive names to be recognized as different. It is certainly not established that all categories *must* have a name in reading; it would seem unlikely that all deaf readers have "names" for words, and everyone responds to some symbols to which they do not give names, such as the punctuation marks.

2. A useful convention adopted here and used henceforth is that references to visual forms of letters or words, that is to the ink marks on the page, will be in *italics,* while the spoken form, or an abstract reference to the word as a category, will be in quotation marks. For example, we can say that *mouse* and *MOUSE* are alternative representations of the word "mouse", and we can say that *h, ℏ,* and *H* are alternative representations of the letter "h".

2

Communication
and Information

Reading is an act of communication in which information is transferred from a transmitter to a receiver, whether the reader is a scholar deciphering a medieval text or a child identifying a single letter on a blackboard. Because of this basic nature of reading, there are insights to be gained from the study of theories of communication and information; there are concepts that are particularly useful for the construction of a theory of reading, and a terminology that can be employed to increase the clarity of its expression.

The present chapter will be particularly relevant to the following aspects of reading: reading is not a passive activity—the reader must make an active contribution if he is to acquire the available information. All information acquisition in reading, from the identification of individual letters or words to the comprehension of entire passages, can be regarded as the reduction of uncertainty. Skilled reading utilizes redundancy—of information from a variety of sources—so that, for example, knowledge of the world and of language will reduce the need for visual information from the printed page.

12

The Communication Transaction

Communication requires the interaction of two participants, who for the sake of generality can be called the *transmitter* and *receiver* of a message. The previous statement should be regarded as more than an assertion of the obvious—that there has to be a listener around for a speaker to get his point across, or that writing has no purpose without a reader. The receiver of a message, whether listener or reader, has to make a contribution at least as great as that of the transmitter if communication is to occur. In fact, the information acquired by a receiver is much more than is actually present in the physical representation of that information in the sound waves through the air or the visible marks on paper.

In some senses, the task of the receiver is more difficult than that of the transmitter. Not only must the receiver have skills of language comprehension equivalent to the skills of language production employed by the transmitter, but he may also need to interpret messages that include elements, structure or content, quite foreign to his own experience. That is, the speaker or writer never has to go beyond his own vocabulary and syntax, and he always should know (though whether this is true is sometimes debatable) what he is talking about. The transmitter can afford to be discursive because he knows the point he is eventually going to make. But the receiver has none of these advantages; everything that the transmitter takes for granted the receiver has to figure out for himself. The receiver has the additional disadvantage that while the transmitter can speak or write at his own pace, the listener can rarely demand a replay or even the slowing down of delivery, and the reader is usually constrained to read in the order in which the writer chooses to present his thoughts and—as we shall see —under time constraints that do not disturb the writer.

We shall make a closer study of the active role that the receiver must play in listening and reading when we consider language and its comprehension. I shall show that there are discrepancies between the sound (or written representation) of language and its meaning that can be bridged only by a contribution from the receiver. But there is one example that can be given without technical detail to illustrate the skill of the listener in perceiving speech; it is known as "the cocktail party problem".[1] The problem is this: how does a listener in a crowd of people all talking loudly at the same time manage to follow what one person is saying and tune out everything else? The communication channel to the listener's ear is full of noise (both literally and technically), yet he can select from within the noise the information coming from one source only. And this "selected" voice is the only one that he hears—unless someone else happens to say something particularly relevant to him, such as his name, in which case he demonstrates that he has really been monitoring all the conversations all the time, "listening without hearing". But as far as the physical input to his ear is concerned, all the sounds from all the speakers are mixed. No one has yet been able to devise a machine that, using the same communication channel, could unscramble more than one voice at a time. Yet the human receiver can separate intermingled messages, and not because they "come in different voices, or from different directions"; it has been shown experimentally that he can follow one message even if successive words are produced by different voices—by following the sense and syntax of the message being attended to. Such a feat can be accomplished only if the listener draws upon his own knowledge of language to extract the message from all the irrelevant noise in which it is embedded.

If a reader is regarded as part of a communication system, then it is useful to borrow concepts and terms from communication theory and related disciplines such as information theory and a rather newer development called *signal detection theory*. In fact, the theory and experience of many researchers and engineers in these fields have proved so relevant to psychologists studying all aspects of perception, whether or not language is involved, that much of the terminology has been adopted wholesale. The result is that treatises on communication systems often make electronic devices like computers and switchboards sound like intelligent humans, while psychological and neurophysiological researches into intelligent human behavior make the brain sound as if it were just a particularly intricate information processing machine.

Among the terms widely used in both communication theory and cognitive psychology that are useful in understanding reading are "transmitter", "receiver", "communication channel", "noise", "information", "uncertainty", and "redundancy". The first two of these terms have already been introduced informally, and we must now look at the others in a little more detail.

The Communication Channel and Noise

The transmitter and receiver may be regarded as the two ends of a communication channel along which information may flow in a variety of ways. In a telephone system, for example, the channel of communication between speaker and listener includes the vocal apparatus of the speaker, the microphone and speaker in each of the telephones, the cable linking the two telephones, and the auditory apparatus of the listener. In passing through this communication channel, a message takes a variety of forms—as a complex sequence of neural impulses organizing the vocal apparatus of the speaker, as wave patterns in the air, as electrical impulses in the telephone cable, and again as sound waves through the air on the way to the listener's eardrum, after which the message goes through a complicated series of changes on the way to being transformed to another set of nervous impulses directed into the listener's brain. At every stage in this channel, the information can be regarded as being embedded in a pattern of events, structured in both space and time. The problem for the receiver is to unravel the final pattern, the sequence of nervous impulses along the auditory or optic nerve, to extract the message.

At each part of the communication process there is the possibility that a message will be changed in some way. Parts of it will be lost because a particular section of the channel is not able to transmit all the information coming into it. The channel may perhaps be incapable of responding to some aspects of the message, just as a loudspeaker may not be sensitive enough to produce with fidelity some of the lowest or highest tones of music. Or parts of a message may be lost because the channel cannot pick up and pass on information as fast as it arrives. The limit on the type or amount of information that can pass through any communication channel is referred to as *channel capacity*. Channel capacity may clearly be independent of the *skill* of the receiver, although the limitation may also be part of the communication channel inside the listener—for example his inability to distinguish more than a certain number of sounds or sights per second.

In addition, extraneous signals called *noise* may degrade or confuse the message. The concept of noise is not restricted to acoustic events, but can be applied to anything that makes communication less clear or effective, such as a difficult-to-read type face for printed material, or poor illumination, or distraction of the reader's attention.

More formally, noise may be regarded as a signal that conveys no information, in contrast to the actual information-bearing signal. The receiver must separate the informative signal from the noise, and whenever he fails to do so part of the message will be lost. Any part of a message that the receiver lacks the skill or knowledge to comprehend obviously becomes noise. A man making a speech in a foreign language may give information to anyone who understands that language but is literally providing only noise for anyone else. And noise cannot be easily ignored; it is not an absence of information but rather a negative, information-reducing component of communication. Because communication channels have limited capacities, noise contributes quite uselessly to overloading the system and prevents the transmission of informative signals.

Because anything that one lacks the skill or knowledge to understand auto-

matically becomes noise, reading is, again, intrinsically more difficult for the novice than for the experienced reader. For the beginner, everything is much noisier.

There are other ways in which the concepts of limited channel capacity and of noise will be relevant to our consideration of both the skilled and the novice reader. For example, we shall see that there is a limit to the speed at which the eye can travel over a passage of text making information-gathering fixations and to the amount of information that can be acquired in a single fixation. Both of these are limitations of channel capacity in the communication system of the reader. We shall also see that one problem for the beginning reader is to discover which aspects of the visual configurations of letters and words actually serve to distinguish them from one another—in other words, which are their "distinctive features". Features that are not distinguishing, which do not make a contribution toward differentiating alternatives, such as the elegant ornamental embellishments of some capital letters, are examples of noise.

Information and Uncertainty

One of the great contributions from the study of communication systems to the study of human behavior has been a clarification of the concept of information—and a technique for quantifying it. We have seen that information assumes a variety of guises as it passes through different portions of a communication channel, but there has been no clue about what remains constant through all these different manifestations. What is this "information" that travels as patterns of sound waves through the air, light waves through space, and pulses through electric or neural cables? The statement that *information is the reduction of uncertainty* may not appear to make much progress toward a definition, until we consider uncertainty in terms of the number of alternatives among which the receiver has to choose. And the answer to a question about the nature of these alternatives is: it does not matter. It is beside the point whether the receiver's decision concerns the classification of objects or events, the identification of an occurrence, or the selection among various paths or possibilities. Information and uncertainty are defined in terms of the *number* of alternative decisions that could be made no matter *what* the alternatives are. However, it is easier to reach an understanding of the concept of uncertainty if particular situations are taken as examples.

Suppose that the message to be transmitted is a single letter of the alphabet. Or to put it in plain English, suppose a child is given the task of identifying a letter written on the blackboard. There are 26 alternatives available to the transmitter and the receiver—the 26 letters of the alphabet. The receiver's uncertainty involves a decision or choice among 26 possibilities. If the situation is the bidding in a bridge game, then the uncertainty may perhaps concern a player's strongest suit, and the number of alternatives will be four. For the simple toss of a coin, the number of alternatives is two. Sometimes the exact number of alternatives cannot be known, for example, if a name or a word is being transmitted. But it may still be possible to determine when this indefinite amount of uncertainty has been reduced—for example, when the receiver learns that the name or word begins with a particular letter, or is of a particular length, either of which will reduce the number of alternative possibilities.

We can now return to the definition of "information" as the reduction of uncertainty. Just as the measure of uncertainty is concerned with the number of alternatives among which the receiver has to choose, so information is concerned with the number of alternatives that are eliminated as a result of reception of the message. If the receiver is able to eliminate all alternatives except one, if he is able to make an appropriate decision, then the amount of information transmitted is equal to the amount of uncertainty that existed. The card player who receives the information that his partner's strongest suit is red has had his uncertainty reduced by a half; if he gets the information that the strongest suit is hearts, his uncertainty is reduced completely. Similarly, the child who knows his letters well enough to decide that the letter on the board is a vowel has had his uncertainty reduced from among 26 alternatives to five. If he correctly identifies the letter, then the "information" in the letter is equal to his original uncertainty.

It is necessary to be a little circumlocutory in associating information and uncertainty with actual numbers, because although both are measured in exactly the same way with respect to the number of alternatives, the measure is not simply the number of alternatives. Instead the measurement is computed in terms of a unit called a *bit,* which is equal always to half the number of alternatives on any particular occasion. Thus the card player who learns that his partner's strongest suit is red gets one bit of information (or has his uncertainty reduced by one bit), and so does the child who is told that the letter he is trying to identify comes from the second half of the alphabet. In the first case two alternatives are eliminated (the two black suits) and in the second case 13 alternatives are removed, but in both cases the proportion of uncertainty reduced is a half, and therefore the amount of information received is one bit.

The uncertainty of a situation in bits, therefore, is equal to the number of times a question would have to be asked to eliminate all the uncertainty if each answer reduced the uncertainty by a half. Thus there are two bits of uncertainty in the card playing example, because two questions will remove all the doubt. Note that these two questions need not actually be specified, or can in fact be posed in a variety of ways—for example,

Q1.   *Is it a red suit?*
Q2.   *If yes, is it hearts? (If no, is it clubs?)*

Q1.   *Is it clubs or diamonds?*
Q2.   *If yes, is it clubs? (If no, is it hearts?)*

Q1.   *Is the suit a six-letter word?*
Q2.   *If yes, is it hearts? (If no, is it clubs?)*

You can see it does not matter how the questions are posed, provided they permit a yes-no answer that will eliminate half the alternatives. The final qualification is important. Obviously, a single lucky question such as "Is it clubs?" will eliminate all the alternatives if the answer is "Yes," but will still leave at least one and possibly more questions to be asked if the answer is "No." The most efficient way of reducing uncertainty when the answer can only be "yes" or "no" is by a binary split, that is, by partitioning the alternatives into two equal sets. In fact the word *bit,* which may have sounded rather colloquial as a term that refers to units of information, is an abbreviation of the words *bi*nary dig*it,* or a number representing a choice between two alternatives.

The uncertainty of the 26 letters of the alphabet lies somewhere between four and five bits. Four bits of information will allow selection among 16 alternatives, the first bit reducing this number to 8, the second to 4, the third to 2, and the fourth to 1; while five bits will select among 32 alternatives, the first eliminating 16 and the other four removing the remaining 16.[2] There is a mathematical formula that shows that the theoretical uncertainty of the 26 letters of the alphabet is precisely 4.7 bits, although, of course, it is not easy to see how one could ask just 4.7 questions.

To explain fully why and how information and uncertainty are measured in terms of the proportion of alternatives eliminated, rather than the actual number, would not be directly relevant to the question of reading, but some more detailed sources for those who might be interested are given at the end of this chapter. For our immediate purposes it will be sufficient to remember that a bit of information reduces uncertainty by a half, and the total amount of uncertainty in a situation is the number of bits required to reduce the alternatives to one.

If we regard reading like any other process of acquiring information, namely the reduction of uncertainty, then we have discovered the first way in which the conventionally disparate areas of letter identification, word identification, and "reading for comprehension" can be considered in the same light. In each of the three aspects of reading, information is acquired visually to reduce a number of alternative possibilities. The exact number of alternatives can be specified for letters, an approximate figure can perhaps be put to the number of words, but the number of alternatives for comprehension, if it can be estimated at all, must obviously be closely related both to the passage being read and the particular individual who is doing the reading. However, it is not necessary to specify the exact amount of uncertainty in order to discuss the informativeness of a message—that is one of the advantages of expressing uncertainty and information as a proportion. We may not know how much uncertainty an individual has about the identity of the sovereign of England in the year 1900, but we do know that his uncertainty must be reduced if he reads and comprehends a message that the sovereign was a woman. In fact we shall see that there are quite reliable ways of estimating the amount of information in a particular statement by using what we know about the channel capacity of the human perceptual systems as a yardstick.

Redundancy

Redundancy is one of the most important concepts that I shall discuss—but, again, it is a concept that occurs very infrequently in the literature on the psychology of reading. Redundancy exists whenever information is duplicated by more than one source. Or we can say—to use the earlier definition of information—that there is redundancy whenever the same alternatives can be eliminated in more than one way.

An obvious way to provide redundancy is to repeat everything; with this method the alternative sources of information are the two successive sentences. A different method of presenting the same message twice would be to present one version to the eye and the other to the ear—an audiovisual or "multimedia" approach. Repetition is an eminently popular technique in advertising, especially in television commercials, exemplifying one of the practical advantages of redundancy that it reduces the likelihood that the receiver will make a mistake, or overlook anything, in his comprehension of the message. There are other aspects of redundancy, however, that are not always as obvious but that play a very important role in the actual process of normal reading.

Very often the fact that some of the same alternatives are being reduced by two sources of information is not apparent. As an example of two overlapping sources of information that also each contain some unique information, consider the following pair of sentences:

1. The letter of the alphabet that I am thinking of is a vowel.
2. The letter I am thinking of is from the first half of the alphabet.

At first glance the two statements might appear to provide complementary pieces of information telling us that the letter is a vowel in
the first half of the alphabet. However, if we look at the alternatives that
each of the two statements eliminates, we can see that they actually contain
a good deal of overlapping information. Statement 1 tells us that the letter
is not *b, c, d, f, g, h, j, k, l, m, n, p, q, r, s, t, v, w, x, y, z*, and Statement 2
tells us that it is not *n, o, p, q, r, s, t, u, v, w, x, y, z*. Both statements tell
us that the letter is not *n, p, q, r, s, t, v, w, x, y, z*, and it is to this extent
(the extent to which the excluded sets of alternatives intersect) that the
statements are redundant. In fact, the only new information provided by
Statement 2 is that the letter is not *o* or *u;* all the other information is already provided in Statement 1.

*There are frequent occurrences of redundancy in reading. As an illus-
tration, consider the unfinished sentence (which could possibly appear at
the bottom of a page of text):*

The captain ordered the mate to drop the an-

*We shall consider four ways of reducing our uncertainty about the remain-
der of that sentence—four alternative and therefore redundant sources of
information. First, we could turn the page and see how the last word
finished—this is what we normally mean by "reading," and we can call
this* visual *information. But we can also make some reasonable predictions
about how the sentence will continue without turning the page. For example, we can say that the next letter is unlikely to be* b, f, h, j, m, p, q, r, w,
or z *because these letters just do not occur after* an *in common words of
the English language; we can therefore attribute the elimination of these
alternatives to* orthographic *(or spelling) information. There are also some
things that can be said about the entire word before turning the page. We
know that it is most likely to be an adjective or a noun, because other
types of words such as articles, conjunctions, verbs and prepositions, for example, are most unlikely to follow the word* the; *the elimination of all
these additional alternatives can be attributed to* syntactic *(or grammatical)
information. Finally, we can continue to eliminate alternatives even if we
consider as candidates for the last word only nouns or adjectives that begin
with* an *plus one of the letters not eliminated by the orthographic information already discussed. We can eliminate words like* answer *and* anagram
and antibody *because although they are not excluded by our orthographic
or syntactic criteria, our knowledge of the world tells us these are not the
kinds of things that captains normally order mates to drop. The elimination of these alternatives can be attributed to* semantic *information. Obviously, the four alternative sources of information about the incomplete
word in the above example,* visual, orthographic, syntactic *and* semantic, *to
some extent provide overlapping information. We do not need as much*

visual information about the next word as we would if it occurred in isolation, because the other sources of information eliminate many alternatives. The four sources of information, therefore, are all to some extent redundant. And the skilled reader who can make use of the three other sources needs much less visual information than the less fluent reader.

It will be helpful to pursue the matter of redundancy a little more deeply, partly because of the importance of the concept of redundancy to reading, but also because the earlier discussion of how *bits* of uncertainty or information were computed contained a rather gross oversimplification that can now be rectified. We shall consider two types of redundancy, known as *distributional* and *sequential* redundancy. The examples given earlier were of sequential redundancy, which will be discussed in more depth in Chapter 10.

Distributional redundancy is associated with the relative number of times each of the alternatives that constitute the uncertainty of a particular situation can occur. Surprising as it may seem, there is less uncertainty when some of the alternatives occur less often, when they are less probable, than others. And because there is less uncertainty when alternatives are not equally probable, there is redundancy. The very fact that alternatives are not equally probable is a source of information that reduces the uncertainty of the set of alternatives as a whole.

The existence of redundancy when alternatives are not equally probable may suggest that uncertainty is greatest when every alternative has an equal chance of occurring. This intuition can be confirmed with a simple example. Consider a coin-tossing game where there are only two alternatives, head or tail; the amount of uncertainty is therefore one bit— provided that the game is fair and there are, in fact, equal chances of a head or tail turning up. The informativeness of knowing that a particular toss of the coin produced a head (or a tail) is indeed one bit, because whatever the outcome, the uncertainty is reduced by a half. But now suppose that the game is not fair, and that the coin will come down head nine times out of ten. What is the uncertainty of the game now (to someone who knows the coin's bias)? The uncertainty is hardly as great as when the odds were 50–50, because then there was no reason to choose between head and tail, while with the loaded coin anyone who knowingly bets tail would be foolish. By the same token, there is likely to be far less information in being told the outcome of a particular toss of the loaded coin. Not much uncertainty is removed if one is told that the coin came down head last time, because that is what was expected all the time. In fact the informativeness of a head can be computed to be just .015 bit compared with 1 bit if the game were fair. It is true that there is much more information in being told that a toss produced a tail—a total of 3.32 bits of information compared with the 1 bit for a tail when heads and tails are equally probable—but we can expect the fall of a tail to occur only once in every ten tosses. The *average* amount of information available from the loaded coin will be nine-tenths of the .015 bit of information for heads and one-tenth of the 3.32 bits of information for tails, which when totaled is approximately .35 bit. The difference between the 1 bit of uncertainty (or information) for the 50–50 fair coin, and the .35 bit for the 90–10 loaded coin, is the redundancy.

The oversimplification in the earlier discussion of information and uncertainty lay in the statements on page 17 that every bit of information halves the number of alternatives, and that the number of bits of uncertainty is the number of yes–no questions that would have to be asked and answered to eliminate all the alternatives. Both of these statements hold only when the alternatives are all equally probable. If some alternatives are less probable than others, then an *average* amount of uncertainty or information has to be computed, which takes into account both the number of alternatives and the probability of each. Because uncertainty and information are at their maximum when alternatives are equally probable, the average uncertainty of situations where this does not occur is necessarily less than the maximum, and redundancy is present.

It is now appropriate to qualify the statement made on page 18 that the uncertainty of the letters of the English language is 4.7 bits. This is a perfectly true statement for any situation involving 26 equally probable alternatives—for example the drawing of any letter from a hat containing one instance only of each of the 26 letters of the alphabet. But the letters of English do not occur in the language with equal frequency; some of them, such as *e, t, a, o, i, n, s,* occur far more often than others. In fact *e* occurs about 40 times more often than the least frequent letter, *z.* Because of the inequality of occurrence, the average uncertainty of letters is somewhat less than the maximum of 4.7 bits that it would be if the letters all occurred equally often. The actual uncertainty of letters, considering their relative frequency, has been computed to be 4.07 bits. The difference of about .63 bit is the *distributional redundancy* of English letters, and a measure of the prospective informativeness that is lost because letters do not occur equally often. In fact if letters were used equally often, we could achieve the 4.07 bits of uncertainty that the 26 letters currently have, with a little over 16 letters; we could save ourselves 9 letters if we could agree (and find a way) to use the remainder equally often.

Words as well as letters have a distributional redundancy. There is nothing in psychology that is more firmly established experimentally and more keenly disputed theoretically than that people need less visual information to identify more common words. A little later in this chapter I shall refer to a promising attempt to explain the phenomenon that has a particular relevance to reading.

It is particularly true in reading that the larger the context, the greater is the redundancy. And the more redundancy there is, the less visual information the skilled reader requires. In passages of continuous text, provided that the content is not too difficult, every other letter can be eliminated from most words, or about one word in five omitted altogether, without making the passage too difficult for a reader to comprehend— provided that he has learned the rules related to letter and word occurrence and co-occurrence.

Hits, Misses, and Criteria

The picture that is being developed is of a skilled reader who does not require a fixed amount of information in order to identify a letter or a word. Such a reader can identify a word on more or less visual information depending on his access to information from other sources, and on the amount of information he demands in order to make a decision.

Exactly how much information a reader will seek before he makes a "decision" about a particular letter, word, or meaning will depend on the difficulty of the passage (which must always be defined with respect to a particular reader), on his skill, and on the "cost" of making a decision.

A useful term for the amount of information that an individual requires before coming to a decision is his *criterion*. If the amount of information about a particular letter, word, or meaning reaches a reader's criterion for making a decision, then he will make a choice at that point, whether or not he has enough information to make the decision correctly.

An important consideration, of course, is how a person decides at what level he wants to establish a criterion—ranging from a supercautious attitude requiring almost an absolute-certainty amount of information before deciding, to willingness to take a chance and make a decision on minimal information, even at the risk of making a mistake. But in order to understand why a particular criterion level is established, it is necessary to understand what the effect of setting the criterion high or low might be.

The concept of criterion developed in the present section comes from a relatively new area of study called *signal detection theory,*[3] which has upset quite a number of venerable ideas about human perception. It is traditional to think, for example, that one either sees an object or one doesn't, and that there is no area of freedom in between within which the perceiver can decide whether or not the object is present. Signal detection theory, however, shows that in many circumstances the question of whether an object is perceived depends less on the intensity of the object —on its "clarity", if you like—than on the attitude of the observer. It is also traditional to think that there is an inverse relationship between correct responses and errors, that the more correct responses on any particular task—for example, the greater the proportion of letters correctly identified—the lower the number of errors must be. Signal detection theory, however, shows that the relationship is quite the reverse, and that in identification tasks (such as reading) the proportion of correct responses for a given amount of information can within limits be selected by the perceiver, but that the cost of increasing the proportion of correct responses is an increase in the number of errors. In other words, the more often you want to be right, the more often you must tolerate being wrong. The paradox can be explained by discussing in a little more detail what the theory is all about.

Signal detection theory was originally concerned literally with the detection of signals—with the ability of radar operators to distinguish between the "signals" and "noise" on their radar screens with the objective of identifying aircraft presumed to be hostile. As far as the actual situation is concerned, there are only two possibilities: a particular blip on the screen is either a signal or noise; an aircraft is present or it is not. As far as the operator is concerned, there are also only two possibilities: he decides that the blip on the screen is an aircraft, or he decides that it is not. In an ideal world, the combination of the actual situation and the operator would still permit only two possibilities: either the blip is a signal, in which case the operator decides that there is an aircraft, or the blip is merely noise, in which case his decision is that there is no aircraft involved. We may call each of these two alternatives *hits* in the sense that they are both correct identifications. However, there are two other possibilities, of quite different kinds, that can be considered errors. The first type of error occurs when no aircraft is present but the operator decides that there is—this situation may be called a *false alarm*. And the other type of error occurs when there is an aircraft present but the operator decides that there is not, that the signal is actually noise—a situation that can be termed a *miss*.

The problem for the operator is that the numbers of hits, false alarms, and misses are not independent; he cannot change the number of one without making a change in the number of another. For example, if the operator is anxious to avoid false alarms, and wants to get maximum information before he decides to report an aircraft, then he will produce more misses. If, on the other hand, he desires to maximize the number of hits, reducing the possibility of a miss by deciding in favor of an aircraft on less information, then he will also produce more false alarms. The situation is rather similar for a sentry on duty on a dark night who hears approaching footsteps but who cannot reveal his own position by asking questions. His alternatives are to shoot or hold his fire. If he shoots and the intruder is indeed hostile, then the sentry will get a medal. If he holds his fire and the stranger is friendly his decision is also commendable. But a miss (letting through an enemy) or a false alarm (shooting a friend) are less desirable consequences. Yet the nature of the world is such that sentries always have to settle for some level of probability for the undesirable consequences; the man anxious to stop every enemy is going to shoot a friend from time to time, while the sentry anxious not to shoot a friend is occasionally going to let an enemy slip through.

Of course, with increased skills of discrimination both the radar operator and the sentry can step up their level of efficiency and increase the ratio of hits to false alarms, just as increased clarity of the situation will make the task easier. But in any given situation the choice is always the same between maximizing hits and minimizing false alarms. Always the perceiver has to make the choice, to decide where he will set his criterion for distinguishing signal from noise, friend from foe, *a* from *b*. The higher the criterion, the more information required before making a decision, the fewer will be the false alarms but the fewer also will be the hits. There will be more hits if the criterion is set lower, if decisions are made on less information, but there will also be more false alarms.

Now we can approach the question of the basis upon which the criterion is established: what makes the perceiver decide to set his criterion high or low? The answer lies in the relative costs and rewards of hits, misses, and false alarms. If the radar operator is heavily penalized for false alarms, then he will set his criterion high, risking an occasional missed identification. On the other hand, if the sentry is highly motivated to eliminate every possible enemy and the slaughter of an innocent friend is leniently regarded, then he will set his criterion low.

The skilled reader cannot afford to set his criterion too high for deciding on word or meaning identification; we shall see that if he demands too much visual information, he will often be unable to get it fast enough to overcome memory limitations and read for sense. This readiness to take chances is a critical matter for beginning readers who may be forced to pay too high a price for making "errors". The child who stays silent (who "misses") rather than risk a "false alarm" by guessing at a letter or word before he is absolutely sure of it, may please his teacher but develop a habit of setting his criterion too high for efficient reading.

The notion of a criterion for identification that can be varied as a function of how much information the reader demands has been used to account for the word-frequency effect referred to on page 22. It has been proposed that readers establish relatively low criteria for deciding in favor

*of words that are common in their experience, but require more informa-
tion if the word is one that appears infrequently.*[4]

References

The most comprehensive yet lucid book on information theory—
and on some of the statistical aspects of language also—is:

J. R. PIERCE, *Symbols, Signals and Noise: The Nature and Process of Communication* (New York: Harper & Row, Publishers, 1961).
Like most books on this topic, it requires a willingness at least to face
mathematical and symbolic expressions and an occasional graph. Rather more
detailed and technical is:

C. CHERRY, *On Human Communication* (Cambridge, Mass.: M.I.T. Press,
1966).

Miller is elegant and informative on information theory; he has introductory
papers in several volumes, including:

G. A. MILLER (ed.), *Mathematics and Psychology* (New York: John Wiley &
Sons, Inc., 1964) (which also contains an extract from citation 3 below on signal detection theory).

G. A. MILLER, *The Psychology of Communication* (New York: Basic Books,
Inc., 1967).

Some original papers on information theory (and language) are reprinted in
another useful and inexpensive compendium:

B. A. FOSS (ed.), *New Horizons in Psychology* (Baltimore: Penguin Books,
Inc., 1966).

Several readable papers on communication, information theory and language
are also included in:

A. G. SMITH, *Communication and Culture* (New York: Holt, Rinehart and
Winston, Inc., 1966).

A more technical source of information about redundancy in language is
available in Chapters 7 and 8 of:

W. GARNER, *Uncertainty and Structure as Psychological Concepts* (New
York: John Wiley & Sons, Inc., 1962).

Notes

1. C. CHERRY, *On Human Communication* (New York: John Wiley & Sons, Inc.,
1961).
2. The number of alternatives that X bits of information will select among is 2^X,
for example, two bits will select among $2^2 = 4$, 3 bits among $2^3 = 8$, four bits among
$2^4 = 16$, and so on. Twenty bits ("twenty questions") are theoretically sufficient to
distinguish among $2^{20} = 1,048,576$ alternatives.

3. J. A. SWETS, W. P. TANNER, JR., and T. G. BIRDSALL, Decision processes in perception, *Psychological Review,* **68** (1961), 301–320.

4. D. E. BROADBENT, The word frequency effect and response bias, *Psychological Review,* **74** (1967), 1–15.

Citations 3 and 4 are both reprinted in R. W. HABER (ed.), *Contemporary Theory and Research in Visual Perception* (New York: Holt, Rinehart and Winston, Inc., 1968).

3

Language
and Reading

Man is a creature who devours information. He spends much of his waking time selecting and acquiring information—and a good part of the time he is asleep organizing it.

Man uses all his sensory systems for acquiring information which he integrates and stores in his brain. In the brain, man constructs a model of the world. The model is a summary of all his past experiences and a basis for all his future activity. In fact, it is not possible to separate the past from the future in either the brain or behavior, because in both the ongoing activity reflects past experience and future expectations.

Man's appetite for information can be regarded as a constant search for regularities in external events—regularities that both explain the past and predict the future. The regularities economize on mental effort because they summarize experience and minimize the necessity to remember a multitude of individual events; they provide the basis for rules for deciding when two events should be regarded as being similar or different. Every discovery of a regularity or application of a rule is an instance of uncertainty reduction. As we shall see, the construction of rules for allocating events to a particular category is an important aspect of learning to read.

In this chapter and the next we shall be looking particularly at the regularities of language and at how a knowledge of them is developed by a child. This analysis is relevant to our primary concern for two reasons: because reading is an aspect of language, only superficially different from the comprehension of speech, and because many of the skills employed by a child in learning the regularities of spoken language may also be employed to learn reading.

Because our coverage of language is limited to a few pages, it must be particularly sketchy to range over such broad (and controversial) areas as grammar, meaning, language production and comprehension, and language acquisition. The discussion will therefore be highly selective and idiosyncratic. It should be remembered that the endeavor is not to provide a comprehensive coverage of linguistics, but to provide a framework for developing a model of reading. The aim in all these preliminary chapters is to work toward a reduction of uncertainty about reading rather than to increase uncertainty about other topics.

The aspect of language with which we shall be most concerned is *grammar*. We shall follow a contemporary linguistic trend and regard grammar not as a set of formal prescriptions for determining whether a sentence is correctly put together or not, but as a set of rules by which sense is made out of language. To understand this dynamic function of grammar, two other aspects of language must first be considered: its sound (or written symbols) and its meaning. Then we shall see how grammar is the link between the two. We can consider the two cases of speech and writing jointly if we regard the words, spoken or written, as the *surface* representation of a message, and the meaning as something *deeper*. These two terms are appropriate as well as convenient, because many linguists and psychologists recently have had a good deal to say (and dispute) about the relation between the *surface* and *deep* levels of language. The surface level refers to the physical manifestation of language as it impinges on the ear or eye, and the deep level refers to meaning or semantic interpretation.

The importance of grammar as a link between the two levels of language lies in the following fact, which is critical for any understanding of language and of reading:

There is no simple correspondence between the surface structure of language and meaning.

You cannot simply take a sequence of sounds or of printed words and immediately derive a meaning from them, because there are aspects of meaning that are not present in the spoken or written words. The fact that there is no simple (or as the jargon puts it, "one-to-one") correspondence between surface structure and meaning is the reason it has proved impossible to construct or program a computer to read and respond to human language in any interesting way, and why human language is so different from any other animal communication system. Computers and animals get confused if signals do not have one-to-one correspondences with meaning; they do not have the language competence to bridge the two.

The Surface Structure of Language

One would think that there could not be too much complication or dispute about the fact that the basic elements of language are sounds. Spoken words are made up of one or more syllables, and syllables are constructed of one or more basic sounds. The word "bed", for example, is made up of the sounds /b/, /e/, and /d/ (it is a useful convention that the sounds of language are printed between oblique // strokes). With some perverse irregularities, the sounds of the language can be represented by the letters of the alphabet, so the number of alternative sounds must be about 26.

Every statement in the preceding paragraph might appear to be reasonable, but basically, every statement in that paragraph is wrong.

English has a few more functionally different sounds than it has letters in the alphabet, about 46. They have the special name *phonemes*. As we shall see later, there is rarely a one-to-one correspondence between a letter and a phoneme, but rather a variety of letters can represent a single phoneme and a variety of phonemes can be represented by a single letter or letter combination.

It is necessary to be tentative in making statements about the number of phonemes because the actual total depends on who is talking and when. Some dialects have more sounds than others. In some regions, for example, there is no difference in the pronunciation of "cot" and "caught", or "god" and "guard". We often think we make distinctions between different words when in fact we do not—the redundancy in the context is usually sufficient to indicate which of the alternatives we mean. Many quite literate speakers do not have sufficient phonemes to distinguish among "Mary", "marry", and "merry"; you may think you articulate each of these three words differently, but to be sure, you should utter them, one at a time, and ask a listener to spell what you have just said. You may find that the listener cannot observe all the differences you think you are making. Phonemes often drop out of casual or colloquial speech. The sound of "th" is a frequent victim; there is often no difference between "think" or "tink," or "then" and "den" in some areas of North America unless the occasion is somewhat formal.[1]

This frequent difference between the phonemes used by different people on different occasions will come to our attention twice more—once when we consider the use of phonic methods, the attempt to teach children "letter-sound correspondences," and once when we consider the question of communication between teacher and pupil.

There is very little about language, either spoken or written, that turns out to be as simple or straightforward as it appears on the surface. It might appear that whatever else we may have to doubt, the fact that spoken language is made up of these clearly distinguishable sounds called phonemes must be 24-carat indisputable. But the idea that language is put together from building blocks of sound just does not stand up under scrutiny.

A phoneme is not so much a single sound as a collection of sounds, all of which sound the same. If that description seems complicated, a more formal definition will not appear much better—a phoneme is a *class of closely related sounds constituting the smallest unit of speech that will distinguish one utterance from another.* We can try to disentangle the definition with an example.

The word "bed" would appear to be constituted of three phonemes by the terms of the italicized definition above. The /b/ at the beginning distinguishes "bed" from words like "fed" and "led" and "red", the /e/ in the middle distinguishes "bed" from "bad" and "bide" and "bowed", and so forth, and the /d/ distinguishes the word from such alternatives as "bet" and "beg". So each of the three elements in "bed" will serve to distinguish the word from others, and each also is the smallest unit that can do this. Each is a *significant difference.* It would not be correct to classify /be/ as a phoneme, because while it certainly distinguishes "bed" from "fad", it can be broken down into smaller units that *make a difference.* It does not matter if the /b/ pronounced at the beginning of "bed" is a little different from /b/ at the beginning of "bad", or if the /b/ in "bed" is pronounced in different ways on different occasions. All the different sounds that I might make that are acceptable as the sound at the beginning of "bed" and "bad", and that serve to distinguish them from "fed" and "fad", and so forth, qualify as being the same phoneme. This illustrates the significance of the first part of the definition of a phoneme: a *class of closely related sounds* constituting the smallest unit of speech, and so forth. For a phoneme is not one sound, but a variety of sounds any of which is acceptable by listeners as making the same contrast. These elementary sounds are called *phones,* and the sets of "closely related" phones that all sound like the same phoneme are called *allophones* of each other (or of the particular phoneme). Allophones are sounds that the perceiver learns to treat as *equivalent,* and to hear as the same.

The distinctions of the previous paragraph may be further illustrated by an analogy with writing, where a comparable situation holds. Just as the word "sound" is ambiguous in speech (depending, for example, on whether we are talking about the sound of a particular phoneme—such as /b/—or the various ways, or phones, by which the phoneme can be produced) so the word "letter" is ambiguous in writing. We call "a" one letter of the al-

phabet, as distinguished from "b", "c", "d", *etc., but we also talk about* a, A, *ạ , etc. as being letters, although they all in a way represent the same* "letter." *In the first case, the letter of the alphabet* "a" *is really a category name for a variety of written symbols such as* a, A, ạ. *For clarity, the 26 category names for the letters in the English alphabet may be called* graphemes, *the written symbols (which are innumerable in their various forms) may be called* graphs, *and the graphs that constitute alternatives for a single grapheme are known as* allographs. *The same defining framework can now be applied to the terms for the elements of speech and writing.*

A phoneme (*grapheme*) is a class of closely related phones (*graphs*) constituting the smallest unit of speech (*writing*) that will distinguish one word from another. The set of phones (*graphs*) in a single phoneme (*grapheme*) class are termed allophones (*allographs*).

Of course, allographs may not seem to have as much in common as allophones; in fact, some allographs, such as a *and* A, *or* g *and* G, *would appear to have nothing in common at all. But they do have a* functional equivalence *in that their differences are not significant for reading, any more than the differences between allophones are significant for comprehending speech. The task for the listener (or reader) is to detect the significant differences, which means first of all that he has to discover what they are. The two terms* "significant differences" *and* "minimal contrasts" *are complementary in the study of language—in both the study of speech and reading. Allophones* (allographs) *are units of sound* (writing) *among which there are* no significant differences, *while phonemes* (graphemes) *are units that represent* minimal contrasts *for distinguishing words in speech* (writing).

There is a very simple way of demonstrating that sounds that we normally hear to be the same can be quite different. If you say the word "pin" into the palm of your hand you will feel a distinct puff of air on the $/p/$; however, the puff is absent when you say the word "spin". In other words, the $/p/$ in "pin" is not pronounced the same as the $/p/$ in "spin"—and both are different from the $/p/$ in "limp". If you now pay careful attention to the way you say the two words, you can probably detect the difference.

Normally, we are not aware of the difference, not because it is not there, but because it is not a significant difference in the language. The $/p/$ in pin (call it $/p_1/$) is "aspirated"—we expel a little extra puff of air on it —while the $/p/$ in spin $/p_2/$ is not. In a language where these two sounds constitute a significant difference—where $/p_1 in/$ would not be heard as the same as $/p_2 in/$—they would be phonemes, but in English it makes no difference if you are one of the minority of people who aspirate the $/p/$ in "spin" or who do not aspirate the $/p/$ in "pin", and so $/p_1/$ and $/p_2/$ are allophones. There are other word pairs that provide a similar demonstration—for example, "kin" and "skin", "team" and "steam". You may also be able to detect a difference between /k/ in "cool" and /k/ in "keen", a difference that is allophonic in English and phonemic in Arabic, or in the /l/ at the beginning and end of "level".

When electronic equipment is used to analyze sounds, quite marked differences can be found especially in consonants, depending on the sound that follows them, although they are heard as exactly the same. For example, the /d/ in "dim" is basically a high-pitched rising sound, while its allophone at the beginning of "doom" is much lower pitched and falling.[2] In fact frequency-analyzing equipment cannot distinguish anything that the two sounds actually have in common. (What they do appear to share is some kind of common preparatory position in the speaker's vocal apparatus, although when he is in this preliminary attitude, he is not actually producing sound. By the time he starts to express something, the configuration of his vocal tract has changed depending on the vowel that is to follow the consonant. So if what the speaker does has anything to do with what the listener hears, the listener must be responding to a portion of the speaker's behavior that is silent!)

A tape recorder can be used to confirm a number of the remarkable findings of speech analysis. As an example, a tape recorder will demonstrate that "dim" and "doom" have no /d/ sound in common. If the two words are recorded, it is impossible to cut the tape in order to separate the /im/ or /oom/ from the /d/. Either one is left with a distinct /di/ or /doo/ sound, or else the /d/ sound disappears altogether. One is left with two quite different kinds of whistle. There is no /d/ except as part of these quite different consonant–vowel combinations. Other phonemes behave in equally bizarre manners. If the first part of the tape-recorded word "pit" is cut and spliced at the front of the final /at/ of a word such as "sat" or "fat", the word that is heard is not "pat", as we might expect, but "cat". The /k/ from the beginning of "keep" makes "top" when joined to the /op/ from "cop" and makes "poop" when combined with the /oop/ from "coop". In short, a phoneme may have no independent or distinctive physical identity of its own; it may be produced in a variety of ways, and vary radically depending on the sound around it, yet still be heard as the same.

A phoneme, then, is not something present at the surface level of spoken language—it is something that the listener constructs. We do not hear different sounds when we are listening to speech, but instead we hear significant differences, phonemes instead of phones. If a pair of sounds does not constitute a significant difference, then we do not hear them as different. That is why Japanese have difficulty in distinguishing between English words such as "link" and "rink"; there is no contrast between /l/ and /r/

in their language, so not only can they not pronounce the two words as different, but they have difficulty in hearing them as different.

It becomes perhaps a little less surprising that scientific instruments cannot isolate the distinctive sounds that we hear as phonemes when we learn that they also cannot detect the beginning and ending of many sounds—or even words—that we hear as quite separate. The actual flow of speech is relatively continuous and smoothly changing, and the segmentation into distinct sounds and words is again largely something that listeners contribute. You can get some indication of this by uttering the two words "west end" and repeating them while listening very carefully to what you are saying. You will probably find that if you introduce any pause at all in the utterance, it will be between the / s / and the / t /—that actually you are saying "wes tend" rather than "west end". Of course, an English speaker would never think that you really said "wes tend". But only because he speaks the language himself and is able to work out—and hear—the sounds you *thought* you were producing. The fact that you need to *know* a language in order to be able to *hear* it properly becomes apparent if you listen to a foreign language—not only can you not distinguish what the distinctive sounds of the language are, but you can not even tell how many words there are. Believe it or not, foreign speakers—and children—have exactly the same trouble with English.

This discussion of some of the phonemic characteristics of language and its reception has been developed at some length (but even so, very sketchily) partly as an illustration of the important contribution that is made by the listener. We shall see in due course that the receiver makes a similarly impressive contribution in perceiving the meaning as well as the sounds of language, and also in the comprehension of written material.

But the major point is a more general one: that of the infinite number of possible and actual differences in the "superficial" physical manifestation of language, only a few are actually significant for comprehension—and many of the differences that are significant (like the pause in "west end") are not actually present. The differences that we hear are those that are significant, whether or not they actually occur. So on the way to demonstrating the original point that there is no one-to-one correspondence between sound and meaning—which suggests that the sound is at the transmitter's end of the communication channel—we have examined evidence that there is actually no one-to-one correspondence between the physical form of a message and its sound, which now becomes located at the receiver's end. It is not that the listener interprets the sound to get the meaning, but that he needs to know the meaning before he can hear the sound.

The point of view just expressed is so different from the way we usually view language perception that it will take a little adjusting to. But we are going to be very deeply involved in the view that reading is not a matter of going from words to meaning, but rather from meaning to words. To read words effectively, you need to have a good idea in advance of what it is that you are reading. This is not as paradoxical as it might seem; broadcasters, for example, like to glance through bulletins before they read them because they know it is much easier to enunciate the words appropriately with prior knowledge of the meaning. The question of what meaning actually is, or what comprehension can be, will be approached and then evaded in the next section, before considering how the receiver might get from raw sound or print to meaning, a function that we have already attributed to grammar.

Meaning—the Reduction of Uncertainty

Most of the discussion of meaning will be postponed because we shall find that whatever meaning is, it must be defined with respect to a listener or reader. For the present it will be adequate (though hardly satisfying) to define meaning in the same way that we have defined other aspects of information, as the reduction of uncertainty. We shall not get involved in the philosophical question of the nature of meaning, as old as Western civilization itself, nor in the equally tenuous question of the nature of the cerebral activity that underlies comprehension.

Instead, we shall simply accept that a listener or reader who has comprehended a message has had a certain set of alternatives reduced. Of course, it is not easy to identify these alternatives when we talk about sentence meaning. If we are concerned with letter or word identification, there is no problem in specifying the alternatives (or at least, their general class). The potential informativeness of a sentence lies in the extent to which it will reduce uncertainty in the listener, while the degree to which the receiver comprehends a sentence lies in the number of alternatives that are eliminated. Such a theory of meaning implies that one cannot discuss the "meaning" of a sentence as such, but only its meaning to a particular listener.[3] This relative approach is not as tidy as an "absolute" one that looks for intrinsic meaning in every possible utterance, but it has the advantage of being rather more practical. If we think of the ways in which we normally test whether someone has actually comprehended a statement, it is not with respect to any intrinsic qualities of the statement but rather with the behavior of the person himself, whether he answers questions in a particular way or pursues a particular course of action. In other words, we expect the behavior of the receiver to be more constrained than it would

be if he had not been presented with the sentence, or had not comprehended it.

However, while refraining from any attempt to give an account of the
meaning of "meaning", or of any abstract meaning of sentences, we can
begin to ask how the meaning of a sentence is made up and how it is com-
municated to the receiver. These are questions relevant both to listening
and reading, and the central problem as we shall face it can be summed up
in a single statement:

The meaning of a sentence is not *the sum total of the meanings of the
individual words of that sentence.*

This is another question that we shall have to approach obliquely; otherwise, we are going to get involved in terribly complex matters such as
what is the meaning of a word. Because although we want to hold that sentences are not made up of word meanings, it would appear that words only
get meaning as a virtue of occurring in sentences. In fact, it is very difficult to see what meaning a word in isolation can have. Even nouns, which
might seem the easiest class of words to account for, present difficulties. It
is certainly far from true that every object has one name and every word
one meaning. Most common words have many more meanings than one, in
fact the more common a word, the more meanings it usually has. Also it is
far from the case that every object has just one name—the family pet, for
example, can be called a canine, a dog, a boxer, Rover, and a variety of
other titles including, of course, "family pet" and "that slavering brute".
What is the "real name" of the animal? There is not one. The appropriate
name for it is like meaning—it depends on the listener, and the extent of
his uncertainty. In talking to a member of the family, the name "Rover" is
adequate, or simply "the animal"; on other occasions no single word
would be adequate and the name would have to be qualified as "that
brown dog over there" or "the large boxer". Everything depends on the
knowledge of the receiver and the alternatives from among which he has to
distinguish Rover. The same animal will also be described in different
ways to the same person depending on the characteristics of other dogs
that are around. What then does a word like "dog" mean? The dictionary
tells us that it means "any of a large and varied group of domesticated animals related to the fox, wolf, and jackal"—but that surely is not the meaning of "dog" in the sentence "Beware of the dog". Let alone such expressions as hot dog, top dog, putting on the dog, dirty dog, lucky dog, or
going to the dogs.

Before we worry too much about the difficulty of finding meaning for
words, we ought to remember that the very existence of words is in some
doubt, and may well be an artifact of the writing system. At least in writ-

ing we can provide a definition of a word—as something with a white space on either side. But in spoken language, as we have seen, there is no natural segmentation of the physical representation of speech into words. Where space does occur in speech it is just as likely to occur within words —"wes tend"—as between them. We shall see that children learning to talk either acquire groups of words that they use as one long word— "allgone", "drinkamilk", "gowalk"—or else single words that they use as entire sentences—"drink", "tired", "no". Children at an age when reading instruction may be begun often cannot say how many words are in a sentence, either spoken or written.

Linguists have the same trouble as children in distinguishing what words are. A word cannot be the smallest significant unit of meaning, because a word like "dogs" has two units—the noun "dog" plus an "s" that indicates the plural. In fact, there is a special word for the smallest significant unit of meaning, morpheme, which functions in many of the same ways as phonemes and graphemes. For example, there are allomorphs, or functionally equivalent forms, for the same morpheme. The plural morpheme can be represented in a variety of ways, "s" (pronounced as either /s/ or /z/), "es", "ren" (as in "children"), as nothing (fish, sheep), and as a change of vowel ("man"–"men"), and so forth.[4]

It is not necessary to pursue the argument about the nature of words, or their meaning, because it is quite clear that sentences may have meanings that are both far more than and far different from the meanings of their component words. For example *The man ate the fish* and *The fish ate the man* contain exactly the same words, yet they have quite different meanings. A *Maltese cross* is not the same as a *cross Maltese,* any more than a *Venetian blind* is a *blind Venetian.* A house that is *pretty ugly* is not exactly ugly, but is certainly not pretty. Obviously, the words in all these examples do not combine in any simple fashion to form the meaning of the whole sentence; in fact the meaning of many of the individual words in the sentence would appear to be quite different from the meaning we would probably say they have in isolation.

However, it is also not adequate to say that the meaning of words in a sentence depends on the order that they are in. Does the phrase "old men and women" refer to *old men* and *old women* or to *old men* and *women of any age?* Does the sentence "Cooking apples can be enjoyable" mean *cooking apples is an enjoyable occupation* or *cooking apples are an enjoyable fruit?* It is sometimes said that the sentences in this paragraph are "ambiguous on the surface level" because their physical representation has more than one meaning. The ambiguity can be removed by bracketing the parts of the sentence together to show how the parts are related:

old (*men and women*) vs. (*old men*) *and* (*women*)
(*cooking apples*) (*can be enjoyable*) vs. (*cooking*) (*apples*) (*can be enjoyable*)

But here are other sentences that cannot be disambiguated by any form of bracketing—there is no way of splitting up "The chicken was too hot to eat" to indicate whether the temperature of the chicken affected its eating or its being eaten. There is no way of clarifying "The shooting of the hunters was terrible" without changing the order of the words.

It would seem that in order to understand the meaning of sentences (whether spoken or written) we need to know much more than the meaning of the words of which they are constructed. There must be certain rules that the speaker uses to produce sentences and that the listener uses to comprehend sentences. These rules, known to both the speaker and the listener, are, of course, vital sources of information for the communication process that is language. There is *no* information in the words that comprise a sentence unless we also have the information about the way they are put together. "Eats fish man the the" are the words of one of our sample sentences in alphabetical order; in this sequence they mean nothing. But the words also mean nothing in the sequence "the man eats the fish" unless we also know the rules by which words are put together. You probably know how difficult it is to read anything in a foreign language, even with the help of a dictionary, if you have not really mastered the grammar.

We have just met the key word—"grammar". Whatever the meaning of a particular piece of language may be—whatever the *deep-level* interpretation of a statement—it is related to the *surface* physical representation— the sound or the sight of the statement—by the rules of grammar.

We shall now consider the function of grammar, or more specifically the rules of syntax, *the rules by which sentences are ordered, which mediate between meaning and surface representation. For the speaker or writer, the rules of grammar are not just the rules that he applies to organize his statements—they are the rules he implicitly assumes the receiver knows in order to be able to extract the meaning from statements. For the listener or the reader, grammar is the key to comprehending language.*

Grammar—The Generator of Language

The following account of grammar could be controversial at a couple of levels. In the first place, the account will be based on one particular approach to grammar that is called both *generative* and *transformational* and is associated primarily with a linguist named Noam Chomsky.

There are linguistic theories that are alternative to Chomsky's; in fact his views have provoked a good deal of disagreement. However, Chomsky's model of grammar is one that has proved stimulating and productive to psychologists endeavoring to understand language as a dynamic human skill, and is particularly appropriate to understanding the process of reading. So the model is being used even though it may be offensive to those linguists who do not agree with Chomsky. But the account of grammar may also disconcert proponents of the Chomsky school because it does not do credit to the depth and intricacy of their ideas and almost certainly because it is not up to date; linguistics as a science is progressing so rapidly that even weekly mimeographed newssheets distributed among the initiates do not fully reflect the shifting theoretical positions and rapid accumulation of evidence. In view of this continual change, and our particular needs in trying to construct a theory of reading rather than explain a theory of linguistics, it is perhaps excusable to be both selective and informal in the manner in which we draw our insights.

The first and most general insight is: *a grammar is a set of rules for distinguishing the grammatical from the ungrammatical sentences of a language.* This is probably what you thought a grammar was all along. But instead of regarding grammar as a static set of rules that provide examples of acceptable and unacceptable constructions, the new view of grammar is of a device that will actually produce grammatical sentences itself, which is rather a different matter. The relatively simple rule that tells us that the head noun and a verb of a sentence *should* agree in person and number is quite different from a rule that will produce only sentences in which such agreement occurs. Yet this is the aim for a dynamic model of grammar, which will distinguish grammatical from ungrammatical sentences in the following way: *a grammar is a device capable of producing all the grammatical sentences of a language and no others.*

It might be asked why there is a need to construct such a *generative* grammar. The answer is that the number of possible sentences in a language such as English is limitless, and that practically every sentence that we hear and produce is one that we have never heard before. Because there is so much novelty in language, the rules of grammar must be capable of producing new sentences; no one could learn how to use a language simply by learning examples of sentences to be used in different situations. A child does not learn to repeat sentences, he learns how to produce them.

One reason that there is no end to the number of different sentences that a grammar must be able to produce is that there is no limit to the length of a sentence. We can make sentences as long as we like without being ungrammatical (although, of course, we may well become incomprehensible for other reasons). Only a manic lawyer would attempt to construct a sentence of 400 words, but there is no *grammatical* reason why everyone should not do so. And if anyone claimed to have produced the ultimate sentence on the basis of length, we could always refute him and produce a longer one by inserting an extra adjective or clause in his own sentence.

As we shall see later in this chapter, a theoretical model of grammar that can produce sentences has a particular advantage in that we can use the model at least as part of an actual model of a language user. If we have a theory of how a set of rules can produce and distinguish only grammatical sentences of a language, then we also have a theory about the linguistic processes of an actual user of the language.

To give a flavor of how a generative grammar might work, I shall start by taking apart a simple sentence in order to make a miniature grammar of a type called *phrase-structure grammars.* Note that it is not necessary to agree with the logical process by which the grammar is devised; the test of whether the grammar is effective lies in the way it works, not in the method by which it was derived. But it is easier to understand what the grammar is about if we begin from the outside and start by analyzing a sentence. The sentence we shall consider is:

The angry dog chases a cowardly man.

We shall analyze this sentence by breaking it into parts that go together. If asked to divide the sentence into two parts, most people would put the break in the place indicated by the following bracketing:

(*The angry dog*) (*chases a cowardly man*).

One logical justification for dividing the sentence in the above manner is that each part can be replaced by a single word while still leaving a complete sentence:

(*The angry dog*) (*acts*)   or   (*Something*) (*chases a cowardly man*).

But it is impossible to make such a simple substitution if the sentence is divided in any other way.

We shall now label the various parts. It does not really matter what we call them; we could call them Part 1 and Part 2, but it will be convenient later if we give them some conventional labels. We shall call the sentence as a whole *sentence* (*S* for short), the first part *noun phrase* (*NP*) and the second part *verb phrase* (*VP*). Using these labels, we have a *rule* for the first subdivision of the sentence:

$S \rightarrow NP + VP.$

This rule is an example of a *rewrite rule,* which means always that the

symbol on the left of the rewrite sign → can be replaced by the symbols
on the right.

We shall not bother to analyze the *NP* any further than to say that it
consists of three parts: the word "the", which we shall call a *determiner*
(*D*); "angry", which we shall call a *qualifier* (*Q*); and "dog", which we shall
call a *noun* (*N*). Again, we are being quite arbitrary in naming the parts; it
would not affect the eventual grammar if we called the three parts *X, Y,*
and *Z.* We can now derive a new rule:

$$NP \rightarrow D + (Q) + N.$$

The *Q* has been put in brackets to indicate that it appears less necessary
in the phrase than the two other parts; we could construct a sequence beginning *the dog* as well as one beginning *the angry dog* and still have a
sentence, but we could not (in this case) drop either the determiner or the
noun. Since the preceding rules have reduced us to the level of individual
words, we can also add

$$D \rightarrow the$$
$$Q \rightarrow angry$$
$$N \rightarrow dog.$$

The words are called *terminal symbols,* because they are not rewritten.
If we attend to the other part of the original sentence, the *VP,* we find that
it subdivides into two parts:

(*chases*) (*a cowardly man*).

The first part seems to be quite a new element, which we shall label *verb*
(*V*). *V* is a new element because we could not use it in place of any of the
other elements, whether the entire *NP* or the *D, Q,* or *N.* However, the
second part of the *VP,* "a cowardly man", clearly contains the same kinds
of elements as the first *NP*—"a" would appear to be a *D* like "the", "cowardly" a *Q* like "angry", and "man" an *N* like "dog". Note that we are allocating these different elements to the same categories, not because they
are the same "parts of speech", but because they are substitutable. Thus
we have the additional rules:

$$VP \rightarrow V + NP$$
$$V \rightarrow chases$$
$$D \rightarrow a$$
$$Q \rightarrow cowardly$$
$$N \rightarrow man.$$

We can combine all the rules we have established into the following set,
which is our miniature grammar:

$$S \rightarrow NP + VP$$
$$NP \rightarrow D + (Q) + N$$
$$VP \rightarrow V + NP$$
$$V \rightarrow chases$$
$$D \rightarrow the, a$$
$$Q \rightarrow angry, cowardly$$
$$N \rightarrow dog, man.$$

Now comes the test of the grammar. By applying the above rules, can we construct only sentences that would be accepted as grammatical by native speakers of the language? We set the device in motion by starting with S and seeing where the rules take us:

> S is rewritten as $NP + VP$.
> NP gives us a D, a Q if we want one, and an N.

Let us arbitrarily select "a" for the D, no Q, and "man" for the N.

> VP gives us a V and an NP.

For V we must choose "chases", for the NP we can select, say, "the angry man" as the D, Q, and N. We can now examine the terminal symbols to see what we have:

> *A dog chases the angry man.*

This is quite different from our original sentence, but still grammatical. We could also have produced a small number of other grammatical sentences—such as the original "The angry dog chases a cowardly man" and "A cowardly dog chases a man" and "The angry man chases a dog" —but no ungrammatical one. In short, we have a sentence producing device.

Of course, the device we have just constructed is rather limited, but we could make it much more powerful by including a few more rules, which we could induce by examining other samples of sentences in the language, and by adding a lot more terminal symbols. We could make it an infinite machine, capable of producing an endless variety of sentences, by the introduction of rules that permit the continual repetition of elements:

> *A very very very very very . . . very angry dog. . . .*

Instead of generating two sentences, such as *The dog chases the man; The man climbs a tree,* we could combine them in a single complex sentence: *The dog chases the man who climbs a tree.* The final example, however, more properly belongs to a more powerful type of rule called a *transformation,* which has certain advantages over the "phrase structure" type of rule that we have considered so far.

Transformational Grammar

There are some basic disadvantages to grammars made up of phrase structure rules only. One disadvantage is that one set of rules would be required to construct sentences of the form

The dog chases a man

and another set to construct a sentence like

A man is chased by the dog;

although one would think that the derivations of both sentences have a good deal in common and that it would be uneconomical not to take advantage of the fact. Furthermore, a phrase structure grammar alone contains nothing that would indicate how the two preceding sentences are related to each other, and to such sentences as "A dog has chased the man", "Does a dog chase the man?", "A dog doesn't chase the man", and so forth.

Transformational rules start with the same basic elements—"dog", "chase", "man" in the above examples—and convert them into different kinds of sentences—active, passive, interrogative, negative, etc.—by imposing a special organization on the elements rather than by rewrite rules. Transformational rules also help to show that some sentences are very different, although this may not be apparent on the surface level. "I was seated by the fountain" and "I was soaked by the fountain" have an identical surface structure, but are basically quite different, as we can see if we try to turn them from passive into active—"The fountain soaked me", but surely not "The fountain seated me". Transformational rules cope with the manipulation of sentence elements to permit sentences to be joined together. In other words, transformations are particular ways of translating the underlying or deep structure of a sentence—the basic elements and their interrelations—into a variety of surface representations without losing account of underlying relationships. Conversely, a knowledge of transformational rules permits the receiver to move from the surface structure of the sentence, which as we have seen lacks a lot of essential information, to the meaning.

Transformational rules might appear to be the key for understanding how we can produce and comprehend language after all, despite the absence of a one-to-one correspondence between sound and meaning.

What Kind of Language Is Reading?

In Chapter 4 we shall examine how a child learns to talk, and see what clues we can derive about the process by which a child learns to read.

For some theorists (and other casual observers) the process of reading is easily explained—reading is a matter of "decoding" printed symbols into sound and then extracting meaning from sound. In a later chapter this simplistic view will be criticized in detail; I shall argue that not only do fluent readers not convert written words into sounds before they can comprehend writing, but that in fact it is generally impossible for them to do so—fluent reading is accomplished too fast for the translation into sound to occur, and the prior comprehension of meaning is a prerequisite for sounding out many sentences.

To some extent it is not inappropriate to regard written language as subsidiary to speech. Speech almost certainly occurred much earlier in man's history than writing, and while every community of men of whom we have a record has a developed spoken language, only a minority have writing systems. Spoken language appears to have developed spontaneously in several areas of the globe—and all known languages have a number of "universal" features in common, suggesting that the capacity to develop and learn language is to a large extent a "natural" phenomenon, reflecting an integral part of man's biological inheritance. But relatively few of the world's languages have an alphabetic writing system such as English, and this system is so "artificial" that it is sometimes claimed that it was invented only once, by the Greeks as an improvement to an earlier Semitic system.[5]

However, while written language may be of recent origin compared with speech, and its original dependence on spoken language is obvious, it does not necessarily follow that language can only be read through the mediation of sound. After all, deaf people learn to read. At the surface level, written and spoken language have little in common beyond the individual words. We may have been taught at school that written language was a model for speech, but we have only to examine written examples of spoken language to see that even the most elegant examples have little in common with the kind of language I am using in this book. We rarely complete sentences in speech the way we almost invariably complete them in print. We are far more repetitious, and much less "polished", in speech than in writing. And we accompany our speech with many nonverbal grunts and shrugs and other gestures that are only slightly an alternative to punctuation in writing. Speech and writing are used for different purposes and make quite different kinds of demands on the receiver. Speech has to be comprehended immediately—the listener generally cannot go back for a sentence he missed the first time, nor has he much control over the rate at which the material is delivered to him; he does, however, have the advantages of being able to ask questions, and he can receive supplementary nonverbal information. The listener can also sometimes provide the speaker with immediate feedback, indicating the extent to which the message is reducing his uncertainty. What the reader loses in supplementary information and immediate feedback he gains by being able to organize the material at his own pace and by being able to read segments more than once. It is probably no coincidence that the speeds at which most people seem to be able to read and listen to language appear to be roughly the same. The average reading speed of about 200 words a minute is probably rooted in the childhood emphasis on oral reading—200 words a minute is an average speaking rate determined largely by physiological factors related to the structure of the vocal system. But even moderately skilled readers can read much faster than 200 words a minute if the material they are reading is "easy" and they are not under any constraint to identify every word, while trained readers can cover (but not read one by one) many thousands of words in a minute.

In a chapter on *phonics,* I shall be at some pains to show that the translation from written symbol to sound is not easily accomplished. In short, written language may quite reasonably be regarded as a manifestation of language quite independent from the spoken form. The two forms are related in that there are complex and somewhat imperfect rules for "mapping" between speech and writing. But it is by no means necessary to believe, although it is widely assumed, that writing is speech (rather than "meaning") written down, and that reading is the conversion of writing to spoken language (rather than a direct conversion to "meaning"). This book takes an opposite view.

Whatever the relation of speech to writing, the fact that almost all children have acquired a good deal of verbal fluency before they face the task of learning to read has a dual significance for understanding the reading process. In the first place children have a basis of language that is obviously relevant to the process of learning to read—the written language is basically the same language as that of speech, even if it has special lexical, syntactic, and communicational aspects. But equally important, study of the manner in which children learn to speak and understand spoken language can provide considerable insight into the manner in which they might approach the task of learning to read.

References

The approach—although by no means all of the detail—of the present chapter derives mainly from the work of two men, Noam Chomsky and George A. Miller. Chomsky should not be read by the novice interested in finding out more about his theories—his linguistic publications are generally very specialized and his output so prolific that he tends to put them out of date within a few months. With these caveats, I shall cite two of his works that are milestones:

N. CHOMSKY, *Syntactic Structures* (The Hague: Mouton, 1957).

N. CHOMSKY, *Aspects of the Theory of Syntax* (Cambridge, Mass.: M. I. T. Press, 1965).

Miller, on the other hand, can be read by a range of audiences and is a facile distiller of information. Essential reading if the questions discussed in this chapter are to be pursued further is:

G. A. MILLER, Some preliminaries to psycholinguistics, *American Psychologist,* 20 (1965), 15–20. Reprinted in a number of places including De Cecco, and Oldfield and Marshall (listed on page 10).

Two fairly elementary collections of papers that will further help to explicate many of the technical terms and topics raised in this chapter are:

JANET A. EMIG, J. T. FLEMING, and HELEN M. POPP (eds.), *Language and Learning* (New York: Harcourt, Brace & World, Inc., 1966).

A. A. HILL (ed.), *Linguistics Today* (New York: Basic Books, Inc., 1969).

A source of rather more specialized papers on language and its psychological aspects is:

S. SAPORTA (ed.), *Psycholinguistics: A Book of Readings* (New York: Holt, Rinehart and Winston, Inc., 1961).

A solid but lucid introductory linguistics tome is:

H. A. GLEASON, *Linguistics and English Grammar* (New York: Holt, Rinehart and Winston, Inc., 1965).

Short, authoritative, and technical at the introductory level of the topic of transformational grammar is:

R. A. JACOBS and P. S. ROSENBAUM, *English Transformational Grammar* (Waltham, Mass.: Blaisdell Publishing Company, 1968).

Finally, a psychologist who writes literately and imaginatively about language (from a pre-Chomskian point of view in the book cited):

R. BROWN, *Words and Things* (New York: The Free Press, 1958).

Notes

1. W. LABOV, Stages in the acquisition of standard English. In R. W. SHUY (ed.), *Social Dialects and Language Learning* (Champaign, Ill.: National Council of Teachers of English, 1965).

2. A. M. LIBERMAN, F. S. COOPER, D. P. SHANKWEILER, and M. STUDDERT-KENNEDY, Perception of the speech code, *Psychological Review,* **54** (1957), 358–368. Reprinted in Haber (listed on page 27).

3. D. R. OLSON, Language and thought: aspects of a cognitive theory of semantics, *Psychological Review* (in press).

4. See page 46 for further discussion of the problem of defining the word "word".

5. L. BLOOMFIELD, *Language* (New York: Holt, Rinehart and Winston, Inc., 1933), Chapter 17 (part of a section also published separately as *Language History,* 1965). Giving the Greeks all the credit is based on a fine point of definition; for example a

good case can also be made for the independent and alphabetic Sanskrit three millennia B.C. It all depends on whether you want to say that an alphabet must have vowel symbols that are separate from but equal to those for consonants. There is more about the development of writing in Chapter 12.

4

The Acquisition of Language

In Chapter 3 the idea was introduced that a grammar of a language may be regarded as a set of rules which, if applied to a relatively small set of elements, will generate an infinite number of grammatical sentences and no others. Although linguists have been unable to provide anything like a complete description of the rules of grammar, the great majority of children develop a set for themselves within the space of about two years. At the age of about 18 months [1] a child produces his first two-word sentence, and by 3½ years he appears to have mastered all the important rules of his language. His vocabulary may not be as rich as that of adults, and he may not talk about such complex events, but the child has constructed for himself a grammar that gives him the competence to produce and comprehend all the possible types of sentences used by the language community in which he lives.

Spoken language is literally self-taught, to a degree far beyond the appreciation of most parents and many specialists in child development. Not even the most accomplished linguists know enough about language to teach a child how to talk, let alone the average parent. If anyone did know enough about language to write a complete description of a grammar, one could program a computer to converse or translate, but this is far from being achieved. Most children learn to speak without any need for formal instruction, therefore there are relatively few books on such topics as

"Teach your child to speak" or "Why Johnny can't talk". The process of first language-learning proceeds in an extremely rapid, smooth, and predictable sequence, indicating that a child is well equipped biologically both to use *and to learn* language. Before looking at how a child learns to speak, and considering its relevance for learning to read, we shall look at some evidence for the view that language learning is largely instinctive (although individual languages, as systems for communicating, are, of course, a cultural invention).

Universal Aspects of Language

One of several different kinds of argument used to support the view that language ability is part of our biological inheritance is that there are many features common to all the languages of the world which one would not expect to occur so frequently by chance. All of the 5000 or so languages that linguists have distinguished contain family resemblances that are not *logically* necessary and that cannot be accounted for by interaction among groups speaking the earliest languages of man. In other words, there could conceivably be many different kinds of language in the world, but there are not. And the reason offered for the absence of many logically possible types of language is that all actual languages fall within a relatively small range of alternatives permitted by biological constraints on the mental activity of man. The features that all known languages have in common are known as *linguistic universals*. For example, all natural languages appear to have both a deep and a surface structure. (The language we learn as children and speak in our everyday life is sometimes referred to as a "natural" language to distinguish it from the "artificial" languages that men have devised to communicate with inanimate objects, such as computers, or with lower animals than man.) It is not logically necessary that this division of levels, separating sound from meaning, should exist, in fact in computer languages it is absolutely essential that all the meaning should be represented in the surface structure because computers do not have an innate biological component that enables them to intuit any aspect of meaning not specifically represented in the input message. Many of the artificial languages devised for computers are logically much less complex than natural languages, and ought to be easier for humans to learn. But common experience is that humans are not very good at learning the rules (the "grammar") of artificial languages, almost certainly because we just are not built the way computers are.

Another universal of natural languages is that they all have a phonology, which again is not absolutely logically necessary. We can communicate visually, and ought to be able to dispense with sound, but no language does. Moreover, the phonology of all natural languages seems to be restricted to within a range of between 20 and 50 phonemes although different languages may have quite different sets. The English language has about 46 phonemes depending on which dialect you speak and how you care to define a phoneme. But there is no logical reason why a language should not have 100 different phonemes—we are capable of producing that number of distinctive sounds, and different languages include quite different kinds of sounds in their own set. Similarly, there is no reason why a language should not get by with only ten phonemes or even two —the Morse code manages with just a dot and a dash.

Contrary to popular view, there are no languages without nouns and verbs. One could imagine a language that does not include these "parts of speech". Nouns and verbs are not given by the way the world is made— you cannot actually distinguish noun-things from verb-events in the physical world, in terms of reference. Instead, grammarians have been forced to define nouns and verbs in terms of their function in a sentence. One could imagine a language that just has nouns, in which events are represented by changes in state, or an all-verb language of happenings, but neither occurs. All languages also seem to have a limitation on the type of rule for the conjunction of subject, object, and verb in simple declarative sentences. There are six possible ways to order the three elements: you could have subject + object + verb, or subject + verb + object, or object + subject + verb, and so forth. But of the six possible different ways in which one could order the sequence only three appear to exist. Associated in a complex but quite systematic way with each of these three alternative subject–object–verb constructions are no fewer than 45 other rules of word order.

Because of such basic similarities of language, the view has been developed that the task confronting a newborn infant is not so much to learn what language is as to learn the idiosyncratic aspects of the actual language spoken in his own community. As we shall see, a child is born ready to start speaking a unique language—which adults denigrate with the name "babytalk"—and that he progressively amends this language until it comes closer and closer to that spoken by his parents. I shall employ the useful oversimplification, adopted by many linguists and psychologists, that a child learning to talk is systematically trying out alternative rules to see which ones apply—that he is "testing hypotheses", literally conducting linguistic experiments, to discover specifically what kind of language is talked around him.

Two other sources of evidence support the view that basic skills in language are innate; they concern the idiosyncratic nature of child language and the fact that its progressive refinement into adult language follows an orderly sequence.[2] Thorough analyses of the verbal productions of infants have shown that the language they speak is neither a miniature adult language nor a deformed one. Very little language learning is attributable to imitation, because very few of the constructions that children utter are arrangements of words that they could possibly have heard their parents utter. In fact one of the most difficult things to ask a child to do is to imitate either a sound or a phrase that he has not already spontaneously produced for himself. Children change their ways to conform to adult language, but they do this by starting with a language of their own, not by starting from nothing.

It has also been shown that the sequence in which language develops in children is not only orderly and systematic, but is closely related to physical and motor aspects of development, which are certainly not associated with the imitation of adult models. For example, babies usually begin to babble—the first stage in their development of language—at the same time that they first hold their heads up, and they say their first "words" like "mama" when they can sit up unsupported. The ability to stand is accompanied by the demonstration of a small set of words, the ability to walk by the expression of small phrases, and running is accompanied by the mastery of prepositions and pronouns.

Learning to read does not appear to have the same orderly sequence of stages as learning to speak, but while the actual skills are different, the processes by which a child sets out to learn speaking and reading have many apparent similarities. In particular, both processes can be viewed as a progressive endeavor to discover the relevant category and equivalence rules. In looking at this process of rule learning more closely, we might start, like a baby, with babbling.

The Development of Language

Although all languages consist of 50 or fewer phonemes, the actual phonemes that are used may vary considerably, depending on the language. The number of possible phonemes is very much greater than the number used in any one language. When a baby starts to babble, at the age of three months, he may produce *all* of the possible phonemes. He does not build up from silence to the sounds of his own language, but starts with all possible language sounds and gradually eliminates those not used by the people around him. For those of us who are not skilled polyglots, the only time that we find it physically possible to utter sounds that are not in our native language is when we are babes in arms.

It is perhaps trivial to point out that the language a child learns is the language of his parents only if it also happens to be the language spoken around him. A child of Chinese parents who is adopted and raised in Boston will speak American with a fluent accent and have as much difficulty as the rest of us in learning Chinese if confronted with the task in his teens.

During the first few years of life children find no particular difficulty in learning *any* language. They are not born more ready to speak one than another. At three months it is impossible to distinguish the babbling of a Chinese child from that of an American. At the age of six months, however, this is not the case. A six-month-old baby may not be able to speak a word of his native tongue, but he is "babbling" in French or German or English. There is experimental evidence that the "native language" of a six-month-old child can be deduced from a tape recording of his babbling. The baby is demonstrating that he has acquired rules for the sounds that are produced around him.[3] But it would be an oversimplification to say that he has learned these sounds by imitating his parents. The baby acquires them the way a sculptor "acquires" a statue—by disposing of surplus material that he originally had available for use if required.

By the age of one year, many children are speaking single words: "drink", "mama", "bye-bye". Are they imitating their parents when they produce these words? Again the answer is that the elements are the result of successive approximation, and not imitation in the sense that the child is aping an adult model. For one thing, many child words are quite unique —the child could not possibly have heard his parent saying them (unless the parent was imitating the child, which is not an infrequent grown-up pastime). Further, the child uses these first words in quite a different manner from the way that adults use them. While adults put words together in accordance with a grammar, one-year-old children do not. Instead, infants use single words to express entire sentences ("holophrases" is the technical term)—an economy beyond the competence of grown-ups. Underlying the single words of the holophrastic stage may be quite complex meanings, "drink", for example, might mean anything from "Bring me a drink" or "Look at that drink" to "I didn't like that drink and so I threw it all over the floor".

Contrary to popular parental belief, the child is not learning words and then finding meanings for them. Instead he is acquiring or inventing words, which may or may not have a close relation to adult language, to meet his own particular requirements and represent meanings which he needs to express.

Even at the holophrastic stage, babies are speaking more language than a chimpanzee could ever learn. While chimpanzee words are literally *signs,* in that there is a one-to-one correspondence between each sound and its meaning, a human infant is already communicating complex underlying thoughts through his single-word utterances. He has the underlying structure, but not the transformations to put words together at the surface level.

By 18 months, however, many children have acquired a powerful syntactic rule. At this age they are producing two- or three-word phrases, like "allgone milk" or "see baby" or "my big truck". Two aspects of this development are significant: first, these short sentences are certainly not imitated from parents (how many adults would say "allgone-milk"?) but are genuinely constructed by the child himself; and, second, the constructions are not random. A child, who may have a vocabulary of two or three hundred words by this time, does not put his words together in random order in his first sentences—he has a system, a rule. This rule is developed by children for their own use, for it does not occur in adult language.

The condition for the first rule is that all words of the vocabulary are ordered into one of two classes, which some researchers call *Pivot* and *Open*. The Pivot class is relatively small and "closed"—new words are not added very frequently—while the Open class, relatively large, is the class to which most new words are added. The first rule can be specified as follows:

$$S \rightarrow (P) + O + (O)$$
$$P \rightarrow allgone, see, my, \ldots$$
$$O \rightarrow milk, baby, big, truck, \ldots .$$

We have already met S (for "sentence"), and the rewrite sign $\rightarrow$; P means a Pivot class word, O means an Open class word, and the brackets indicate that the item is optional—we can include it or not. The rule can thus be interpreted as follows:

A sentence can be written as an Open class word optionally preceded by a Pivot class word and optionally followed by another Open class word. Among the sentences that can be produced are "allgone big truck", "see milk", "my baby" but not "big truck allgone", "milk see", or "baby my".

The words in each class vary, of course, from child to child, and a word that occurs in one child's Pivot class may be found in another child's Open. But all children appear to go through the same first-rule stage, although no children are explicitly taught it. The acquisition of the rule is one of the universals of language development in children.

It might be asked what justification there is for asserting that children have such a rule as $S \rightarrow (P) + O + (O)$. Obviously, children do not tell the researchers that they have it, or that they have the two classes to which all their words are allocated. The explanation is that the researchers have formulated the rule themselves as a method of describing child language at that period; they have observed the manner in which words appear to occur systematically in a particular child's early sentences, and tested the rule by predicting that certain sentences that they have not already heard could occur, but that other combinations of words which infringe the rule could not occur, and then tested their predictions against the sentences they have subsequently heard the child make. When the researchers' rule successfully predicts the child's performance, then it is regarded as a reasonable reflection of the implicit "rule" that the child himself uses to produce the sentences.

From the first coarse-grained Pivot–Open class distinction, children go on to make successive differentiations within each class, progressively making their language more complex and gradually bringing it closer and closer to that spoken by adults. While a child is speaking a rule-governed language of his own, he at no time throws words together randomly, and at no time can he be said to be slavishly imitating an adult model.

Sometimes it is very clear that a child is not imitating. One very revealing example of the manner in which children discover rules rather than copy examples lies in the highly predictable sequence in which almost all children utter *incorrect* forms of very common verbs after they have apparently learned the correct forms. The phenomenon occurs among "strong" verbs like "come", "go", and "drink" which occur frequently in the language and which have irregular past tense inflections such as "came", "went", and "drank". Frequently a child produces these past tense constructions correctly until he discovers the + *ed* rule for the "regular" construction *walk–walked, climb–climbed, laugh–laughed.* As a demonstration that he has learned the past tense rule, the child suddenly begins to lose the correct forms *came, went, drank* and to overgeneralize the + *ed* rule and say *comed, goed, drinked.* These are obviously not forms that the child has heard his parents or anyone else utter—he is trying out a new rule, and does not use it correctly until he gets the information that certain words such as *come, go,* and *drink* are exceptions.

In fact it can be shown that imitation of adult speech is one of the hardest tasks that can be set. If an adult says to a child at the Pivot–Open class stage *Say "the milk is all gone",* the child will reply *allgone milk* or whatever construction has the same meaning according to his own rules. It is not simply that the child cannot repeat the utterance he hears the adult make—it is unlikely that he actually *hears* the difference between what the adult says and his own version. Unless he is specifically listening for the sounds, rather than the meaning, he will "hear" the adult phrase in the terms of the rule that he himself would use to express a similar meaning. The same principle applies with the sounds themselves. If a child calls an engine an *oing-oing,* then nine times out of ten when an exasperated parent says to him *Now listen carefully, say "engine"* the child with the best will in the world will respond: *oing-oing.* The phenomenon is reminiscent of the view in linguistics that differences are detected only if they are contrastive—which in some circumstances might be interpreted as meaning that one cannot hear distinctions that one does not oneself make. The dilemma of the speech therapist is that very often the problem is not that the child will not *produce* the particular phonological or syntactic form that is required, but that he cannot *hear* it. We shall see that the same problem occurs in classrooms where teacher and students speak different dialects. A child who pronounces "guard" and "god" in exactly the same way is likely to experience nothing but frustration and confusion when his teacher says "Do not say 'guard', say 'god' ", because he cannot hear any difference between the two.

The rules that a child acquires for constructing and pronouncing his language are also the rules that he uses for interpreting (and actually hearing) the language of others.

The picture that has been presented shows a child from the very beginning of his life looking for rules that will provide him with the key to the language community in which he finds himself. The child has rules for learning rules, and he tests to see which particular rules apply. We shall see in due course that precisely the same kind of argument may be applied to reading—that basically a child is equipped with every skill that he needs in order to read and to learn to read; all that he needs to discover is the particular rules that apply. When we view the role of the child in this new light, we also see a different role for the adult in the language-learning process. We can perhaps gain some insights into the task of the reading teacher if we understand the function of adults when a child is learning how to speak.

The task for the language-learning child is to find out what are the rules of grammar—to uncover the structure that lies beneath the surface of every utterance and that bridges the gap between sound and meaning. What the child does is try out alternative rules for constructing the kinds of sentences that he hears. He never "just repeats" a sentence that he hears an adult utter; what would be the point of that? He never tries to learn by rote the sentences that adults produce; that would also be pointless, because almost every sentence we hear and use is a new one. What the child needs to learn is how to produce and understand all the potential sentences of his language, that is to say, to learn the rules by which the sentences of his language are produced. And, of course, that is something that no mother even attempts to teach her child. The child in effect performs a detection task—he hears a sentence and tries to determine a possible rule by which it could be produced. Then he tests whether the rule is correct, by using it to produce a few sample sentences and seeing whether they are acceptable as sentences of the language. This is what is meant when it is sometimes said that a child is "testing hypotheses".

In this light, the responsibility of parents becomes rather clear, although it is quite different from the role traditionally attributed to them. First, a child must be given credit for knowing more about learning language than an adult does. It is one of the paradoxes of growing up that as we learn to speak one language we lose our facility for learning others together with all memory of what it was like to learn our first language. But we can make use of a child's apparent knowledge of the best way to learn by keeping him exposed to plenty of adult language. The adult who does not help his child is the one who tries to speak "baby talk", which is as about as helpful to a child trying to master adult language as speaking English in a phony French accent would be to a Frenchman trying to learn our language.

Second, the primary role of the adult is to provide a child with information when he needs it. The child does not want, and cannot use, little snippets of information thrown at him arbitrarily in a formal learning situation. What a child needs is feedback to tell him whether he is observing the significant differences of his language in a particular situation. The simplest way to provide feedback at the right time is perhaps to regard every utterance made by a child as having a double function: the first being the expression of a need or feeling, and the second the test of a rule. In fact very often only the "test" situation applies; children frequently play "language games", with adults, with each other, and by themselves, in which there is no real concern with communication at all but simply a running through of programs or possibilities for constructing words and sentences.[4] The nonsense noises that the child makes up, like the new words or nonsense sounds that adults themselves may produce when asked, invariably reflect the rules (the regularities) of the language.

If the preceding discussion makes the task of the adult sound too vague, there is one simple rule of thumb: a child wants information about a sentence when he uses it. Many parents follow this rule unknowingly when they engage in the game that has received the technical name of "expansions".[5] In this transaction, parents take a sample of child speech and expand it into adult form, for example when the child says "want milk"; the parent "expands" the statement into "You want some milk, do you?" or "I want a glass of milk, please, Mummy".

An adult expanding child language is providing an adult language surface structure for a deep structure that the child already has in his mind. It is not simply a matter of "correcting" an item of child language, but of giving information so that the child can verify a rule that he has just applied, at a time when he can relate it to the appropriate deep structure.

It is worthwhile to consider why a child should bother to learn language in the first place, especially when babies are usually so very well looked after and the progressive accomplishment in language is accompanied by diminution of adult care. If a child can get everything he wants without speech, why should he take the trouble to learn; especially at the ages of two and three and four when he is notoriously distractable and obstinate and unteachable? The answer to this question may provide us with further insights into how, and why, a child might learn to read.

A facile answer to the question of why a child learns to speak is that he is "wired up" to do so; he learns to speak for the same reason that he learns to walk, this is the way he is built. But a deeper and more significant answer is that his life from the time of his birth is a constant endeavor to impose regularity and predictability on the world, and the only way he can do this is to develop rules that will reduce the load on his memory. Imagine if a child were restricted to learning language in the way that even the most intelligent chimpanzees are almost certainly restricted —associating a single unchanging meaning with every word. The child would have to learn a new word for every meaning, and his internal "dictionary" of words would grow every time he wanted to express a new meaning. Instead, as we have seen, a child appears to give up the notion of establishing a holophrase dictionary by the middle of his second year, when he starts to put words together into two- or three-word sentences. The dramatic discovery that words can be combined to form meanings not expressible in existing single words must be a great relief for the infant's memory. With only 100 words, for example, 20 Pivot and 80 Open class, the child could produce 1600 different two-word sentences.

But then why, if "phrase structure" rules like $S \to (P) + O + (O)$ are so powerful, should a child go on to develop transformations? The motivation may be the same as that of the linguists who proposed transformational grammar in the first place. Transformations are very powerful rules because they increase enormously the number of sentences that can be produced with only a minimal increase in the number of rules, and because they show the connection between many sentences that otherwise might appear quite unrelated, such as "The boy reads the book", "Does the boy read the book?" and so forth.

A child learning to talk looks for rules that will reduce some of the uncertainty of the world around him. In the normal progression of development he should go on to apply these same rule-discovering skills to the task of learning how to read. In what circumstances does he look for information? What does he do with the information that he gets? In the next chapter we shall look at two competing psychological theories, one which offers some answers to the first question, and the other which provides some insights into the second.

References

Notable among the first scholars to study and interpret children's language in the analytic manner illustrated in this chapter—rather than simply by counting words—are David McNeill, Roger Brown, Martin Braine, and Susan Ervin-Tripp. (It would be more accurate to say that such researchers rediscovered a method and approach that was fruitful in Europe fifty or more years ago, and that fell into a long period of disrepute and disuse—as did many other aspects of studying the human "mind" with the ascension of the austere psychology of behaviorism in the United States.)

McNeill, whose approach to the development of grammar has perhaps been most closely followed, has written readable contributions to several volumes, for example:

D. MCNEILL, Developmental psycholinguistics. In F. SMITH and G. A. MILLER (eds.), *The Genesis of Language* (Cambridge, Mass.: M. I. T. Press, 1966).

G. A. MILLER and D. MCNEILL, Psycholinguistics. In G. LINDZEY and E. ARONSON (eds.), *Handbook of Social Psychology* (Reading, Mass.: Addison-Wesley Publishing Co., 1968), Vol. 3.

The idea that the ability to learn and use language is part of the innate biological inheritance of the human child is most fully developed in a somewhat technical work:

E. H. LENNEBERG, *Biological Foundations of Language* (New York: John Wiley & Sons, Inc., 1967).

There are several interesting chapters on language and language acquisition in an articulate introductory text:

R. BROWN, *Social Psychology* (New York: The Free Press, 1965).

All of the above authorities are widely reprinted—for example, in Oldfield and Marshall (listed on page 10).

Notes

1. There are wide individual differences in the time, but not the sequence, in which language is learned. The hypothetical child whose language progress is discussed in this book is the well-known statistical artifact whose behavior, if it existed at all, would fall precisely on the mean of the behavior of all actual children. A child who does not produce a two-word sentence until 24 months is no more likely to be a verbal problem than the 12-month-old conversationalist is a linguistic prodigy; both fall within the normal range of variation for child language development.

2. J. H. GREENBERG, Some universals of grammar with particular reference to the order of meaningful elements. In J. H. GREENBERG (ed.), *Universals of Language* (Cambridge, Mass.: M. I. T. Press, 1966).

3. RUTH H. WEIR, Some questions on the child's learning of phonology. In F. SMITH and G. A. MILLER (eds.), *The Genesis of Language* (Cambridge, Mass.: M. I. T. Press, 1966).

4. RUTH H. WEIR, *Language in the Crib* (The Hague: Mouton, 1962).

5. COURTNEY CAZDEN, *Environmental Assistance to the Child's Acquisition of Grammar*. Doctoral thesis, School of Education, Harvard University, 1965.

5

Learning (1): Habits

There is no theorist without prejudice. An occasional ascetic statistician may accumulate facts and figures without trying to impose a point of view upon them, but bias is unavoidable the moment one tries to explain the data. The theorist's method of contributing to knowledge is to organize data into a coherent system—to cut them to fit, and to suggest implications. In such circumstances it is necessary to have preconceptions.

There are basically two alternative psychological theories about learning, the extremes of which are diametrically in opposition. I shall refer to them as *behaviorist* and *cognitive*. The behaviorist view is that all learning is *habit formation,* and that the only data of importance are the observable circumstances in which habits are established. The cognitive view is that learning involves the *acquisition of knowledge,* and that what is interesting is the unobservable manner in which information is acquired and organized by the brain.

One or the other of these two theoretical standpoints is represented in almost all of the psychological and educational literature. All the interesting books are theoretical—they interpret data. The pure data are deadly dull and quarantined in reference books where they can safely be ignored.

Which of the two theories is likely to be the true one? The question is irrelevant; theories can be judged only by their utility. And the very fact that behaviorist and cognitive theories have coexisted for over 50 years, in a variety of forms and despite every new discovery, is a reasonable indication that both have something to offer and that neither is "better" or "more correct".

Learning to speak and read defy analysis if only a single theoretical point of view is adopted. In this book, the behaviorist approach will be used where it seems most appropriate, namely in discussing the establishment and maintenance of those aspects of behavior that are most conveniently viewed as habitual, in other words, motivation. But a cognitive vantage point will be adopted for analysis of what is learned, rather than why learning takes place.

The most famous contemporary exponent of behaviorism is B. F. Skinner, whose very name has become a conditioned response to the box (actually a cage) that he invented and in which many of the principles of behaviorist theory have been analyzed and elaborated. In the Skinner box the behavior of rats, pigeons, fish, worms, and other living organisms have been studied and extrapolated—with considerable success—to account for the behavior of the most interesting of all organisms, man. Behaviorists assert that all behavior can be understood—in Skinnerian terminology "predicted and controlled"—in terms of *habits* established by the *reinforcement* of a *response* in the presence of a particular *stimulus*.

A response, quite simply, is a piece of observable behavior; not an idea, or a complex, or an emotion, or a memory—all of these are unobservable constructs—but an explicit movement or physical change. A stimulus, also quite simply, is an occasion for a response. A red light is the stimulus for stopping a car; the words "pass the salt, please" are the stimulus for passing the salt; a baby is a stimulus for protective and nurturant behavior, and a red flag is a stimulus for a variety of emotional reactions. Learning is the establishment—or conditioning—of a bond between a particular stimulus and response, the establishment of a habit. The actual nature of the habit is determined by S–R (stimulus–response) contingencies. If a pigeon is conditioned to peck at a disk when a red light shines, then the S–R bond will be formed between the red light and a peck at the disk. If a student has a gastric disturbance when the word "examination" is presented, and conditioning takes place, then an S–R bond will be established that the student will have a gastric disturbance whenever an examination is mentioned. In the language of behaviorism, the response (of a gastric upset) is under control of the stimulus (the word "examination").

Reinforcement determines whether conditioning actually takes place. A particular S–R bond will be established only if the behaving organism is reinforced in a particular way while responding in the presence of a stimulus. Technically, reinforcement is defined operationally—positive reinforcement is anything that increases the probability that a response will recur in the presence of a particular stimulus, negative reinforcement reduces that probability. In everyday life positive reinforcement is associated with reward, negative reinforcement with punishment. (However, there are some aspects of punishment that make it clear that it is something more than simply negative reinforcement. Negative reinforcement, such as the withholding of a reward, reduces the probability that a type of behavior will recur in a particular situation. Punished behavior, however, is very likely to recur as soon as the punishment is stopped; the removal of punishment is positively reinforcing.)

After that slab of definition, examples are in order. I shall offer two: one animal and one human. Imagine a rat in a box equipped with stimulus, response, and reinforcement apparatus—a Skinner box, in other words. In this particular box there are two stimuli—a red light and a green light—and two available responses in the form of levers that the rat can press, one on the left and one on the right. The reinforcement apparatus is a chute down which a pellet of food may be dropped. Ignoring for a moment the question of how the rat first learns to make the right kinds of responses, we shall watch the acquisition of an S–R habit. The rat is at 85 percent of its normal body weight, so it is no surprise that a pellet of food is positive reinforcement. The rat pushes one of the levers when no light is on, and nothing happens. A red light comes on, but it pushes the "wrong" lever, and still nothing happens. Eventually, the rat pushes the "correct" lever when the red light comes on, and it receives positive reinforcement, the reward of a pellet of food. But if it pushes the same lever when the green light comes on, there is, of course, no pellet. Very soon the rat is pushing one lever every time the red light comes on, and the other lever for the green. Quite a complex piece of discriminative behavior has been conditioned. Similar behavior can be conditioned in quite a different way, by negatively reinforcing the animal if the correct response is not made—for example, with a mild electric shock.

The second example reveals a child in a classroom also equipped with stimulus, response, and reinforcement apparatus, but not called a Skinner box. The stimulus apparatus is called a teacher, who asks questions, and the response apparatus is the child's voice. The child is not at 85 per cent of his normal body weight, but then he will not be reinforced with pellets of food (although candy is a remarkably effective reinforcer particularly where there is an initial difficulty, as with autistic children). The stimulus apparatus holds up a card bearing the word *cat,* and the child responds by gazing mutely out of the window. There is no reinforcement. The child responds by uttering the word "dog". There is no reinforcement. Eventually he utters the word "cat", and is reinforced—the teacher smiles, or says "Correct" or "Very good" or "Go out and play now", or stops referring to him sarcastically as a genius, or does something else that is a reinforcer by our operational definition. This increases the probability of the child saying "cat" when he is confronted with the printed word *cat*.

Anyone who thinks that the classroom example is too simplified really to account for a human learning situation should reflect on the technology of machine and computer-assisted instruction, which is flourishing throughout all areas of education and training, based on the continual combination of the three basic elements: stimulus, response, and reinforcement.

The type of conditioning just described is generally called *operant* (or occasionally *instrumental*) to distinguish it from the *classical* (or *respondent*) conditioning paradigm formulated by the Russian physiologist Pavlov. A typical Pavlovian conditioning situation, you may recall, involved the simultaneous presentation to a harnessed dog of both a reinforcer (in this case called the *unconditioned stimulus*), say some meat powder, and a *conditioned stimulus,* say a buzzer. The dog's *unconditioned response* to the meat powder, namely salivating, gradually became a *conditioned response* to the buzzer, because eventually salivation would occur when the meat powder was not presented at all. A significant difference between the Pavlovian and Skinnerian paradigms should be noted. For Pavlov, the reinforcer has to be presented before occurrence of the behavior that is to be conditioned, while for Skinner the reinforcement occurs afterwards. For Pavlov the critical piece of behavior has to be *elicited*—the salivation is produced by the presentation of the meat—while for Skinner the behavior must first be *emitted* if reinforcement is to occur.

Given that "reading" or "learning to read" are responses that should be established, how can these habits be conditioned? Behavior has to be "emitted" before it can be reinforced; but how can a child be motivated to learn in the first place (how is the rat brought to press the lever so that the first reinforcement can occur)? And how can lever pressing be compared with the very fine discrimination and complex chains of behavior involved in reading? It is not always convenient or practical to provide reinforcement on every trial, and even an underweight rat must have a limit as to how much food it will work for; so how can the desired behavior be maintained in the absence of reinforcement? And if habitual patterns of behavior are established only when reinforcement occurs, what could have established the irrelevant and even punishing behavior patterns that humans so often display? The behaviorists show that insights into these questions are available from studies of rats and birds in Skinner boxes.

The process of setting up the exact kind of behavior that it is desired to reinforce is known as *shaping.* The term is appropriate—the behavior is literally molded into shape by a process of *successive approximation.* Consider again the lever-pressing rat, from the moment an untrained animal

—"naive" is the felicitous term employed—is first put into the box. The experimenter in control of the apparatus first has to show the rat how it is to be reinforced; he drops a pellet of food down the chute into a food tray, and the rat eats and looks for more. The next problem is to get the rat to focus attention on the lever. If the experimenter waited until the rat actually pushed the lever, it might take all day. Instead, the experimenter reinforces the rat for a very rough approximation, namely entering the end of the box at which the levers are situated. Very quickly the rat "learns" [1] that it is reinforced only at that end of the cage, but by then the experimenter reinforces only if the rat comes to the corner where the levers are. The rat concentrates its attention on that particular corner and inevitably bumps against one of the levers, for which again it is reinforced. As soon as the experimenter has got the rat to push the lever, he begins the serious business of reinforcing only when the rat pushes the right lever at the right time. The whole process takes an experienced trainer less time to accomplish than to describe. Training a naive rat to lever-press to a particular light or a sound is a five-minute laboratory demonstration. And once the shaping has been accomplished the rest of the training and data collection can be controlled quite automatically, programmed circuits organizing S–R contingencies so that every move by the conditioned animal is inexorably followed by a predetermined consequence.

The reverse of the principle of successive approximation is used very effectively in a burgeoning new field of clinical endeavor called behavior therapy. *The objective is to free a person of an inappropriate pattern of behavior—for example, a morbid fear of snakes. (A "phobia" to a psychoanalyst is simply a bad habit to a behavior therapist, who does not believe that mysterious "causes" underlie the symptoms.) The therapeutic process is one of desensitization to more and more direct confrontations with the feared object. First the patient is helped to attain a state of deep relaxation, then exposed to a manifestation of a snake in its most innocuous form—perhaps just a photograph, or the word on a card, or a model of a snake, or a real snake far away. The "threat" is removed as soon as the slightest tension occurs, but gradually the patient is conditioned to tolerate closer and closer approximations to the desired end, which may be handling and fondling a live snake. The trick is not to advance to a new stage until the patient is completely desensitized at the present stage, and can confront the feared object at that particular degree of closeness without tension.*

The principle of shaping—which is, of course, the method by which circus trainers develop the most complex tricks in their animals—can produce or demonstrate incredibly fine powers of discrimination. A pigeon that has been reinforced to peck at a key only when it sees a particular shade of green, but no other, can "tell" the experimenter just how fine is its ability to distinguish two similar colors and in which areas it might be color blind.[2] Pigeons conditioned to peck at a key only when a color slide containing a human has been projected have demonstrated that they can detect human figures so well concealed in the surrounding scenery that the experimenter has failed to observe them.[3] It is as easy to manipulate the rate at which behavior will be emitted as the occasions on which it will occur.

By an associated process called *chaining,* quite elaborate sequences of behavior can be built up out of small elements. As a rather trivial example, pigeons can be trained to play table tennis. In both shaping and chaining the underlying principle is the same, made quite explicit in the terminology of the behaviorist experimenter—first get one piece of behavior *under control.* Once a system is established by which an organism will respond in order to receive reinforcement, the schedule of reinforcement can be adapted to develop the particular pattern of behavior required.

Is there not some limit to how much reinforcement can be given? What happens when the rat gets too fat on all those constant pellets of food, or a teacher runs out of rewards for the child? But the remarkable fact is that the actual reinforcer comes to play only a minor part in the conditioning process once behavior has been brought under control. In fact the conditioning of really complex behavior is accomplished in the absence of reinforcement. Once reinforcement is expected, the experimenter works on the expectation. Pie in the sky is the most effective reinforcer of all.

For an example, we may return to the lever-pressing rat. Once the experimenter has shaped its behavior to the point that it presses the correct lever, he begins to withhold the reinforcement on occasional trials. At first the rat may respond to this unexpected deprivation by trying alternative responses, or by running excitedly around the cage, but these are behaviors that never produce a reward. The rat returns to the response that does pay off from time to time—pushing the right lever when a particular light is on. Inexorably, the experimenter (or his automatic equipment) cuts down on the rate of reinforcement—once every five correct responses, once every ten. A battle of wits develops which the rat is doomed to lose. The rat appears to "realize" that it has to make ten responses before every reinforcement, and tends to respond rather slowly after every reward, speeding up only as he reaches the end of a ten-response sequence. Quickly the experimenter takes control again and instead of reinforcing every tenth trial, he reinforces an *average* of one in ten, sometimes rewarding successive responses, sometimes only one in 20. The rat has lost its information about when the reinforcement will be delivered, and does not vary the rate at which it will respond. Under this kind of *variable rein-*

forcement schedule, rats and pigeons have been observed to make thousands upon thousands of responses without the return of a single reinforcing event.[4]

If you think that humans would never operate a lever thousands of times in a totally deluded expectation of eventual profit, you have overlooked the example of the "one-armed bandit" gambling machine. And, incidentally, it is not necessary to be hungry to perform the conditioned behavior—the only reason the rat or pigeon is starved initially is to help to get the desired behavior under way. Once the habit has been established, the animal will respond for the nominal "reward" of a pellet that rarely comes even though a dish full of food pellets is beside it.[5] Chimps working at a one-armed bandit will throw their occasional candy jackpots on the floor in annoyance because they interfere with the execution of the habit.

An interesting aspect of conditioned responding that has attracted experimenters is termed *superstitious behavior*. The term applies to a response that was initially produced adventitiously and became associated with a stimulus quite by chance. A rat reinforced for its first correct lever push might coincidentally have had its left back leg raised in the air at the same time. The experimenter may have thought he was reinforcing the rat for the lever push, but for the rat, the raised leg might seem just as good a reason for a reward as anything else. The result is a rat with a tendency to walk on three legs in the superstitious belief that it is this ritual that somehow brings reward or keeps it safe from punishment. The moral for human reinforcers is to be sure about which behavior pattern is being conditioned. A child making an inappropriate response at the time the whole class is reinforced may have his behavior conditioned just as much as anyone else.

Habits, good or bad, useful or disruptive, obviously have their own momentum. The very exercise of habitual behavior seems to reinforce and consolidate the habit, irrespective of the initial incentive or motivation. The world is particularly rich in reinforcers for humans, who in addition to an almost limitless susceptibility to praise (external or self-administered) will also learn and work for novelty, curiosity, challenge or the simple pleasure of doing anything at all. The opportunity to engage in a habit is a most effective reinforcer. Psychologists regard "drives" for competence or mastery or knowledge as effective as motivations for behavior as any physical hunger. But just as learning patterns can be conditioned and maintained by appropriate schedules of reinforcement, so desirable behavior can be stifled and extinguished *if the reinforcement contingencies are inappropriate. A child negatively reinforced for "making a mistake" in speech or reading, even though he is in effect only testing a potential rule, is a little less likely to risk testing a new rule in the future. Willingness to risk errors, to test hypotheses, is as we shall see one of the most critical aspects of learning to read.*

A sudden change of terminology may have been observed toward the end of the previous paragraph. While the behaviorist idiom of "stimulus" and "response" and "reinforcement" was employed to discuss motivation for learning, a different lexical gear was engaged for a description of how the learner might behave, such as "risk errors, test hypotheses". The gear that has been engaged is the cognitive one, because we shall now look at learning from the point of view that is more concerned with the process of learning than with its motivation.

References

Skinner rejects everyone else's technical jargon, introduces relatively few new terms himself, and so his writing is usually a model of unadorned plain English. Two representative examples, one old and one new, are:

B. F. SKINNER, *Science and Human Behavior* (New York: The Macmillan Company, 1953).

B. F. SKINNER, *The Technology of Teaching* (New York: Appleton-Century-Crofts, 1968).

Skinner on language is neither concise nor lucid. His epic tome on this topic was salvaged by a far more readable (but no less one-sided) review by his linguistic antithesis, Chomsky. The review is abridged in De Cecco (listed on page 15); reading it has the grim fascination of watching a shark tearing bites from the hulk of a whale.

N. CHOMSKY, Review of B. F SKINNER, *Verbal Behavior* (New York: Appleton-Century-Crofts, 1957). *Language, 35* (1959), 26–58.

Notes

1. It is difficult to avoid using anthropomorphic terms such as "learns" and "knows" and "chooses" even when writing about a rat, but it should be obvious that the use of these metaphors does not imply the sense of conscious awareness that would apply for a human. Only behaviorists would disagree with the previous statement, and that is because they would insist that the language of voluntary and conscious behavior is just as inappropriate for the human as for the rat.

2. D. S. BLOUGH, Spectral sensitivity in the pigeon, *Journal of the Optical Society of America,* **47** (1957), 827–833.

3. R. J. HERRNSTEIN and D. H. LOVELAND, Complex visual concept in the pigeon, *Science,* **146** (October 23, 1964), 549–551.

4. C. B. FERSTER and B. F. SKINNER, *Schedules of Reinforcement* (New York: Appleton-Century-Crofts, 1957).

5. A. J. NEURINGER, Animals respond for food in the presence of free food, *Science,* **166** (October 17, 1969), 399–401.

6

Learning (2): Knowledge

A difference in vocabulary is only one of the ways in which a behaviorist may be distinguished from a cognitive psychologist. Behaviorists are interested in creatures of habit, while cognitivists focus their attention on creatures who think. The fact that these creatures may be the same (although cognitivists usually cannot get very excited about rats, however talented) suggests that each side is looking at only part of the picture.

Cognitive psychologists see human beings as "informavores", or consumers of information. Reinforcement affects behavior, they say, because it is informative. People scale mountains, just to see what is on the other side, not from force of habit; they read books, just to find out what they contain.

In particular, cognitive psychologists assert that language skills cannot satisfactorily be explained as habits established by the conditioning of S–R bonds. To start with, there is no simple correspondence in language between stimulus and response, between sound and meaning. The response of comprehension must be based on the understanding of rules rather than the development of habits. Besides, skill in language production and comprehension cannot have developed through the establishment of S–R bonds because practically all the sentences we make or meet are novel ones.

"Cognition" means "knowing", and this is what cognitive psychologists believe living and learning is all about. They believe that what is interesting—and what needs explaining—about individual behavior is the selective manner in which information is sought, acquired, organized, retrieved, and used. The word "selective" should be noted; cognitivists hold that individuals do not learn about the world haphazardly or by chance, but that they *look for* the information they want. The cognitivists believe that individuals acquire information to make a "model" of the world—a complex internal representation—which is both a summary of their past experience and a basis for predicting how events will turn out in the future.

The similarity between the description of the internal representation and my earlier comments about the nature of theories is not coincidental; the cognitivists believe that the individual's internal store of information about the world is in fact a *theory* of what the world is like, and that all of our mental life—our perceptions, attitudes, plans, expectations—is colored by this constantly changing internal theory of the world. Individuals do not respond habitually according to the reinforcement schedules of the environment, they make *decisions* on the basis of two kinds of evidence: *current* information received from the environment by their receptor systems, and the *stored* information that is available in memory.

The last sentence bears paraphrasing, because it summarizes both the cognitive view in general and the particular approach that will be adopted in the consideration of reading in later chapters. All perception is the result of a decision-making process that reflects past experience and future expectations as well as the information being received at the moment. A reader or listener, for example, extracts meaning from the environment (reduces his uncertainty) on the basis of the visual information (the surface structure of language) and all the deep structure of language and knowledge of the world at large that is contained within his brain. It has already been argued that language could not be comprehended unless the receiver made this critical, active contribution. But it will also be asserted that the process of reading would be a physical impossibility even if all the information were concentrated into the words on the printed text. The visual system is not capable of getting information into the brain fast enough to take all the responsibility for reading. There is a limited-capacity short-term memory that creates a bottleneck in the transmission of visual information to the comprehension processes of the brain; therefore, it is essential that the brain provide more information from its side of the eyeballs than the eyes pick up from the page.

The following sections of this chapter will pay particular attention to the way in which knowledge of the world is organized and to the transformation of visual information into perceptions.

Cognitive Organization

Normally, we perceive the world so effortlessly that we take the process for granted, as if everything that we see, hear, touch, taste, or smell makes its presence known to us directly, without any contribution on our part. We are rarely aware that there is a decision-making process involved in seeing a tree, distinguishing a dog from a cat, recognizing a face, or reading a word. Later the physiological evidence will be discussed that perception is not instantaneous; for the moment we shall be concerned with the process itself, with the fact that perceptual skills have to be learned, and that perception is not determined by incoming information alone—by the information picked up from the stimulus by the receptor system of the eye or ear, and so on—but is molded by knowledge of the world that we have already acquired and organized. Perception can, in fact, be regarded as a process of inference; if we pause and close our eyes we find that we just do not have the information that we thought we had when our eyes were open. We did not actually notice the pattern on our friend's shirt, although we are sure he was wearing one; nor can we confirm that he wore shoes; we missed the fact that he had shaved off his beard again, and the hat that we thought was brown was actually blue. But we were not aware of any gaps in our perception—the information that we did not pick up we supplied ourselves, or simply ignored. This is one of the central tenets of the cognitivist position—that perception, like remembering, is a *constructive* process. We build our percepts and our recollections out of minimal information, filling in the empty spaces in the direction of what we expect, or want, the missing parts to be. If we "know" that all fire engines are red then we tend to see red vehicles as fire engines whether or not they really are. If we "know" that Chinese are furtive and inscrutable, then we see all Chinese in that way. Recall again the linguistic assertion that we only perceive those differences that are significant. A child beginning reading instruction may have no reason to distinguish *a* from *b, cat* from *dog,* unless he is given some motivation to discriminate each pair. If he does not have some good reason to look for significant differences he will see letters and words as the same kind of meaningless squiggle.

It is not often that the perceptual events of our lives surprise us. Our experience rarely confronts us with a science-fiction something that we cannot identify in one way or another. We may be uncertain about a precise identification—"Was that a 1949 Thunderclap convertible or a 1948 Thunderclap convertible?"—or doubt whether an identification was accurate—"Was that really a camel I saw in the back of that truck?"—but we are rarely at a loss for any kind of recognition—"What was that noisy mass of colored metal and chrome with transparent inserts, four circular appendages, and flashing lights at the corners?" Moreover, there is usually no surprise about the manner in which the events that we experience are constituted. We see 1949 Thunderclap convertibles on highways, not in trees; hear babies crying but not telegraph poles; and find that oranges smell like oranges. We are not surprised by any of these occurrences because they conform to what we have learned to expect. When we do encounter something surprising, we can usually say why. An automobile with three front wheels, a flowering telegraph pole, a lavender-scented orange, all would confound our expectations in a perfectly explicable way.

What we expect and what is surprising to us are clearly determined by our prior conceptions of the world. The fact that so little is surprising says something about our fund of knowledge as well as about the predictability of the world; it says that we are very good at extracting general rules from specific incidents to predict how events will occur in the future. The very process of recognition, of object identification, must depend on these rules; we must be able to say "There is a Thunderclap again", or how could we ever give something a name? Our fund of knowledge about the world and its ways is given a variety of technical names, such as "cognitive schemata" or "cognitive structure" or "cognitive maps", but essentially the reference is to the rules we acquire and use to predict and interpret events in the world around us, the order that we ourselves impose on our environment.

The perceptual process clearly involves components of prediction, identification, and interpretation as well as the subjective experience of "seeing" or "hearing" or "feeling" that is the final stage of the process. Prediction is obviously involved because of the way events can confirm or confound our expectations. We shall see later that the more skilled a reader is, the less visual information he needs from the page—the more he is able to *predict* what the unread material will be. Perception involves identification because we do more than just discriminate one object or event from another—we recognize that they are familiar, and can identify them. From this identification, we are able to make assumptions that are not given in the event themselves—we know that a particular cloud formation means rain, a particular facial expression means anger, a crowded bus means a missed train. All of this—the prediction, the identification, and the interpretation—is part of the final percept. The beginning of the process is an unidentified and uninterpreted "happening", the impact of information from the world on our receptor systems. This unstructured raw material is what is generally called the *stimulus;* for many of our examples it will be referred to as the *visual array* or—especially for reading—the *vis-*

ual configuration, and when the discussion is more informal, it will be called an *event.*

The human organism is particularly adapted to impose organization on the world around it, or more precisely, on the information that it receives from the world through its receptor systems. It organizes this information into categories and relationships that can be expressed in terms of rules. These rules reflect the manner in which events occur in the world, and can therefore be used to identify, interpret, and predict. Each category may be defined operationally by the rules employed to allocate an event to that category. And everything that is allocated to that category is treated as equivalent. This ability to treat different events as equivalent permits one to draw inferences about how particular events recur in particular circumstances, which is to say, that this ability permits the construction of rules that are theories of how the world is organized.

Very crudely, we might regard the content of our internal cognitive world as a filing system with two kinds of rules: one set concerned with how incoming information should be allocated to particular files, and another set concerned with relations among the files themselves. In talking about the cognitive world, the files are usually referred to as *categories.*

Consider the identification of the 1949 Thunderclap convertible. The recognition of the visual configuration, its allocation to the appropriate cognitive category, must take place according to certain rules that we have acquired for distinguishing this particular event from all other possibilities. We do not put all convertibles into this particular category, not even all Thunderclap convertibles, but only the 1949 models. The rules by which we make this distinction must be related to *significant differences* that we have detected between 1949 Thunderclap convertibles and all possible alternatives. You will probably recognize the term "significant differences" from the earlier discussion of how linguistic elements are distinguished from each other, and recall that a difference that is not significant is rarely perceived. Obviously, if we have not learned to distinguish 1949 from 1950 Thunderclaps on the basis of that distinctive strip of chrome molded on the door panels, then this is a difference that is not significant (for us) and we shall not normally be aware of it. Since the rules by which events are allocated to cognitive categories must refer to characteristics of the categories themselves, the categories may be regarded as having property lists, each set of properties constituting a category definition. One of the properties of the category of 1949 Thunderclap convertible would be the distinctive strip of chrome—we would not allocate anything to that category (we would not make that particular identification) if the particular property were absent.

Categories can relate to each other in a variety of ways. Some categories are mutually exclusive—our Thunderclap could not be identified both as a 1949 convertible and a 1948 convertible; but both the 1949 and 1948 categories are hierarchically related in the larger category of Thunderclap convertibles, and these models are part of the larger categories of all Thunderclaps and all convertibles, which in turn are members of a single category of automobiles which may be a subcategory of such superordinate groupings as upholstered mobile people-containers and potent sources of atmospheric pollution.

The way in which we organize our categories clearly reflects our personal interests and experience as well as the way in which the world is constructed. We are likely to have a complex network of categories and richness of category relations in those areas where fine differences are significant to us—postage stamps for philatelists, snow for skiers and Eskimos, word configurations for skilled readers.

The particular category to which we allocate an event depends on what we want to distinguish it from. That object in the street is an automobile if we want to distinguish it from other modes of transport; it is a convertible if we want to distinguish it from coupes and sedans and wagons, a Thunderclap if we want to distinguish it from other models, and a 1949 model to distinguish it from Thunderclaps made in other years. The level selected depends on the nature of alternatives that should be eliminated. This rule of category allocation with respect to the elimination of alternatives applies both to perception (how we view an object or event) and description (how we believe a listener or reader would want his uncertainty about alternatives reduced). It would be as inappropriate to send a telegram to one's father: "Rush home. 1965 Green and mauve Intaglio fastback sedan with optional wheelcovers and rose tinted windshield hit mother, broke both legs" as it would be to inform the highway patrol "Get the car that hit mother 20 minutes ago". A more relevant example is that we see *words* if we are checking a directory for names, but *letters* if we are looking for a spelling—what we see depends upon the nature of the alternatives we want to exclude.

The assertion that the level of specificity chosen in selecting cognitive categories depends upon the number of alternatives to be eliminated provides a clue to the actual function of categories; their utility is that they permit us to separate our experience into events that we wish to consider as equivalent and those that we wish to differentiate. As far as father is concerned, the make and year of the car that hit mother is not a significant difference but the highway patrol wants as much differentiation as possible. If we live in temperate zones, then one category for snow may be adequate, but skiers and Arctic residents require much finer discriminations.

In order to cope with the world, to be able to predict and identify those aspects that are important to us, we need to differentiate experience into categories, but not indefinitely. If every event, every perception, were to be absolutely unique, then we could never summarize our experience or predict from one event to another. We can only derive the rules that we require if we discover those differences that are significant (which help us to make reasonable predictions about the future) and ignore those that are not. For example, for the skill of reading letters we have to discover that certain differences between *A* and *H* are significant (because we want to allocate them to different letter categories) but not the differences between *A* and *a* (although differences between *A* and *a* do become significant if we want to distinguish upper case from lower case letters).

Not only may the same event be allocated to a different category depending on the nature of the alternatives to be eliminated, but exactly the same stimulus event may be allocated to quite a different category depending on the nature of the perception that is required. As a very pertinent example, one may look at some printed marks on the page (a visual array) and read them as the word "cat" (which means, allocate it to one of our categories for words) or else as a sequence of letters "c", "a", "t" (allocate the array to the relevant letter categories).

A particular visual array may be interpreted as individual letters or as words, but not as both at the same time. This is one piece of evidence for the assertion that word identification does not necessarily proceed through letter identification. A related example of the way in which the same array of visual information can be allocated to different categories can be demonstrated by asking someone to read the number 76055 2 or the word e mbossed . You may not have noticed that the configuration boss was exactly the same in the middle of both the number and the word, but even when this is pointed out, you still cannot read the ambiguous section in both ways at the same time. The way in which we perceive the world depends on the manner in which we categorize the incoming information, not simply on the characteristics of the incoming information itself.

We can now attempt to describe *learning* from the cognitive point of view. There are three aspects of learning, all interrelated: the establishment of new categories, the development of relations among categories, and the refinement of rules for the allocation of events to categories.

A child is constantly required to establish new categories in his cognitive structure, and to discover the rules that limit the allocation of events to that category. He has to learn that not all men are "dada", but that one man is. A child learning to sight-recognize the printed word *cat* has to establish a visual category for that word. The establishment of a category must involve establishing a property list by which the category is defined and distinguished from other categories—for example the property list for the 1949 Thunderclap would include all the properties of the 1948 model plus the streak of chrome along the door. For skilled readers there must be a property list for every letter of the alphabet and also for every word that can be identified on sight, together, possibly, with lists for frequently occurring syllabic groups of letters. This process of learning to establish categories involves detecting significant differences—the only reason to establish a new category is to make a new differentiation in our experience, and the learning problem is to find the significant differences that should define the category. The child has to learn that the significant difference that defines "dada" from all other men is not the fact that he has a moustache or wears odd socks, because he will then mistakenly allocate other people with moustaches or odd socks to the category of "dada". He has to find sufficient significant differences so that only one person is allocated to that category, and that person invariably. In other words, he has to find a rule. The eventual property list for the category becomes the rule.

The second aspect of learning involves establishing relations between categories—for example, associating the category for the printed word with the sound of the word and with all the associations or meanings that have already been associated with the sound. Merely establishing a category for the sight-recognition of *cat* permits the discrimination of that word from other words, it establishes a difference. But in order to be identified, the word has to have a name, and in order to be meaningful, the word has to be plugged into a network of associations. An obvious way of establishing a network of associations for the printed word would be to connect it with the associations already established for the spoken word; this sight–sound association does not, however, imply that words are subsequently identified or comprehended through the mediation of their sound. Rather I shall propose that with the visual category and its associations established, one can move from the printed page to meanings directly. Very often the sounds of written words could not be accurately produced unless the meaning of the words had already been determined.

Related to this point of whether words have to be identified through the mediation of their sounds, it might be objected that children could not possibly learn to associate sounds with printed words (to "name" words) without making use of the alphabetic principle by which words are spelled according to rules roughly corresponding to their sounds. In Chapter 12 I shall argue that it is, in fact, impossible to learn the sounds of words by building up from the sounds of letters; for the moment it is sufficient to assert that such a procedure is in any case unnecessary. It is by no means an impossible task to associate names quite unsystematically with thousands of visual configurations that "do not spell their names"; human beings, and especially the young, have the facility to do this to an extraordinary extent. With relatively few exceptions, such as function words, every one of the several thousand words in the vocabulary of a five-year-old child must be associated with a category that does not spell its own name. Children easily learn that the category of trees is called "trees", dogs are called "dogs", red is called "red" and running is called "running", and so on. Besides, the alphabetic writing system that we use is an exception; most of the world's languages that have visual representations do not have an alphabet, but people learn to read them.

The third aspect of cognitive learning involves the discovery of more and more of the cues by which actual events can be allocated to categories. Note that despite their obvious relationship, these cues—the "features"—are not the same as the property list. To start with, the features must be specific to the receptor system that identifies them—the visual system cannot detect "strip of chrome" but rather looks for certain features of the stimulus array that have been learned as cues for chrome. The features of particular letters must be in the actual ink marks on paper; it is a convenient fiction to regard them as properties of letters such as circles and lines and angles which are actually part of the response, part of the percept that we "see".[1] In addition, alternative sets of features may exist for identifying particular categories. There may be a tail ornament on a 1949 Thunderclap convertible that distinguishes it just as reliably as the strip of chrome on the side. In this case we might say that both the strip of chrome and the tail ornament provide *functionally equivalent* distinctive features of the 1949 Thunderclap. Any set of features that will serve to categorize an object I shall term a *criterial set*. As we learn, we discover more and more ways in which to make the decision that a particular event should be categorized in a certain way—the number of functionally equivalent criterial sets gets larger. We shall also discover that with learning comes the ability to make use of less and less featural information to make an identification. We shall run into many examples of the use of functionally equivalent criterial sets of features in our discussion of the processes of reading. We shall find that most skilled readers can read words that have had large parts (many features) obliterated, such as HAPPINESS. This is possible because we have learned to make optimal use of the information that is available, both visually and from our acquired knowledge of the language and of the way fragments of words go together. The beginning reader has less prior knowledge of the featural structure of words and fewer skills at making identifications based on minimal information, and, consequently, is unable to read a word like HAPPINESS under so much visual impoverishment, even though he can read the word when it is presented normally.

Every aspect of reading can be seen as a process of categorization. The

identification of letters involves allocating the incoming of visual informa-
tion (from the marks on the page) into a set of 26 pre-established catego-
ries, each associated with the name of a letter of the alphabet. The identi-
fication of words involves allocating the visual information to a much
larger set of categories, each of which has the sound of the word as a name
and also a number of related semantic connections or associations. Read-
ing for comprehension (which I shall also term the identification of meaning) *involves the allocation of visual information to category structures*
that represent meaning to the reader. In every case the same visual infor-
mation is utilized, but it is allocated cognitively in a different way.

There is one explanation for the twin phenomena that visual items can
be identified on minimal information, and that the same visual information
may be allocated to different categories on different occasions. The expla-
nation is that the intake of visual information is supplemented by the addi-
tional information (redundancy) that the reader has already stored as a
consequence of his previous experience and analysis of his language. This
preacquired fund of knowledge is organized and stored in his long-term
memory. Some aspects of long-term memory will be discussed in the fol-
lowing section, where I shall describe the process of visual identification as
information passes through several levels of memory.

Three Faces of Memory

While behaviorists reject as a nonexplanatory myth the notion
that any kind of internal store of information is filed away inside our
heads, many cognitive psychologists assert that there are, in fact, no fewer
than three kinds of memory: [2]

(1) A *sensory store* (sometimes referred to as a visual image) in which
the raw material of perception is briefly retained while information-processing operations begin. (Perception is not instantaneous; the decision-
making process of integrating incoming information with what is already
known and expected takes a significant amount of time—a quarter of a
second or more.) Information in the sensory store decays very rapidly, perhaps in less than a second, and is erased by a new intake of information
through a receptor.

(2) A *short-term memory* in which raw information is held temporarily
while it is processed. (The ubiquitous word "processing" can be loosely regarded as meaning "identified" or "categorized". For example, the configuration of black marks on a white page that forms the letter *A* has not
been fully processed until the letter is, in fact, identified, or categorized, as
an "A".) There is much less information in short-term memory than in

sensory store, in fact it can hold only about four or five separate items, and this information is lost unless it is constantly renewed by some form of internal rehearsal. Because its capacity is very limited, short-term memory is disrupted if new information comes in before the information it contains has been disposed of. Unlike sensory store, then, there is no absolute limit to how long information can be kept in short-term memory, but because we constantly want to pass new information through the bottleneck of its limited capacity its effective duration is only a few seconds at the most.

(3) A *long-term memory* which appears to have no storage limitations at all—anything that ever gets into long-term memory stays there permanently. The verbal probes of psychoanalysts and the stainless steel probes of brain surgeons can revive childhood experiences long thought forgotten. There are, however, two limitations on long-term memory that prevent us from using it as effectively as we might: the first is that it takes time to get information into it (aggravating the short-term memory bottleneck), and the second is that we need special retrieval procedures (or rules) for getting the information out. The reason we so often "forget" knowledge we once had is not that it has left our long-term memory, but that we have lost the means of access to it.

In reading, as in any perceptual event, all three aspects of memory must be involved. Visual information is picked up from the printed page and held for less than a second in a sensory store. Much of the information in the sensory store must necessarily be lost, but some is transferred to short-term memory, where it can be held for a few seconds while further information from the sensory store is acquired. New visual information effectively wipes out the content of the sensory store immediately (which is supporting evidence for the view that most of the time we have our eyes open we are not taking in any information at all).[3]

How much information gets into short-term memory depends on its form. Short-term memory may contain only four or five elements at any one time, but each of these elements may be a single letter or a single word or possibly a meaning extracted from several words. Since sentence meaning cannot be determined on a sequential word-by-word basis, it is obvious that information from several printed words has to be held in short-term memory at any one time. The load on short-term memory can be reduced by "chunking" information in larger units [4] (for example, by storing words rather than letters) but this involves making use of syntactic and semantic information that must already be stored in long-term memory. In fact, nothing could be identified—which means nothing could be perceived—if a contribution were not made by long-term memory, because it is there that is lodged the knowledge of the world to which all incoming information must be referred.

The skilled reader usually keeps his eyes four or five words ahead of his voice while he is reading—a record of your eye movements if you were reading the present sentence aloud would have shown that your voice was only up to here/ when your eyes were here /. In other words, a skilled reader probably keeps his short-term memory fully loaded while he is reading. The short-term memory bottleneck also suggests why even the slightest distraction is enough to make us lose the thread of what we are reading.

To continue the reading example, the processed elements in short-term memory must be disposed of—either lost altogether or transferred to long-term memory. Getting something into long-term memory is not an easy task, however. We can probably only get items into long-term memory at the rate of one every five seconds.[5] Of course, by "chunking" we can make sure that each of these items is larger than a single word (many psychological experiments have shown that we remember meanings much better than we remember actual words), but even so, a good deal of information must be lost between short- and long-term memory, just as a good deal was earlier discarded between the sensory store and short-term memory. A good reader (in fact, the good perceiver) is the individual who can ensure that the information lost in the perceptual process is that which is least important. How can he know in advance what information will prove to be the least important? He knows because he already has acquired, as part of his knowledge of the world, the competence to predict just what the nature and relevance of incoming information is likely to be. We shall be very concerned with a discussion of this skill when we discuss the nature and use of redundancy in reading.

Again, it should be remembered that the verbs "know" and "predict" and "decide" are used in the present context in a very metaphorical sense. No one actually suggests that the perceiver is *aware* of making so many "decisions" in the process of acquiring and organizing information; quite the reverse. The subjective experience of perception can not occur until selections among alternative possibilities have been made at a preconscious level.

References

Bruner, perhaps, writes with the most erudition and persuasion on perception as a process of inference. Two of his papers are essential reading for a further understanding of this approach to cognition:

J. S. BRUNER, On perceptual readiness, *Psychological Review,* **64** (1957), 123–152.

J. S. BRUNER, On going beyond the information given. In *Contemporary Approaches to Cognition* (Cambridge, Mass.: Harvard University Press, 1957). Both papers are widely reprinted—for example, in the following useful collection:

R. J. C. HARPER, C. C. ANDERSON, C. M. CHRISTENSEN, and S. M. HUNKA, *The Cognitive Processes: Readings* (Englewood Cliffs, N.J.: Prentice-Hall, Inc., 1964).

Two more technical volumes, the first on the development of perception and the second on concept formation, are:

J. S. BRUNER, R. R. OLVER, and P. M. GREENFIELD, *Studies in Cognitive Growth* (New York: John Wiley & Sons, Inc., 1966).

J. S. BRUNER, J. J. GOODENOUGH, and G. A. AUSTIN, *A Study of Thinking* (New York: John Wiley & Sons, Inc., 1956).

The works by Neisser and Gibson listed on page 10 are valuable next steps, and rich veins of further reference for those interested in the information-processing approach to cognition or to perceptual development, but both would require at least an introductory-level prior experience in psychology to be digestible. Both books are relevant to many of the topics to be treated in the remaining chapters—for example Gibson on letter identification and Neisser on pattern recognition.

A reasonably straightforward alternative source of supplementary information on some of the topics covered in the present chapter, well summed-up by its title, is:

D. A. NORMAN, *Memory and Attention: An Introduction to Human Information Processing* (New York: John Wiley & Sons, Inc., 1969).

Notes

1. At this point the use of the term "feature" as an element of the stimulus is necessarily imprecise; the conceptual nature of features will be discussed in more detail in Chapter 9.

2. The statement that there are three "kinds" of memory is somewhat contentious, although many psychologists find it useful to hold this view—"as a model"—to reflect what appear to be distinct stages in the process of memory. An authoritative (but technical) discussion of this question from all sides is in a special issue of a journal: A. W. MELTON (ed.), *Journal of Verbal Learning and Verbal Behavior,* **2** (1963), 1.

3. There is more information about sensory storage in Chapter 7.

4. G. A. MILLER, The magical number seven, plus or minus two: Some limits on our capacity for processing information, *Psychological Review,* **63** (1956), 81–92. A classic paper, extensively reprinted—for example, in Haber (listed on page 27) and also in: G. A. MILLER, *The Psychology of Communication* (New York: Basic Books, Inc., 1967).

5. H. A. SIMON, *The Sciences of the Artificial* (Cambridge, Mass.: M. I. T. Press, 1969), Chapter 2.

7

What the Eye Tells the Brain

The cognitive picture of man is of an active and selective information-gathering individual who acquires and interprets new knowledge on the basis of rules already stored in his brain. This picture is particularly appropriate in the case of language activities such as listening and reading, where there is insufficient information in the signal from the outside world for the transmission of knowledge without a significant contribution on the part of the receiver.

As an organ, the brain itself is not very communicative. In appearance it is a soft and crumpled homogeneous mass, a multitude of interconnected nerve tissues without any clear separation into functional parts. A substantial amount of relatively gross information is being accumulated about the differing contribution of various areas, and exciting things of a chemical nature are being learned at the microscopic level; but the most relevant knowledge about the role of the brain in our perception of the world is made without physically prying into its depths at all. This knowledge is acquired through controlled observation of the brain as an "input–output device", by comparing what it produces—perceptions and changes in behavior—with the different kinds of information that might be fed into it. A considerable amount is being learned about how messages pass between the brain and its sole sources of information, the receptor organs. The brain depends on these organs—the eyes, ears, skin, and so forth—

for all the information that it gets; it has to, for the brain itself is sealed in darkness and silence in the cavern of the skull. To speak metaphorically, the brain is quite blind and deaf, it has no direct contact with light or sound, but instead has to acquire all its information about the state of the outside world in the form of pulses of bio-electrical activity pumped in along bundles of nerve fibers from the external surfaces of the body, its interface with the environment. All the receptor systems pass their messages back to the brain in the same form, as bursts of nerve firings. The receptors are transformers of information, converting light rays into nerve impulses, sound waves into nerve impulses, chemical stimulation into nerve impulses—all of which can vary only in the temporal sequence in which they are fired.

But at the center of this undifferentiated network of neural freeways sits the brain, majestic coordinator and alchemist. One part of the brain reads the stuttering neural code from the ear and orchestrates it into sounds with tone and timbre, pitch, volume, and melody. Another part receives a similar bombardment along six inches of optic nerve fiber and transforms it into light, color, shade, texture, and form. Scientists and philosophers still have no inkling of how this vision that we "see" is constructed; in fact it is a question that may never be answered because we can never observe the image that another person sees.

It does no harm to pause occasionally and pay respect to the awesome but usually overlooked instrument in our heads. But the ultimate metaphysical mystery does not prevent us from learning a good amount about what passes between the receptors and the brain. A study of the visual system is particularly illuminating because the eye can be so informative about what it does and does not do—for example, during the reading process.

The present chapter is intended to make two major points. First, the visual system is primarily constructive, the information contributed by the brain being very much greater than the information it receives from the eye. This point leads to a paradox that will be presented in due course that reading should not be regarded primarily as a visual process. Second, our eyes are not continually open to information from the world, but rather they take sporadic "gulps" of information that the brain digests over time; most of the time we are seeing, our eyes are functionally blind. Chapter 8 will consider the control that the brain exercises over the eye. The eye does not acquire and transmit information randomly, but instead functions according to very precise instructions received from the brain. We shall see that much can be learned about this executive role of the brain in vision by a study of eye movements, especially during the process of reading.

The Visual Pathway

Vision—the subjectively experienced and private "image" of what we see—is a *response* to external stimulation. Very probably the processes that construct the images of our dream and fantasy worlds are also employed in the "veridical" perception of actual events in our environment, but in normal vision the constructions of our "imaging" processes are constrained by the stimulus information received through the eyes. However, the fact that vision normally is a response to stimulation, and therefore constrained by the incoming information, does not mean that there is a "one-to-one" correspondence between the stimulus and the response—that what we "see" is exactly and only that which enters the eye.

In Chapter 7 I pointed out how much of perception is "constructive"—we structure and fill in the gaps of our visual world more on the basis of what we expect than on what is actually there. At a rather different level of analysis, it would be unreasonable to expect that a one-to-one correspondence could exist between the information that goes into the visual system and the rich percept that comes out. What goes into the eye is a diffuse and continual bombardment of electromagnetic radiation, minute waves of light energy that vary only in their frequency, amplitude, and spatial and temporal patterning. The rays of light that impinge on the eye do not in themselves carry the color and form and texture and movement that we see; all of these familiar and meaningful aspects of perception are generated by the brain itself—they are the response that has no one-to-one correspondence with the stimulus.

Many examples of the way in which the brain imposes order and meaning on what is presented to the eye are provided by what psychologists call the visual constancies. For example, we always see a known object as a constant size; we do not think that a person or automobile moving away from us gets smaller as the distance increases, although the actual size of the image on the receptive surface of the eye is halved as the distance doubles. We do not think the world changes color just because the sun goes in, or see a lawn as two-tone grass because part of it is in the shade. The constancy of the visual impression belies the variations in the light information received by the eye. We "see" plates and coins as round, although from the angle at which such objects are usually viewed the image hitting the eye is almost invariably one form of oval or another. A cat that hides behind a chair is recognized as the same cat when it comes out again, although that information is certainly not present in the input to the eye. In fact, the distinctive forms of cats, chairs, and all other objects are not present in that input—we can distinguish them because we already know the forms we want to separate. Why else should we perceive Th as T and h and not as T^r and n or any other combination of parts?

One might think that at least the perception of movement is determined by whether or not the information that falls on the retina is moving, but that is not the case. If our eyes are stationary and a moving image falls across them, we do indeed normally see movement. But if a similar movement across the eyes occurs when we move our eyes voluntarily—as we do when we read across a line of print or glance around a room—then we do not see the world as moving, our perception of whether something is moving or not depends as much on the knowledge we have about what our eye muscles are doing as on the visual information being received by the eye. We can easily fool our own brain by sending it false information—if we "voluntarily" move an eye from left to right by the use of our eye muscles, we do not see the book or wall in our field of vision as in motion, but if we move the eye in the same way by poking it with a finger—moving the eye without moving the eye muscles—then we do see the book or wall in movement. The brain "thinks" that if the eye muscles have not been actively involved, then the changing image on the eye must mean external movement, and constructs our perception accordingly.

This absence of a one-to-one correspondence between the stimulus and response in vision is not the result of a single operation by which the input is transformed into quite a different output. The information that passes through the eye to the brain undergoes a number of analyses and transformations on the way. The patterned array of light that falls on the eye and the structured percept that is produced by the brain are linked by a train of nervous impulses that itself has no simple correspondence with the occurrences at either extreme of the visual system.

The image that falls on the eye is actually lost the moment it gets there. The light sensitive area of the eyeball, the *retina,* consists of millions of cells that transform light energy into neural impulses in a very complex (and quite time-consuming) way.

There are actually two visual systems in the eye, involving two distinct types of receptor cell that are called (because of their shapes) *cones* and *rods.* There are about ten million cone receptors in each eye, the majority of them packed into a central area called the *fovea* where vision is the most acute. Cones apparently permit us to discriminate form and to determine color—that is why we tend to center our gaze on an interested object so that its image falls directly on the fovea. But cones are relatively insensitive at low light intensities, which is why we do not see much color at dusk. Rods are very good at picking up information in low illumination, but not at distinguishing what they detect—they are sensitive to change rather than form, movement rather than color, transmitting information about where something is rather than what it is. There are over a hundred million rods, which are not represented in the fovea at all. Anyone who has to detect objects in poor illumination knows the trick of looking at a point somewhat removed from where the object actually is, thus ensuring that the image is more likely to fall on the more sensitive region of the eye.

When we consider the role of the eye in reading, we shall see that information received in the periphery of the eye helps to guide the movement of the eye to the next fixation point. In other words, the rod system of the eye is part of the guidance mechanism that directs the more precise cone system to where it should pick up information.

Where are the separate streams of information from the two visual systems of the eye integrated? Where indeed are all the signals received from the eyes analyzed and organized into the final "message" that the brain interprets in order to generate our perception of the visual world? There is no simple answer to these questions because there is no simple connection between eye and brain—there is no one-to-one link between the light-sensitive cells in the eye and the ultimate receptors of the information in the visual areas of the brain. Not one nerve fiber runs directly from the eye to the brain, instead there are at least six interchanges where impulses along one nerve may—or may not—cause an impulse to be transmitted along another in the next section of the pathway. At each of these neural relay stations there are large numbers of interconnections, some of which determine that a single impulse arriving along one section may set off a complex pattern of impulses in the next, while others may relay the message only if a particular combination of signals arrives. Each interconnection point is, in fact, a place where a complex analysis and transformation of signals takes place.

Three layers of interconnections are located in the retina of the eye, which is in terms of both function and embryonic development an extension of the brain. A tremendous compression of information takes place within the retina itself. When the pathway of nerve fibers eventually leaves the eye on its journey to the brain (as the pencil-thick bundle of nerve fibers collectively called the *optic nerve*) the information from about 120 million light-sensitive cells in the retina where the neural messages originate has been reduced over a hundred-fold; the optic nerve consists of barely a million neural pathways.

An interesting facet of this part of the visual system is that the retina of the eye would appear to have been constructed "the wrong way round"— probably because of the requirements of the process of constructing the retina from an extension of the similarly multilayered brain surface during prenatal development, beginning as early as three weeks after conception. All of the eye's three layers of nerve cells and their interconnections, together with the vessels that provide the retina with its rich blood supply, lie *between* the light-sensitive surface of the eye and the lens. The light-sensitive cells face the world through their own cell bodies, through two other layers of nerve cells, millions upon millions of interconnecting neural networks, and the curtain of their own neural processes as they converge upon one spot (the "blind spot") to pierce the shell of the eye at the beginning of the optic nerve.

The actual nature of the message that passes along this complex cable of nerves is also very different from our perception or belief of what the visual stimulus is really like. Every nerve in our body is limited to convey only one type of signal—either it fires, or it does not. The speed of the impulse may vary from nerve to nerve, but for any one nerve it is fixed; the response is "all or none". The nerve impulse is relatively slow; the fastest rate, for some of the long thick nerves that travel several feet along the body, is perhaps 300 feet a second, but the smaller nerves, such as those in the visual system and brain, transmit at only a tenth of that speed (about 20 miles an hour, compared with the 186,000 miles a second at which light travels to the eye).

Not all nerves respond to stimulation in the same way. Very few nerve cells fire for as long as stimulation is present; instead, the majority respond only to change, and in quite distinctive and specialized ways. Some cells fire only when a stimulus arrives and then remain inactive. Others fire only when a stimulus is removed. Still others respond to any kind of change—when a light goes on, and when it goes off. Many cells are intimately connected to their neighbors—if one is firing, those around it will not fire. Some visual cells fire only in the presence of moving objects, others only at contours, others only for lines in certain orientations. All the way down the visual pathway from the eye to the brain, nerve cells react and interact to transmit a constantly changing coded message.

The most dramatic "distortion" of the visual message—and demonstration of the constructive role of the brain—has not yet been mentioned. To appreciate this final example, it is necessary to say a little more about the architecture of the brain.

The human brain is a tightly packed and intricately convoluted mass of interconnecting nerve cells, far more densely furrowed and folded than any of the animal brains that you might have encountered. It is among the myriad interconnections on the extensive surface area of the brain—more than a yard square if all the folds were spread out flat—that the major associative activities of our higher mental processes appear to take place. The deepest and straightest "fold" in the surface is actually a sharp division that runs straight along the midline from front to back, effectively dividing the brain into two parts that are cross-connected only at relatively limited and deep areas. If you imagine a vertical line traced up the ridge of your nose, over the forehead and crown, and down the back of your skull, you will have traced the dividing line that separates the two parts. In some circumstances the two parts can work as quite independent brains, with independent activities, knowledge, and thoughts.[1] The half of the brain behind the left eye is known as the *left hemisphere,* and the half behind the right eye the *right hemisphere.*

For almost all parts and functions of the body there is a particular relationship with the brain known as *contralaterality.* All the muscle groups on the left side of the body—shoulder, arm, hand, leg, fingers, and toes— are controlled by the right hemisphere of the brain, while the control of the right side of the body resides in the left hemisphere. Similarly, the major part of all the incoming neural information from the skin and trunk and limbs of each side of the body crosses over to the opposite side of the brain. Any observable effect of injuries or illnesses or strokes on one side of the brain is manifested in loss of sensation or control of limbs on the opposite side of the body.

Many remarkable experiments have been conducted to demonstrate the independence of the two hemispheres of the brain. If critical optical and other cross-connecting pathways are severed, one-half of the brain may acquire knowledge through one eye that the other half of the brain is quite ignorant of. A cat in such a condition may learn with its right eye closed to avoid a particular object that gives a mild electric shock, but will be unable to demonstrate that knowledge if it subsequently views the world through the right eye alone. Because of the division in its brain, the cat is restricted to learning with one hemisphere through one eye and cannot pass new information to the other hemisphere.

One notable activity that is not contralaterally represented in the human brain is language. All our knowledge about language—how to speak, listen, read, and write—seems to be located in different areas of only one hemisphere, usually the left. Damage to the left side of the adult brain frequently results in one form or another of language impairment, while damage to the other side does not. If the left side of a victim of a stroke or injury is paralyzed and he also loses some of his power of speech, we know he is an exception, and that his language skills are located in the right hemisphere.

At least one unfortunate case of a human "split brain" is on record—a Boston policeman who lost major interconnections between the two hemispheres as a result of illness and surgery. One consequence of his condition was that he could spell with his right hand (connected to language centers in the left hemisphere) but not with his left, although he was able to use either hand to tap out individual letters on a typewriter.[2]

The hemispheric division of the brain sets the scene for discussing the complex and peculiar manner in which contralaterality is manifested in vision—a final example to demonstrate the extent to which the world as we perceive it has very little one-to-one correspondence with the manner in which incoming information is distributed to different areas of the brain.

The primary visual areas of the brain, the parts that are the first recipients of most of the high-level "cognitive" information from the eyes, are located at the back of the brain. There is one primary visual area at the back of the left hemisphere, and another at the back of the right. In front of each primary area is a secondary "association" area to which information from the primary area is directed and where the integration of visual and other information seems to take place, culminating in the sensation of "seeing".

It might be noted that the only condition necessary for us to see is neural activity in these relatively circumscribed areas of the brain. It is not necessary for light to stimulate the eyes for a visual sensation to be experienced; anything that activates the visual areas of the brain, such as a blow on the back of the head, may produce a visual sensation, while light falling on the eye will not result in vision if a neural message does not get back to the appropriate areas of the brain.

There is, then, an area of the brain specializing in vision at the back of the left hemisphere, and a similar visual area at the back of the right hemisphere, *with a deep division between the two sides.* Two questions might be asked—how is information distributed from each eye to each of these two areas, and how is this information integrated spatially to form a single unitary percept? The first answer is that visual information is distributed in quite a surprising (and seemingly illogical) manner, and the second is that we have not the faintest idea. To understand why there is so much mystery about how the brain constructs our view of the world, we must consider the manner in which each hemisphere gets its information from the eyes.

At first glance, the tidy manner in which the bundle of fibers called the optic nerve leaves each eye and travels back into the brain seems to be perfect in its simplicity. The optic nerve, seen from above, is arranged in the form of an X, with the bundle from the left eye entering at the top left, and the bundle from the right eye entering at the top right, and with the lower left side feeding into the left hemisphere and the lower right side distributing to the right hemisphere. Such an arrangement would appear to be a straightforward example of contralaterality, information from the left eye going to the right side of the brain and information from the right eye going to the left side. Because both eyes provide a roughly similar view of the world, each side of the brain would receive the same information about the world. But as it happens, this "straightforward" arrangement is not the way the visual system is organized at all. At the point where the two legs of the optic nerve intersect (at the optic *chiasma,* or crossing) a peculiar redirection of some nerve fibers takes place, as a result of which each side of the brain receives only half of the total picture.

It is true that each eye provides roughly the same view of the world (with some discrepancy due to the difference in viewing angle at close distances). Because of the way in which light rays are focused by the lens of the eye—or the lens of a camera—those from the left side of the field of view cross to the right while those from the right cross to the left; the image on the retina therefore is reversed from the way things are organized outside. But this reversal is quite irrelevant to the brain, which is concerned only with the relation of parts of the image to each other, with the angles of objects to walls and floors, rather than with how the entire picture is oriented. The brain "knows" from long experience with touch and other senses which side is left and which right. In a number of perceptual experiments, many men and animals have been fitted with special spectacles which completely distort the information received by the eye, switching top to bottom, or left to right, or distorting form or color. But within a very short while the brain "adapts" and the perceived world reverts to its normal appearance. No further distortion is perceived until the trick spectacles are removed, whereupon the "normal" pattern of stimulation produces a topsy-turvy percept which persists until the brain readapts.

There is very little difference in the information that flows back from the eyes down each leg of the optic nerve until it reaches the intersection at the chiasma. If we could examine the image in a cross section of each side of the optic nerve anywhere between the eye and the chiasma, we would see information from the left side of each eye's image on the left side of each leg of the optic nerve, and from the right side of the image on the right of each leg. The severance of one leg between eye and chiasma would result in blindness in one eye but have no effect on the complete field of view available from the other. But at the optic chiasma itself, the inside half of each leg of the optic nerve crosses over to pass to the other side of the brain, while the outside half continues to the same side as the eye from which it came. In other words, each eye sends the inside "nasal" half of its information to the opposite side of the brain and the outside half to the same side. This "semi-intersection" at the crossing point of the optic nerve distributes all the information from the left side of our field of view to the right hemisphere, and all the information from the right side to the left hemisphere. If one of the lower legs of the optic nerve were severed, somewhere between the chiasma and the brain, we should still see with both eyes, but in each eye we would be restricted to only half of the normal field of vision, and we would lose the same half of our field of view in each eye.

To summarize: the left side of the brain receives information only about what goes on in the right half of our field of view, and the right hemisphere receives information only from the left. And there is no surface connection between the respective visual areas of the two hemispheres. But though the visual areas are spatially separate, we "see" the picture as one. We never find that the left half of our field of view is out of alignment with the right, nor can we detect a seam between the two halves, however hard we try. Yet as far as their knowledge of the physical arrangements of the brain is concerned, scientists have no idea how the two halves of the image are brought together.

The intention of this neurophysiological excursion has been to demonstrate that in matters visual, events are by no means what they seem. The way the brain goes about its work is very different from our intuition of what it does. We must credit the brain with being much more active and involved in perception than perhaps we thought. Now we shall examine some evidence that constructing the visual world takes time. Not only does the brain select and organize the information that is available through the eyes, but for most of the time that we are seeing the services of the eyes are dispensed with altogether.

Visual Selectivity

The fact that the eye is open and exposed to stimulation by light is no indication that visual information is being received and processed by the brain. The eye is exposed to much more information than the brain can possibly use, and the brain selects and processes only as much as it can handle. And while the brain is busy constructing one percept the system appears to be closed to new information that might be arriving from the eyes. Yet just as we see no spatial discontinuity at the point where the separate visual experiences from the two halves of our field of view are brought together, so we are unaware of the discontinuity over time that occurs with a visual system that is in effect "taking snapshots" of the world no faster than four times a second.

To understand the research that has provided information about many aspects of vision relevant to the reading process, it is necessary to acquire some familiarity with a venerable piece of psychological instrumentation and with a rather precise way of talking about very small units of time. The small unit of time is a *millisecond,* usually abbreviated to msec. One millisecond is a thousandth part of a second, ten milliseconds is a hundredth of a second, 100 msec is a tenth, 250 msec a quarter, 500 msec a half a second, and so forth. Ten milliseconds is about the amount of time the shutter of a camera requires to be open in normal conditions to get a reasonable image on a film. It can also be sufficient time for information to be exposed to the eye for a single perceptual experience to result. Much more time is required for a message to get from the eye to the brain, or for the brain to react with a response.

The venerable piece of psychological equipment is the *tachistoscope,* a device that can present information to the eyes for very brief periods of time. The tachistoscope has enabled psychologists to learn that information need be present for 50 msec—and sometimes much less—for the eye to register it, but that it takes about five times that long for the brain to identify and react to it.

In its simplest form, a tachistoscope is a slide projector that throws a picture upon a screen for a controlled amount of time, usually only a fraction of a second. One of the first discoveries made through the use of the device during the 1890s was that the eye had to be exposed to visual stimuli for very much less time than generally thought. If there is sufficient intensity, an exposure of 50 msec is more than adequate for all the information that a subject can acquire in a single fixation. This does not mean that 50 msec is adequate for identifying everything in a single glance; obviously it is not. You cannot allow someone to inspect a page of a book for less than a second and expect him to have seen every word. But 50 msec is a sufficient exposure for all the information that the viewer can pick up from a single fixation. It will make no difference if the stimulus is removed after 50 msec or left for 250 msec, he will still report the same amount of information.[3] Eyes pick up usable information for only a fraction of the time that they are open, and as we shall see in the next chapter, they can pick up new information no faster than four times a second.

The second significant finding from the tachistoscopic studies was that what could be perceived in a single brief presentation depended on what was presented and on the viewer's prior knowledge. If random letters of the alphabet were presented—a sequence like *BKFTLR*—then only four or five letters might be reported. But if words were presented, two or three might be reported comprising a total of perhaps 12 letters. And if the words happened to be organized into a short sentence, then four or five words, a total of perhaps 20 letters, might be perceived from the one exposure.[4]

How does it happen that the number of letters that can be identified in-
creases from four to five to 12 and even 20, depending on whether they
are organized into words? This finding is obviously a very relevant one for
reading. It would look as if viewers make use of the largest units possible,
words rather than letters, and meanings rather than isolated words. This
historic evidence is often cited in support of the view that words must be
identified as units, therefore reading should be taught by the sight method.
We shall consider later what it can reasonably mean to assert that words
are identified "as whole". First we shall look rather more closely at what is
going on in the tachistoscopic situation; we shall see that there appears to
be a limit to the amount of information that can be acquired in a single
exposure or fixation.

Sixty years after it was discovered that the amount of information that
could be acquired in a single visual event was about four items (whether
unrelated letters or a related series of words), another series of tachistoscopic studies showed that the picture was not as uncomplicated as it ap-
peared to be. It was discovered that the four-item limitation was not im-
posed by any inability of the eye to pick up more information, but rather
by a log jam in the processing of what initially is a considerably larger
amount of information.

It had been known for sometime that subjects in tachistoscopic experiments felt they were not able to report back everything they saw. They believed that they saw much more than four or five items in the presentation,
but that the image faded before they could finish naming them. The valid-
ity of the subjects' objection has been well established in recent years by
an experimental technique called *partial recall,* in which a large number of
items—say 12 unrelated letters—is presented for a brief period of time,
after which the viewer is asked to say what a sample set of four letters
was.[5] In other words it is not required that the viewer's response exceed
the limitation of short-term memory. There is, however, a reasonable test
of whether information about all the items is, in fact, available, because
the subject does not know before the stimulus is removed which four letters will be asked for. The experimental technique involves presenting the
12 test letters in three lines of four letters each. Very soon after the 50-
msec presentation has been turned off, a tone is sounded. The subject already knows that a high tone indicates that he is to report back the letters
that were in the top line, a low tone calls for a report of the bottom line,
and a middle tone the middle line. When this method of partial recall is
employed subjects can normally report back all the letters requested, indicating that the limitation on report is set either by the speed of processing
or the limited capacity of short-term memory. The fact that subjects can
report back only about four letters does not mean that they do not have an

"image" of all twelve; but simply that four or five is all they have time to report before the image fades. If the cue tone is delayed more than half a second after the stimulus has been removed, the number of items that can be reported falls away sharply. The image, the "sensory store" of vision, does not persist in any useful form for much longer than half a second.

How long does it take to read out four or five letters from the visual image? Certainly less than a second, because in less than a second the image is gone. But it is not difficult to show that processing is not instantaneous. The time required to "read out of the visual image" can be demonstrated through a phenomenon called *masking.* The statement that a subject can report four or five letters from a display of 50 msec or less duration requires the qualification that he is given a rather longer time to "process" the information that has gone into his visual image. A second package of information presented to his eyes shortly after the first will interfere with his report. The "masking display" is typically another array of letters or other kind of visual interference that has the effect of erasing the first visual image. If the masking presentation is not given until 50 msec after the first "target" presentation, then it does not normally interfere with a three-item report. But if it is presented earlier, then the number of items that can be reported is reduced. So it takes about 50 msec to process three or four items—letters or words—out of the sensory store and into short-term memory. This is a much faster rate than the speed at which we can say three items (or rehearse them subvocally) so that the items that are read out of the visual image must be held in another kind of buffer store until they can be articulated.

Items have to be held a very long time for entry into long-term memory, which requires about five seconds an item. The only way to retain items that long seems to be verbal rehearsal. It is no wonder that we usually cannot recite a sentence word for word after a delay of more than a few seconds. Unless we have been able to concentrate on an "echoic" rehearsal of the individual words from the time we got them out of sensory store until the actual time of report, we remember *meanings,* not words. We can say what a statement was about, but only in a paraphrase. There is a good deal of psychological research to show that what we normally perceive and recall of language, both spoken and written, is its gist, its meaning, rather than the exact words. We can perhaps now see that this inability to be word perfect is a necessary consequence of the processing bottleneck between short- and long-term memory, just as the limitation of four or five items on the immediate report of a single perceptual event is a consequence of the processing bottleneck between the sensory store and short-term memory.

The knowledge that has been gained from tachistoscopic studies could make an enormous contribution to understanding what goes on behind the eyeballs during reading—and provide particularly important insights into the difficulties of a child who is learning to read. And yet the results and their implications are not widely known. At this point three conclusions can be drawn that would seem to have inescapable implications for understanding the reading process:

(1) The reader has to be fast—the information that he gets from the page is not available to him continuously, but is delivered "in packages" about four times a second to a sensory store, the visual image, where it stays for not much more than half a second.

(2) The reader must be selective—it doesn't matter how much information enters the visual system, he can get only four or five items through the processing bottleneck into short-term memory. So, in addition to being fast, he must choose the four or five items that will best meet his information needs.

(3) The reader must be able to use prior knowledge—in order to process the information that is available to him in larger and larger units. He will not be able to read fast enough if he reads letter by letter—by the time he has reached the end of one word he will have forgotten what he had read earlier—because he cannot hold more than four or five items in his short-term memory. But the items in short-term memory need not be individual letters, or even individual words; they can be larger units of "meaning" (a matter that will be gone into later). It is only by reading in these larger units that the limited capacity of the system can be overcome. It is a common experience that when a passage is so difficult that we have to read it word by word, we have to reread it afterwards in order to acquire the actual meaning.

In later chapters the limitations of visual processing will be presented in a somewhat different way: in order to overcome the limited capacity of the system, the reader has to rely on less and less visual information from the printed page. The "contribution" that the fluent reader makes is that he knows so much about his language that he does not need so much information from the page. In due course we shall see that the fluent reader needs less visual information than the beginner to identify letters, less to identify words, and less to extract meaning.

Before we move into a very specific discussion of letter, word and meaning identification, there is one more chapter to be devoted to the eye. In the present chapter we have considered briefly how the brain selects from the information that the eye has collected—how it "scans" the visual image. But the eye itself is under the control of the brain, and we can gain a few more insights about the way in which the brain prefers to operate if we consider how it actually directs the eye to pick up information from the environment.

References

Basic background information about the physiology and function of the brain and the visual system is available in almost all introductory psychology texts, and is presented in rather more detail in:

C. T. MORGAN, *Physiological Psychology* (New York: McGraw· Hill, Inc., 1965).

E. GARDNER, *Fundamentals of Neurology* (Philadelphia: W. B. Saunders Co., 1963).

Neisser (listed on page 10) goes quite extensively into the recent literature on visual information processing, and a number of original papers are included in Haber (listed on page 27).

Notes

1. R. W. SPERRY, Hemisphere deconnection and unity in conscious awareness, *American Psychologist,* **23,** 10 (1968), 723–733.

2. N. GESCHWIND and EDITH KAPLAN, A human cerebral deconnection syndrome, *Neurology,* **12,** 10 (1962), 675–685.

3. F. SMITH and P. CAREY, Temporal factors in visual information processing, *Canadian Journal of Psychology,* **20,** 3 (1966), 337–342.

4. J. MCK. CATTELL, *Man of Science, 1860–1944* (Lancaster, Penn.: Science Press, 1947), Vol. 1. (A valuable collection of Cattell's published work.)

5. G. SPERLING, The information available in brief visual presentations, *Psychological Monographs,* **74,** 11 (1960), Whole No. 498.

8

What the Brain
Tells the Eye

Our eyes are continually in movement—with our knowledge
and without it. If we pause to think about it, we know that our eyes are
scanning a page of text, or glancing around a room, or following a moving
object. These are the movements we can see if we watch another person's
face. These movements are only very rarely random—we would be very
quickly alarmed if our own eyes or someone else's began rolling around
uncontrollably—but instead the eyes move systematically to where there is
the most information. These are the movements of the eye that are controlled by the brain, and we shall be looking at them in some detail in this
chapter because by examining what the brain tells the eye to do, we can
get a good idea of what kind of information the brain is looking for.

But first we shall consider quite a different kind of eye movement, one
not apparently under the direct control of the brain, nor one that is noticeable either in ourselves or others, but which nonetheless can help to underline a point about the constructive nature of vision. Regardless of whether
we are glancing around the environment or following a moving object or
maintaining a single fixation, the eyeball is in a constant state of very fast
movement. This movement, or *tremor,* occurs at the rate of 50 oscillations
a second. We do not notice the tremor in other people, partly because it is
so fast, but also because the movement covers only a very short distance; it
is more a vibration about a central position than a movement from one

place to another. But although the movement is normally unnoticeable, it does have a significant role in the visual process; the tremor ensures that more than one group of retinal cells are involved in the reaction to any one piece of stimulus information. The tremor provides another illustration of the now familiar point that there is no one-to-one correspondence between stimulus and response anywhere along the line. The image of the stimulus is constantly shifting back and forth across neighboring areas of the retina, and if the perceptual experience were a simple reproduction of whatever fell upon the retina, then all we should ever see would be a giddy blur.

Instead, it can be shown that the constant tremor of the eye is essential for vision—cancel it and our perception of the world disappears almost immediately. The cancellation is accomplished by a neat procedure called *stabilizing the image* on the retina.[1] To stabilize the image, the information coming to the eye is made to oscillate at the same rate and over the same distance as the movement of the eye itself. The fluctuation of the image is accomplished by mounting a small mirror on the eyeball by means of a kind of contact lens, so that every time the eye moves, the mirror moves also. The stimulus can be reflected through the mirror so that its image always falls on the same position on the retina, no matter what the eye is doing. The consequence of stabilizing the image on the retina is not that the viewer suddenly perceives a super-sharp picture of the world; on the contrary his perception disappears.

What is important for our present purpose is not so much the fact that the stabilized image disappears as the way in which it goes. The image does not disappear instantaneously, nor does it fade slowly like a movie scene. Instead, whole parts drop away in a very systematic fashion. If the outline of a face has been presented, then whole parts will go, one by one, first perhaps the hair, then an ear, then perhaps the eyes, the nose, until the only thing remaining may be, like the Cheshire cat, the smile. Geometrical figures break up in a similarly orderly way, losing extremities first, and then one side after another. The word *BEAT* might first disintegrate by the loss of its initial letter, leaving *EAT,* and then by dissolution to *AT* and *A.* By itself the letter *B* might lose one loop to become *P* and then another to leave *I.* The phenomenon should not be interpreted to mean that the cells of the retina themselves respond to—and then lose— whole words and letters or forms; rather it shows that the brain holds on to a disappearing image in the most meaningful way possible. Presumably the overworked retinal cells, deprived of the momentary respite the tremor can give them, become fatigued and send less and less information back to the brain, while the brain continues to construct as much of a percept as it can from the diminishing material that it receives.

The phenomenon of tremor deserves description because it provides yet another example of the way in which the brain makes the most of minimal information. We shall later look at a phenomenon that might be called stabilization in reverse; if the amount of information permitted to fall on the retina is gradually increased from a very low level, the brain will construct images as suddenly and as systematically as it loses them in the stabilized image phenomenon. I shall discuss evidence that words projected at very low intensities do not reveal themselves to our recognition a fragment of a letter at a time, but that the entire word or letters suddenly become quite clear percepts. Such letters are perceived on much less visual information than would be required for their identification if they were presented alone.

There are other kinds of eye movement which will not detain us. There is a kind of slow drift, a tendency of the eye to wander from the point of fixation. The slow drift is probably not very important because, as we saw in Chapter 7, the eye has picked up all the useful information it is going to get in a fixation during the first few milliseconds. There are "pursuit" movements that the eye makes when it follows a moving object. The only time that the eye can move smoothly and continuously from one position to another is in the course of a pursuit movement. The notion of looking a person up and down with a single sweep of the eyes occurs only in fiction; it is impossible for the eye to move without jerkiness across a static scene. Just try to move your eyes slowly across this page from left to right without leaping directly from one side to the other or making a number of distinct jumps; you will find it possible only if you give yourself a moving target to lock your eyes on to, such as your fingertip.

The eye movement that is really of concern in reading is, in fact, a jumpy, irregular, spasmodic, but surprisingly accurate leap from one position to another. It is perhaps a little inappropriate to call such an important movement a jump, so it is dignified by the far more elegant-sounding French word saccade *(which translated into English means "jerk").*

A saccade is by no means a special characteristic of reading, but is rather the way we normally sample our visual environment for the information about the world. We are very skilled in making saccadic movements of the eye. Guided by information received in its periphery, the eye can move very rapidly and accurately from one side of the visual field to the other, from left to right, up and down, even though the point upon which the fovea will fall is by no means in clear focus—or even in our awareness—before the movement begins.

In reading, saccades are generally regarded as proceeding from left to right across the page, although, of course, our eye movements also take us from the top of the page toward the bottom and from right to left as we proceed from one line to the next. Really skilled readers often do not read "from left to right" at all—they may not make more than one fixation a line and may skip lines in reading down the page. We shall consider in a later chapter how such a method of reading can be possible. All readers, good and poor, make another kind of movement that is just another saccade but that has got itself something of a bad name—a *regression*. A regression is simply a saccade that goes in the opposite direction from the line of type—from right to left along a line, or from one line to an earlier one. All readers produce regressions—and for skilled readers a regression may be just as productive an eye movement as a saccade in a forward, or progressive, direction. There will be more about regressive movements later in the chapter. For the moment, we are more specifically concerned with how the eye moves than with the sequence in which it picks up information.

During the saccade, while the eye is moving from one position to another, very little is seen at all. The leaping eye is practically blind. Information is picked up in between saccades when the eye is relatively still—during fixations. The qualification "relative" still has to be made because the eye is never absolutely stationary—there are always tremors and drifts. But neither of these types of movement seems to interrupt the important business of picking up information. The sole purpose of a saccade, in whatever direction, is to move the eye from one position to another in order to pick up more information.

It seems possible to pick up information only once during a fixation—for the few hundredths of a second at the beginning when information is being loaded into the sensory store. After that time, the backroom parts of the visual system are busy, perhaps for the next quarter of a second, processing the information. In order to get another input of information into the visual store, it is probably necessary under normal conditions (that is, excluding the rather artificial case of successive tachistoscopic presentations of differing stimulus arrays) for the eye to move—or to blink. The statements that the eye picks up useful information for less than 50 msec of every 250-msec fixation, and that there is little vision during the saccadic movement itself, do not imply that every part of the visual system is "blind". We are, of course, never aware of these blank periods in our perception because continuity is provided by the brain. It is the input to the brain that is interrupted by the exigencies of the visual process, not the brain's perceptual output.

Saccades are fast as well as precise. The larger saccades are faster than the small ones, but it still takes more time to move the eye a long distance than a short one. The movement of the eyes through 100 degrees, say from the extreme left to the extreme right of the visual field, takes about 100 msec—a tenth of a second. A movement of only a twentieth of that distance—about two or three words at a normal reading distance—might take 50 msec. But the fact that a saccade can be made in 50 msec does not mean that we can take in new information by moving the eye 20 times a second. There seems to be a limit on the speed at which we can usefully move from one fixation to another, and that would appear to be set by the processing requirement of about 200 msec for every new input. That is why there can be little "improvement" in the rate at which fixations are made during reading. We shall see in a moment that there is very little difference in the rate or duration of fixations between fluent readers and beginners; what does distinguish the men from the boys in reading is the use made of information that is picked up during a fixation.

There are some interesting analogies to be drawn between eye movements and hand movements. The top speed of movement for eye and hand are roughly similar, and like the eye, the hand moves faster when it moves over a greater distance. The hand performs the same kind of activity as the eye. It moves precisely and selectively to the most useful position, and it starts "picking up" only when it has arrived. But although the hands of children may move almost as fast and accurately as those of adults, they cannot be used so efficiently—children lack the grasp of the more mature adult.

The number of fixations varies with both the skill of the reader and the difficulty of the passage being read, but not to any remarkable extent. In fact, fixation rate settles down by about Grade 4. There is a slight tendency for skilled readers to change fixations faster than unskilled readers, but the difference is only about one extra fixation a second; adults may average four while the child just starting to read changes fixation three times a second. For any reader, skilled or unskilled, reading a difficult passage may cut about one fixation a second off the fastest reading rate.

This minimal difference in fixation rate between skilled and unskilled readers, between easy and difficult passages, should not surprise us. We have seen that a single intake of visual information requires about a quarter of a second to process, and that by half a second the sensory store may have decayed to the extent that much of its content is lost, so there would seem to be fairly tight functional constraints on the rate or duration of fixations.

There is also not a dramatic difference between children and adults in the matter of regressions. Children do tend to make more regressions than fluent readers, but not so many more, perhaps one for every four progressive fixations compared with one in six for the adult. Once again, the rate of occurrence is determined as much by the difficulty of the passage as by the skill of the reader. Faced with a moderately difficult passage, the skilled reader will produce as many regressions as the beginning reader with a passage that he finds relatively easy. The reader who does not make any regressions is probably reading too slowly—he is not taking enough chances. And when a child makes a lot of regressions it is a signal that he is having difficulty rather than a cause of his difficulty. The number of regressions that a reader makes is a cue to the difficulty of the passage he is trying to read.

I shall leave detailed discussion of regressions aside for the moment but we shall come back to them in some detail before we are finished. We still have to build up a picture of a skilled reader as a person who will make use of the minimum of visual information from the page. Of course, the reader who relies minimally on visual information—and who does not read word for word—will tend to check back occasionally. We shall see that the fluent reader who is reading a passage that is not too difficult does not read word for word or from left to right, and that it is perfectly natural that the manner in which he samples the visual information should occasionally take him in what might appear to be "a reverse direction".

In short, the duration of fixations and the number of regressions are not reliable guides for distinguishing between good and poor readers; they are more an indication of the difficulty of the passage being read. What does distinguish the fluent from the less-skilled reader is the number of items, the number of letters or words, that can be identified in a single fixation. As a result, the really meaningful way to distinguish the eye movements of a poor reader and a skilled one is to count the number of fixations required to read a hundred words. The skilled reader needs far fewer than the beginner because he is able to pick up more information on every fixation. A skilled reader at the "college graduate" level might pick up enough information to identify words at an average rate of over one a fixation (including regressions) while the beginner might have to look twice for every word. These averages are reasonably representative of the number of fixations per 100 words, ranging from around 200 in first and second grade to 90 for college students.

There is an obvious parallel to be drawn between the fact that a skilled reader can pick up more information in a single fixation and the fact that the tachistoscopic "span of apprehension" referred to in Chapter 7 increases depending on the nature of the stimulus material. Both these statements are oversimplifications; the span of apprehension does not depend solely on the way the material is arranged—it depends rather on the knowledge of the perceiver. If four or five words are presented in a foreign language that we do not speak, then we shall obviously not be able to identify them as words, and we shall read only a few letters. The point of the span-of-apprehension experiment is not that more letters are identified if they spell words, but that the way in which information from a single glance can be utilized depends on the knowledge of the reader. Obviously, the greater the knowledge of the reader, the more he will identify in a fixation and the faster he will be able to read. And because of the tendency of visual information to decay rapidly, and be forgotten, if it is not processed, the more skilled and faster reader clearly has an advantage over the more laboring beginner.

The other oversimplification may have caught your attention. You may have wondered how a skilled reader can pick up so much more information in a single fixation than the beginner when there appears to be such a rigid constraint on how much information can be channelled through the visual system every quarter of a second. The oversimplification has been the suggestion that the skilled reader does, in fact, pick up more information. He does not—the skilled reader picks up no more *visual information* when he identifies four words in a single glance than the beginning reader who requires two fixations for a single word (or than the skilled reader himself when he is presented with an unrelated series of letters). The skilled reader needs no more visual information to identify a string of words than the beginner needs to identify a couple of letters because all the additional information that the skilled reader requires is contributed by his prior knowledge of the language. To return to the earlier definition of information as the reduction of uncertainty, the reason a skilled reader does not require as much visual information as a beginner to identify a word is that he already knows so much more, therefore his uncertainty is much less to begin with.

When the fluent reader encounters a passage that is difficult to read—because it is poorly written or crammed with new information—the number of fixations (including regressions) that he makes every 100 words increases, and, of course, his reading speed goes down. Because of the additional uncertainty in the situation, he is forced to pick up more visual information about every word. That the size of the span of apprehension varies with the difficulty of the material can be demonstrated experimentally. Subjects are presented tachistoscopically with a line of letters and asked to report the center one (the position of which has already been indictated by a "fixation point" on the screen) and as many letters as possible on either side. Sometimes there are only two alternatives for these other letters—for example, each may be either *A* or *B*—sometimes there are four alternatives, and sometimes more. On each trial the subject knows how many alternatives there are. And the more alternatives there are, the fewer letters the subject is able to identify on either side of the fixation point. When there are very many alternatives, he can identify only two or three letters in a very narrow field of view, a condition that is known as *tunnel vision.*[2]

The explanation for tunnel vision is that the more alternatives there are, the greater is the viewer's uncertainty of what each letter might be. The greater the uncertainty of every letter, the more information every letter conveys. And because the amount of visual information that can be picked up in a single glance is limited, fewer of the more informative letters will be identified from a single exposure. The phenomenon is sometimes summed up in a single memorable slogan: *information overload causes tunnel vision.* The implication is that the less you already know about a stimulus situation, the smaller will be the area that you will be able to apprehend in a single glance. The phenomenon applies in all areas of visual perception— the expert "sees" a situation in a single glance while the novice's greater uncertainty produces tunnel vision.

I can now make a statement that will help us to understand a little more the difficulties a child faces in learning how to read: the beginning reader is afflicted by tunnel vision. And in view of the need to process information as fast as possible (because there is very little flexibility in the rate at which fixations can be made), tunnel vision is a severe handicap. When a child is having difficulty, plodding laboriously over words in an attempt to read a passage, it may well be advantageous for him to speed up in an endeavor to grasp more of the sense of the passage, reduce uncertainty, and increase his span of apprehension.

There is no one best reading rate; that depends on the difficulty of the passage and the skill of the reader. The optimal rate also depends on the reading task itself—on whether the reader is trying to identify every word, for example, in order to read aloud, or whether he is "reading for meaning" only. It is claimed that some speed readers can read ten thousand words a minute, which would imply about 50 words a fixation. Since there is no evidence at all that it is possible for anyone to identify 50 words in a fixation, the speed reader must be *scanning,* that is, sampling the text for meaning rather than to identify words. A reasonable word-by-word rate for silent reading might appear to be 500 words a minute— two-word identifications in every fixation at the rate of four fixations a second—but, in fact, most practiced "college-level" students do not get beyond half that rate. The constraint here seems to be that we cannot "think words" faster than we can actually say them, and even the most accomplished news announcer rarely reaches a speaking rate of 300 words a minute. There would appear to be no doubt that in order to read fast, one should not read word for word. There would also appear to be good grounds for trying to read as fast as possible, because the larger the size of the unit that can be processed at any one time, the less is the strain on the critical but limited short-term memory capacity.

What can be said about how the eye directs the brain? The conclusion is that the brain moves the eye through the text as fast as it can process the incoming information; if one or two words can be identified in every fixation, then the reading rate will be relatively fast, but if tunnel vision is occurring, then the rate will be relatively slow. Tunnel vision indicates that the brain—not the eye—is having trouble.

The brain tells the eye when it has got all the visual information it requires from a fixation, and directs the eye very precisely where to move next. The saccade will be either a progressive or regressive movement, depending on whether the next information that the brain requires is further ahead or further back in the page.

The brain always "knows" where it is sending the eye, in reading as in other forms of vision. Trying to control eye movements in reading may often be like trying to steer a horse by its tail. If the eye does not go to what we think is an appropriate place in reading, it is probably because the brain does not know where to put it, not that the reader is unskilled in transferring his gaze to the right place at the right time.

References

Basic sources for eye movements in reading are:

G. T. BUSWELL, Fundamental reading habits: a study of their development, *Supplementary Educational Monographs* No. 21, 1922.

M. A. TINKER, Recent studies of eye movements in reading, *Psychological Bulletin,* **54** (1958), 215–231.

Classic experiments on the span of apprehension were conducted by Cattell, whose 1885 work is reprinted in the volume cited in Footnote 4 on page 95.

Summaries of relevant work on the span of apprehension, on eye movements in reading, and in many other related areas are in:

R. S. WOODWORTH and H. SCHLOSBERG, *Experimental Psychology* (New York: Holt, Rinehart and Winston, Inc., 1954). (Even more basic detail of early studies is included in the original 1938 Woodworth edition published in New York by Holt.)

Notes

1. E. G. HECKENMUELLER, Stabilization of the retinal image: a review of method, effects and theory, *Psychological Review,* **63** (1965), 157–169. Reprinted in Haber (listed on page 27). R. M. PRITCHARD, Stabilized Images on the Retina, *Scientific American,* **204** (1961), 6, 72–78.

2. N. H. MACKWORTH, Visual noise causes tunnel vision, *Psychonomic Science,* **3** (1965), 67–68, reprinted in Haber (listed on page 27).

9

Letter
Identification

In crossing a complicated terrain, the shortest route may not be the most direct. Now that we are getting deeper into the analysis of reading an indirect approach will be adopted. The point we are heading for is that fluent reading does not normally require the identification of individual words or letters, but the most convenient route to that goal begins with a discussion of letter identification. Letter identification focuses on one aspect of reading where at least the problem can be concisely stated and specified: what is the process by which anyone who knows the alphabet can discriminate and name any one of the 26 alternatives that is actually presented to him?

Unlike the reading of words, the question does not arise whether letters are read a bit at a time or all at once. Individual letters cannot be "sounded out" like words; they do not spell their names. And there is relatively little problem about their "meaning"; we "comprehend" a letter when we can say its name, and that is that.

Yet despite this simplification, letter and word identification are alike in one important aspect, they both involve the discrimination and categorization of a visual configuration. Later we shall see that the way that letters are identified may be of special relevance to an understanding of the identification of words.

Before we move ahead, a pause may be in order to explain the somewhat arbitrary use of the terms "identification" and "recognition" as labels for the process by which a letter or word (or meaning) is discriminated and allocated to a particular cognitive category. The dictionary definitions of the two words are particularly tortuous but it is clear that the words are not, strictly speaking, synonymous. "Identification" involves a decision that an object now confronted should be treated in the same way as a different object met before; that the two should be put into the same category. There is no implication that the object being identified should itself have been met before. "Recognition", on the other hand, literally means that the object now confronted has been seen before, although it does not require identification. We *recognize* a person when we know we have seen him before, whether or not we can put a name to him. We *identify* a person when we put a name to him, whether or not we have met him before.

Experimental psychologists and reading specialists usually talk about letter and word *recognition,* but the use of the term seems doubly inappropriate. First, they would hardly consider a word to be recognized unless its name could be given; they would not consider that a child was recognizing a word if all he could say about it was "That's the very same squiggle I couldn't read yesterday". Second the skilled reader can very often attach a name to a visual array that he has never met before. As a rather extreme case, do you "recognize" or "identify" the visual stimulus *rEaDiNg* as the word "reading"? You almost certainly have never seen the word written that way before. The weight of evidence would seem to favor "identification," and the term is therefore used for formal purposes such as chapter headings. But having made a point of the distinction, we need not be dogmatic about it; "identify", "recognize", "categorize", "name", and "read" will, in general, continue to be used interchangeably.

Theories of Pattern Recognition

Letter identification is a special problem within the broader area of "pattern recognition"—the process by which any two events are "cognized" to be the same. The process of recognition is of classical philosophical concern because it has been realized for over two thousand years that no two events are ever exactly the same; the world is always in flux, and we never see an object twice in exactly the same form, from the same angle, in the same light, or with the same eye. A topic of very general interest to psychology is what exactly determines whether two events shall be considered to be equivalent. The equivalence decision clearly rests with the perceiver and not in any property of the objects. Are *J* and *T* the same? Many might say yes, but a printer would say no. Are two green

1949 Thunderclap convertibles identical? Possibly to everyone except their owners. *It is the perceiver, not the object, that determines equivalence.* We organize our lives and our knowledge by deciding that some things we will treat as equivalent—these are the things that we put into the same category—and some as different. Those differences between objects or events that help us to place them in more than one category may be called by a variety of names, such as "defining attributes" or "criterial attributes" or "criterial properties"; in essence, they are the differences that we choose to make *significant*. The differences that we choose to ignore, the ones that do not influence our decision, are often not noticed at all. Obviously it is more efficient to pay attention only to significant differences, particularly in view of the limited information-processing capacity of the human perceptual system. It is, therefore, hardly surprising that we may overlook differences that we are not looking for in the first place, like the sudden absence of our friend's beard, or the pattern of his tie, or the misspelling in the newspaper headline. Man owes his pre-eminent position in the intellectual hierarchy of living organisms not so much to his ability to perceive his world in so many different ways as to his capacity to perceive things as the same according to criteria that he himself establishes, selectively ignoring what might be termed superficial differences. The intellectual giant is not the man who has a distinctive name for every individual animal in the zoological gardens, but the one who can look past the individual differences and group them into "equivalent" species and families on a more abstract and systematic basis.

The process that determines how particular letters or words are treated as equivalent has become a renewed focus of theoretical attention as a consequence of its particular application to computer technology. There is an obvious economic as well as theoretical interest in designing computers to read. The construction of a computer with any fluent degree of reading ability is currently impossible for a number of reasons, one of which is that not enough is known about language to give a computer the necessary basic information. Another difficulty is that nobody can provide a computer with rules for identifying letters, let alone words or meanings, at least not with anything like the facility with which humans can identify them. If we consider the problems of pattern recognition from the computer point of view, we may get some insight into what must be involved in the human skill.

There are two basic ways in which a computer might be constructed to recognize patterns, whether letters, words, texts, numbers, faces, fingerprints, voiceprints, signatures, diagrams, maps, or real objects. The ways are essentially those that appear to be open theoretically to account for the recognition of patterns by humans. The alternatives may be called *tem-*

plate matching and *feature analysis;* the best way to describe them is to imagine trying to build a computer capable of reading the 26 letters of the alphabet.

For both our models, the template matching and the feature analysis devices, the ground rules have to be the same. We shall consider them to be equipped with exactly the same input and output mechanisms. At the input end is an optical system—a light-sensitive electronic "eye" to scan visual stimuli and "ask questions" about the arrangement of light and shade— and at the output end a set of 26 responses, namely the possibility of printing out (or even "speaking" with preprogrammed equipment) each of the letters of the alphabet. The aim, of course, is to construct a system between the input and output mechanisms to insure that when E is presented to the scanner, "E" will be produced in the output.

For a *template-matching* device, a series of internal representations will be constructed to be, in effect, its reference library for the letters it is required to identify. We might start with one internal representation, or "template", for each letter of the alphabet. Each template is directly connected with the appropriate response, while between the eye and the templates we shall put a "comparator" or matching mechanism capable of comparing any input letter with all of the set of templates. Any letter that comes into the computer's field of view will be internalized and compared with each of the templates, at least until a match is made. Upon "matching" the input with a template, the computer will perform the response associated with that particular template and the identification will be complete.

There are obvious limitations to such a system. If the computer is given a template for the representation $A,$ what will it do if confronted with A or Ꙕ not to mention Ā or even H or $4?$ Of course, some flexibility can be built into the system. Inputs can be "normalized" to iron out some of the variability—they can be scaled down to a standard size, adjusted into a particular orientation, have crooked lines straightened, small gaps filled, and minor excrescences removed; in short a number of things can be done to increase the probability that the computer will not respond "I don't know" but will instead match an input to a template. But, unfortunately, the greater the likelihood that the computer will make a match, the greater the probability that it will make a mistake.[1] A computer that can "normalize" Ā to make it look like the template A will be likely to do the same with 4 and H. The only remedy will be to have more than one template for every response, and to keep adding templates to try to accommodate all the different styles and types of lettering the device might meet. Even then, such a computer will be unable to make use of all the supporting knowledge that human beings have; it will be quite capable of reading the word *HOT* as *AOT* because it does not have any "common sense" to apply in the elimination of alternatives.

The critical limitations of template-matching systems, for both computer and human, lie in their relative inefficiency and costliness. A single set of templates, one for each response, is highly restricted in the number of inputs that it can match, but every increase in the number of templates adds considerably to the size, expense, and complexity of the system. But the template-matching model does work, in fact the only existing practical system for character recognition by computers is based on this technique. The system copes with the diversity of input representations by cheating its way around the problem. Instead of providing the computer with templates to meet many different styles of character, it makes sure the computer eye meets only one style, like the "bankers' numbers" ⅃0⅄2   that are becoming so familiar on our checks.

The alternative method of pattern perception, *feature analysis,* dispenses with internal representations completely. There is no question of attempting to match the input with anything, but instead a series of tests are made directly on the input. The results of each test eliminate a number of alternative responses until, finally, all uncertainty is reduced and identification is achieved. The "features" are properties of the stimulus that are subjected to tests to determine which alternative responses should be eliminated. Decisions about which alternatives each test shall eliminate are made by the perceiver (or computer designer) himself.

To clarify the explanation, let us again imagine constructing a computer for the identification of letters, this time using feature analysis. Remember, the problem is essentially one of using rules to decide into which of a limited number of categories might a very large number of alternative events be placed—in other words, this is a matter of establishing equivalences.

At the receptor end of the system, where the computer has its light-sensitive optical scanner, we shall establish a set of "feature analyzers". A feature analyzer is a specialized kind of detector that looks for—is sensitive to—just one kind of feature in the visual array, and which passes just one kind of report back. For the sake of illustration, we might imagine that each analyzer looks for a particular "distinctive feature" by asking a question; one analyzer asks "Is the configuration in front of the scanner curved?" another asks "Is it closed?" a third asks "Is it symmetrical?" and a fourth asks "Is there an intersection?" Every analyzer is, in fact, a test, and the message it sends back is binary—either "yes" or "no", signal or no signal. Without looking too closely at the question of what constitutes a distinctive feature, we can say it is a property of the stimulus configuration that can be used to differentiate it from others. By definition, a distinctive feature must be common to more than one object or event, otherwise it could not be used to put more than one into the same category. But, on the other hand, if it were present in all objects or events, then we could not use it to segregate them into different categories; it would not be "distinctive". In other words, a feature is an element of stimuli which if detected permits the elimination of some of the alternative categories into which a stimulus might be allocated.

As an example, a "no" answer to the test "Is the configuration curved?" would eliminate rounded letters such as *a, b, c, d,* but not other letters such as *i, k, l, v, w, x, z.* A "yes" answer to "Is it closed?" would eliminate open letters such as *c, f, w,* but not *b, d,* or *o.* The question about symmetry would distinguish letters like *m, o, w* and *v* from *d, f, k, r.* Different questions eliminate different alternatives, and relatively few tests would be required to distinguish between 26 alternatives in an alphabet. In fact, if all tests eliminated about half of the alternatives, and there was no test that overlapped with any other, only five questions would be needed to identify any letter. The logic of the previous statement is set out in the discussion of information theory in Chapter 2. No one would actually suggest that as few as five tests are employed to distinguish among 26 letters, but it is reasonable to assume that there need be many fewer tests than categories—that is one of the great economic advantages of a feature system.

With an input bank of say ten or a dozen feature analyzers built into the letter-identification device, a link has to be provided to the 26 responses or output categories; "decision rules" must be devised so that the results of the individual tests are integrated and associated with the appropriate letter names. The most convenient way to set up the rules is to establish a *feature list* for each category—that is, for each of the 26 letters. The construction of the feature lists is the same for every category, namely a listing of the analyzers that were set up to examine the stimulus configuration. The feature list for every category also indicates whether each particular analyzer should send back a "yes" or "no" signal for that category. For the category *c,* for example, the feature list should specify a "yes" for the "curved?" analyzer, a "no" for the "closed?" analyzer, a "no" for the "symmetrical?" analyzer, and so forth. Feature lists for a couple of the categories might be conceptualized as looking like Table 1 (the " + " sign indicates "yes").[2] Obviously, every category would be associated with a different feature list pattern, each pattern providing a specification for a single category.

The actual wiring of the letter-identification device presents no problems—every feature analyzer is connected to every category that lists a "yes" signal from it, and we arrange that a categorizing decision (an "identification") is made only when "yes" signals are received for all the analyzers listed positively on a category's feature list.

Table 1   Feature Lists for Letters

Category "A"		Category "B"	
Test 1	—	Test 1	+
2	+	2	+
3	+	3	—
4	+	4	+
5	—	5	+
6	+	6	—
7	—	7	—
8	—	8	—
9	+	9	+
10	—	10	+

And that, in a very simplified and schematic form, is a feature-analytic letter-identification device. The system is very powerful, in the sense that it will do a lot of work with a minimum of effort. Unlike the template model, which to be versatile requires many templates for every decision that it might make together with a complex normalizing device, the feature-analytic device demands only a very small number of analyzers compared with the number of decisions it makes. Theoretically, such a device could decide among over a million alternatives with only "20 questions" ($2^{20} = 1,048,576$); in practice even fewer than 20 feature analyzers would be required to discriminate among such a large number if the device could take into account not just the presence or absence of features, but also their position relative to each other. A million alternative words (which is between 10 and 20 times greater than the sight vocabulary of most literate readers) could be reduced to just one with only ten analyzers if the tests and feature lists took account not only of the presence or absence of features but asked their questions specifically about the beginning and ending of the word.

There are other and very important advantages of a feature-analytic system for pattern recognition that help to commend it as a model for the human letter- or word-identification process. But it should be noted that all these advantages are strictly theoretical—*that is why no practical feature-analytic pattern-recognizing device has actually been built. The main problem concerns the actual specification of the distinctive features of different letters (in different writing or printing styles); we shall return to this question later. But even theoretical advantages are of interest when we are con-*

sidering processes as abstract and complex as those involving the human brain, and so before turning specifically to a consideration of the two models for the human pattern recognizer, we shall list some of the additional strengths of the feature-analytic alternative.

A considerable advantage of the feature-analysis model over template matching is that the former has very much less trouble in adjusting to inputs that ought to be allocated to the same category but which vary in size or orientation or detail, for example *A, 4, A, A*, and *A*. The types of tests that feature analyzers apply are far better able to cope with distortion and "noise" than any device that requires an approximate match. But far more important, very little is added in the way of complexity or cost to provide one or more alternative feature lists for every category. With such a flexibility, the system can easily allocate not only the examples already given, but also forms as divergent as *a* and *a* to the category "A". The set of alternative feature lists for a single letter response might then look something like Table 2.

Table 2   Functionally Equivalent Feature Lists

	Category "A"		
Test 1	−	+	+
2	+	+	+
3	+	−	−
4	+	−	+
5	−	+	−
6	+	−	+
7	−	−	+
8	−	+	−
9	+	+	−
10	−	−	+

The only adjustment that need be made to the battery of analyzers is in wiring additional connections between them and the categories where the feature lists require positive tests, so that an identification will be made on any occasion when all the specifications of any of the alternative lists are satisfied.

I shall call any set of features that meet the specifications of a particular category a *criterial set*. With the type of feature-analytic device being outlined, more than one criterial set of features may exist for any one category. Obviously, the more criterial sets that exist for a given device, the more efficient that device will be in making accurate identifications of different kinds of visual configuration.

It will also be useful to give a special name to the alternative criterial sets of features that specify the same category—we shall say that they are *functionally equivalent.* A, 𝒶 and 𝒶 are functionally equivalent for our imagined device (and for the human pattern recognizer) because they are all treated as being the same as far as the category "A" is concerned. Of course, they are not functionally equivalent if we want to distinguish the configurations on a basis other than their membership of the alphabet; a printer, for example, might want to categorize them into type styles. But as I pointed out earlier, it is the prerogative of the perceiver, not a characteristic of the stimuli, to decide which differences shall be significant—which sets of features shall be criterial—in the establishment of equivalences. Functional equivalence can be determined by any systematic or arbitrary method that the pattern recognizer cares to choose. All he has to do to establish functional equivalence for quite disparate kinds of stimuli is to set up alternative feature lists for the same category.

Another powerful aspect of the feature-analytic model of pattern recognition is that it can work on a flexible and probabilistic basis. If a single feature list specifies the outcomes of ten analyzer tests for the categorical identification of a letter of the alphabet, a considerable amount of redundant information must be involved. Redundancy, as I have noted in Chapter 2, exists when the same information is available from more than one source, or when more information is available than is required to reduce the actual amount of uncertainty. Ten analyzer tests could provide enough information to select from over a thousand equally probable alternatives ($2^{10} = 1024$), and if there are only 26 alternatives, information from five of those tests could be lacking and there might still be enough data to make the appropriate identification. Even if analyzer information were insufficient to enable an absolutely certain selection between two or three remaining alternatives, it might still be possible to decide which of the alternatives is more likely, given the particular pattern of features that is discriminated. By not demanding that *all* the specifications of a particular feature list be satisfied before a categorical identification is made, the system can greatly increase its repertoire of functionally equivalent criterial sets of features. Such an increase significantly enhances the efficiency of the device at a cost of little extra complexity.

The fact that different criterial sets can be established within a single feature list provides an advantage that was alluded to in the previous paragraph—a feature-analytic system can make use of *redundancy*. Let us say that the system already "knows" from some other source of information that the configuration it is presented with is a vowel; it has perhaps already identified the letters *THR*... and it has been programmed with some basic knowledge of the spelling patterns of English. The device can then exclude from consideration for the fourth letter all those feature lists that specify consonant categories, leaving considerably reduced criterial sets for selection among the remaining alternatives (three tests might easily distinguish among five or six vowels).

A final powerful advantage of the feature-analytic model has also already been implied; it is a device that can easily *learn*. Every time a new feature list or criterial set is established, is an instance of learning. All that the device requires in order to learn is *feedback* from the environment. It establishes—or rejects—a new feature list for a particular category (or category for a particular feature list) by "hypothesizing" an association between a feature list and a category, and testing whether that association is, in fact, appropriate.

You may have noticed that as soon as learning processes are discussed, the feature-analytic description slips easily into the information-processing terminology of cognitive psychology. It is evident that the more efficient and sophisticated we make our imaginary letter-identifying device, the more we are likely to talk about its realization in human rather than computer form. It is time for the analogy to be discarded, and to adopt a more specific focus on the human pattern recognizer.

The Human Letter Identifier

The analogy is discarded; it is time to make the specific proposal that the process by which letters are identified by readers is feature analytic. It is proposed that we learn to identify the letters of the alphabet by establishing feature lists for the required 26 categories, each of which is associated with a single name "A", "B", "C" and so forth. It is proposed that the visual system is equipped with analyzers that respond to those features in the visual environment that are distinctive for the alphabetic discriminations that are to be made, and that the results of the analyzer tests are integrated and directed to the appropriate feature lists so that letter identifications can occur.[3] It is proposed that the human visual perceptual system is biologically competent to demonstrate all the most powerful aspects of the feature-analytic model outlined in the last section—to establish manifold criterial sets of features with functional equivalence, to function probabilistically, to make use of redundancy, and to learn by testing predictions and receiving feedback.

Support for the preceding propositions is available on logical, physiological, and empirical grounds. The exposition of these grounds will be facilitated by a preliminary analysis of what must be involved in letter identification.

Two aspects of letter identification can be distinguished. The first aspect is the allocation of visual configurations to various cognitive categories—the discrimination of various configurations as *different,* as not functionally equivalent. A good deal of learning is involved in finding out what exactly are the distinctive features by which various configurations should be categorized as different from each other, and what are the sets of features that are criterial for particular categories. The second aspect of letter identification is the establishment of the categories themselves, and especially the allocation of category names to them, such as "A", "B", "C".

To distinguish the two aspects of letter identification, we must ask how new categories might be established and associated with a particular response, such as the name of a letter of the alphabet. The first point to be made is that the association of a name to a category is neither necessary nor primary in the discrimination process. It is quite possible to segregate visual configurations into different categories without having a name for them—we can see that *A* and *&* are different, even though we may not have a category name, or even a specific category, for *&* . In fact we cannot allocate a name to *&* unless first we acquire some rules for discriminating it from *A* and from every other visual configuration with which it should not be given functional equivalence. There are intermediate steps involved in the allocation of a new name to a configuration. At one extreme there is the necessity to learn that one configuration at least does not fit into any existing categories—it has no functional equivalences—and to discover the differences that are significant in keeping it out of existing categories. We shall not learn a name for *&* if we cannot distinguish it from *A*. At the other extreme is the learning of a response (such as the articulation or recognition of the name "ampersand") for a new category. The motivation for the establishment of a new category may come from either direction— either a configuration such as *&* cannot be fitted into any existing category, or a new response such as "ampersand" cannot be associated with an existing visual category. The intermediate steps that tie the entire system together are the establishment of the first feature lists and criterial sets for the category so that the appropriate analyzer tests and the categorical response can be connected.

Not only is the association of a name to a category not necessary— discriminations can be made without names—it is not primary. Discriminations must be made before names can be applied. And not only is the association of a name to a category not primary, it is not difficult. The complicated part of learning to make an identification is not in remembering what is the name to be associated with a particular category, but in discovering what are the criterial sets of features for that category. This fact, which has already been commented upon in Chapter 6, is no less significant because it is difficult to explain. We do not know *why* human beings seem to have this infinite capacity for associating quite arbitrary names to functionally equivalent sets of objects or events, but they do. Children at the age when they are often learning to read are also learning hundreds of new names for objects every year—names of friends and public figures and automobiles and animals—as well as the names of letters and words. And note the method by which a child is taught names—the instructor usually points to an object and says "That is an 'X' ". The instructor rarely tries to explain the equivalence rules for putting various objects into the category that is to be called "X"; it is left for the child to work out what the significant differences must be. The complicated part of learning is the establishment of functional equivalences for the categories with which names are associated.

The reason that "learning names" is frequently thought to be difficult is that the intermediate steps are ignored and it is assumed that a name is applied directly to a particular visual configuration. Of course, a child may find it difficult to respond with the right name for b *or* d *(or for* house *and* mouse) *but this is not because he cannot put the name to the configuration—that is not the way the visual system works. His basic problem is to find out how the two alternatives are significantly different. Once he can make the discrimination, so that the appropriate functional equivalences are observed, the allocation of the correct verbal label is a relatively trivial problem, because the label is associated directly with the category. In the following sections I shall be talking only about the question—the big question—of how visual configurations are discriminated into functional equivalence within a category, not how the categories get their name.*

Some logical support for the feature-analytic model has already been given in the comparison of my second imaginary letter-identification computer with the earlier template-matching device. I shall not recapitulate the arguments.

Some of the physiological evidence for the feature-analytic model has also already been indicated. There is no one-to-one correspondence between the stimulus information impinging on the eye and anything that goes on behind the eyeball. The eye does not send an "image" of the stimulus back to the brain; the stammering pattern of neural impulses is a coded representation of discrete features detected by the eye, not the transfer of a "picture". In the brain itself, there is no way of storing a set of templates, or even acquiring them in the first place. The brain does not deal in veridical representations; it organizes our knowledge and behavior by shunting symbolic information through its complex neural networks. It is true that one aspect of the brain's output, our subjective experience of the world, is generated in the form of "percepts" that might be regarded as pictures, but this experience is the consequence of the brain's activity, not something the brain "stores" and compares with inputs. Our visual experience is the product of the perceptual system, not part of the process.

How then does the visual system acquire and manage its information? The evidence is that the input end does, in fact, consist of specialized detectors whose task is to sample and test the visual environment for particular features, and that there are indeed several banks of "analyzers" along the neural route that optical information follows. You will recall from Chapter 7 that the information from each light-sensitive cell of the eye does not travel directly along a single nerve to its destination within the brain, but that there are six interconnecting points on the way. Each interconnection is in effect a relay station or decision point where a complex analysis takes place, where information from the preceding stage is collected and integrated and distributed.

Exciting neurophysiological evidence has been acquired about specialized detectors and analyzers in the visual systems of animals less complex than man. One pioneering group of experimenters examined *What the frog's eye tells the frog's brain,* and wrote a well-known technical paper with that title (which, in turn, inspired the headings for Chapters 7 and 8).[4] Their method was to isolate and place electrodes upon single fibers in the optic nerve bundle—in effect to "bug" a particular nerve channel and overhear the message that it sent to the brain. The message was always the same, of course, a stream of nerve impulses; the important question concerned the occasions on which the message was sent. What was going on in front of the frog's eye at the time when the tapped nerve was firing? What was the overheard message really telling the brain?

The delicate operation that placed the monitoring electrode within the optic nerve was conducted without affecting the general operation of the visual system. The frog, wired so that the activity of the monitored nerve could be continually recorded, could be positioned so that it was able actively to observe all the events taking place on a rear-projection screen. Behind the screen the experimenters organized a shadow play for the frog, recording all the while the response of the monitored nerve to the information provided for the eyes. As a result of many patient studies with a large number of frogs the investigators concluded that there were four different kinds of detectors in the frog's eye, and that each of these detectors caused a message to be relayed back to the brain only if a particular kind of visual event occurred. One kind of detector, for example, was responsive only to the edges of objects; it did not fire when an object was present, nor when it was absent, but only when a "line" crossed its field of view. Another unit responded only to variations in light and shade, while a third fired only if there was a general dimming of illumination. One intriguing detector responded only to objects that were both small and moving in an erratic fashion. Messages sent back from the "small moving object" detector actually elicited a reflex movement of the frog's tongue—the unit was, in fact, a very specialized "flying object detector".

The frog studies support everything that I have said about the function of the visual system—it does not send "pictures" back to the brain, but instead transmits discrete pieces of "coded" information about changes and relations among particular aspects of the visual scene. The function of the eye is to answer the brain's questions, and the brain does not ask "What is it?"—that is a decision only the brain can make—instead it asks for information about specific "features" to help it make a decision.

Other experimenters have made similar studies of the visual systems of higher animals like cats and monkeys, sometimes monitoring the system much further back than the optic nerve, in the visual centers of the brain itself. The further back they go, the more limited is the kind of visual stimulus that seems to produce a response, supporting the view that the function of the successive interconnections is to make more and more complex analyses. Some brain areas respond only to straight or curved lines in particular orientations—they will show activity for | but not for /. Other areas will respond only to movement in a particular direction.[5]

There is little direct evidence about the actual nature of the detectors and analyzers in the human visual system, but there is no reason to think them different in any significant way from those in the frog or cat. The only difference in man is in the overall complexity of the system. Man can do so much more with the information that he gets.

The Letter Identifier in Action

We have come to the final question of the present chapter: the empirical evidence in support of the feature analysis model of the human visual system. If there is little direct physiological evidence about the visual analyzer system in man, how can we tell whether it does indeed function in the manner suggested? To bring us right back to the issue under consideration, we shall examine evidence for the feature-analytic model from letter-identification experiments.

The basic assumption to be tested is that letters are actually conglomerates of features, of which there are perhaps a dozen different kinds. The only way in which letters can differ physically from each other is in the presence or absence of each of these features. Letters that have several features in common will be very similar, while letters that are constructed of quite different feature combinations will be quite dissimilar in appearance. How does one define "similarity"? Letters are similar—they are presumed to share many features—if they are frequently confused with each other. And letters that are rarely confused with each other are assumed to have very few features in common.

Of course, we do not very often confuse letters, and when we do the character of the error is usually influenced by nonvisual factors. We might, for example, think that the fourth letter in the sequence *REQF* . . . is a *U* not because *F* and *U* are visually similar but because we normally expect a *U* to follow *Q*. However, large numbers of visual letter confusions can be generated by experimental techniques in which the stimulus letter is so "impoverished" that the viewer cannot see it clearly, although he is forced to make a guess about what it probably is. In other words, the subject has to make a letter-identification decision on minimal information. The experimental assumption is that if the viewer cannot see the stimulus clearly, he must be lacking some vital information; and if he is lacking some vital information, then he must be unable to make some feature tests. And if he is unable to make certain feature tests, then the tests that he is able to make will not reduce all his uncertainty about the 26 alternative responses. He will still be left in doubt about a few possibilities that can be differentiated only by the tests that he has been unable to perform.

The actual method of impoverishing the stimulus is not important. The presentation may be tachistoscopic, or it may involve a stimulus that has very little contrast with its surroundings—projected by a lamp at a very low intensity, or printed on a page under several layers of tissue paper, or hidden behind a lot of visual noise, like ⫻. The smaller a letter is, or the further it is away from the viewer, the less information there is assumed to be. As soon as the subject starts making "errors" one can assume that he is not getting all the information that he needs to make an identification. He is receiving something less than a criterial set of features.

On the face of it there are only two possibilities if a subject is forced to identify a letter on insufficient information; either his guess will be completely random, or he will respond in some systematic way. If his guess is random, there can be no prediction of what his answer will be; he will be just as likely to respond with the letter presented or with any of the other letters of the alphabet. If we examine the record of his "confusions", the occasions when he has reported a letter incorrectly, we will find that each of the other 25 letters is represented about equally often. If his response is systematic, there are two possibilities, both of which limit considerably the number of confusions likely to occur. One possibility, which is not very interesting, is that he will always say the same thing if he cannot distinguish a letter; he might say "That's a 'k' " whenever he is not sure; fortunately, such a response is easy to detect. The other and more interesting possibility is that the subject will select only from those alternative responses that remain after the features that he can discriminate in the presentation have been taken into account. In such a circumstance it is to be expected that the confusions will "cluster"—instead of 25 types of confusion, one for all the possible erroneous responses, there will be only a few types.

All the evidence—and a good deal of it is accumulating—can be summarized in a few words: letter confusions fall into tightly packed clusters, and over two-thirds of the confusions for most letters can be accounted for by three or four confusion types. If a subject makes a mistake in identifying a letter, the nature of his erroneous response is highly predictable. Typical confusion clusters can be very suggestive about the kind of information the eye must be looking for in discriminating letters. Some typical confusion clusters are (*a, e, n, o, u*), (*t, f, i*), (*h, m, n*).[6]

The specific conclusion that is drawn from the kind of experiment just described is that letters are indeed composed of a relatively small number of features. Letters that are easily confused, like *a* and *e,* or *t* and *f,* must have a number of features in common, while those that are rarely confused, like *o* and *w,* or *d* and *y,* must have few if any features in common. The general conclusion that may be drawn is that the visual system is indeed feature analytic. Letter identification is accomplished by the eye examining the visual environment for featural information that will eliminate all alternatives except one, thus permitting an accurate identification to be made.

What Is a Feature?

The entire discussion of letter identification by feature analysis has been conducted without actually specifying what a feature is. A formal definition can be offered: a distinctive feature is a discriminable element common to more than one and less than all of a set of configurations. However, there is still no statement about what a feature looks like. The omission has been deliberate, because nobody knows what the distinctive features of letters are. We do not know enough about the structure of the human visual system to say exactly what is the featural information that the system looks for.

Of course, general statements about features can be made. There have been a number of attempts to do this, with statements like "The only difference between *c* and *o* is that *o* is 'closed'; therefore, being closed must be a feature" or "The only difference between *h* and *n* is the 'ascender' at the top of *h;* therefore, an ascender must be a distinctive feature". This kind of deductive reasoning is quite illuminating, and it is true that one can make predictions about which pairs of letters might be confused on the basis of such an analysis. But such features are proposed on the basis of logic, not of evidence, because we really do not know whether, or how, the eye might look for "closedness" or for "ascenders". It can be argued that these hypothesized features are really properties of whole letters—we actually cannot tell whether something is closed or has an ascender until we see the letter as a whole, and it is far from clear how a property of the whole could also be an element out of which the whole is constructed. It is obviously a reasonable assertion that the significant difference between *h* and *n* has something to do with the ascender, but it is an oversimplification to say that the ascender is the actual feature.

Another good reason for avoiding the specific question of what the features are is that one always has to make the qualification "It depends". The significant difference between *A* and *B* is not the same as the significant difference between *a* and *b,* and the features of A must be quite different from the features of *a.* In fact one cannot predict what letters will be confused in an identification experiment unless one knows the type face that is being used, and whether the letters are capital or lower case.

Fortunately, it is not necessary to know exactly what the features are in order to learn something about the identification process or to teach a child to discriminate letters. We can trust the child's visual system to give itself the information it requires, provided the appropriate informational environment is provided. The appropriate informational environment is the opportunity to make comparisons and discover what the significant differences are. Remember, the primary problem of identification is to distinguish the presented configuration from all those to which it might be equivalent but is not; the configuration has to be subjected to feature analyses and put in the appropriate category. Presenting h *to a child 50 times and telling him it is "h" because it has an ascender will not help him to discriminate the letter. The presentation of* h *and* n *and other letters in pairs and groups, together with the feedback that they are* not *functionally equivalent, is the kind of information required for the visual system and brain to find out very quickly what the distinctive features really are.*

References

The fascinating problems of pattern recognition have stimulated workers in a number of fields, including many concerned with the design of sophisticated computer programs and the stimulation of higher human mental processes—for example, Simon (listed on page 80, note 5). An excellent starting point for surveying the field is Neisser (listed on page 10).

A more technical volume, with a useful introductory chapter by the first editor, is:

P. A. KOLERS and M. EDEN, *Recognizing Patterns: Studies in Living and Automatic Systems* (Cambridge, Mass.: M. I. T. Press, 1968).

More specifically, the feature analytic approach to letter recognition was led by Eleanor J. Gibson whose book (listed on page 10) is basic on the development of perceptual skills. Her approach to reading, in detail quite different from that of this book, is set out in the following two papers:

ELEANOR J. GIBSON, Learning to read, *Science,* **148,** 3673 (1965), 1066–1072.

ELEANOR J. GIBSON, The ontogeny of reading, *American Psychologist,* **25,** 2 (1970), 136–143.

Notes

1. This is the signal detection dilemma mentioned on page 24.

2. Readers should resist any temptation to figure out what are the particular features or tests specified in my imaginary feature lists—they should not try to deduce what feature should be marked − on Test 1 for "A" and + on Test 1 for "B". This caution is not offered to discourage anyone from indulging in the important and fascinating game of speculating upon the distinctive features that different letters might have in common, but because the examples in *Understanding Reading* have been constructed quite arbitrarily; my aim is not to assert what particular features "actually are". Some of the reasons for my reluctance were given on page 120.

3. I do not want to suggest that there are visual analyzers that function solely to collect information about letters of the alphabet. Rather I am proposing that information used in letter identification is received from analyzers involved in a wide variety of visual activities, of which those concerned with reading are only a small part. The same analyzers might contribute information in different circumstances to the identification of letters, digits, words, geometric forms, faces, or any other set of visual categories, as well as to the apprehension of meaning. This view that the perceptual system makes specialized use of very general receptor equipment permits statements to be made about analyzers "looking for" alphabetic features without the implication that a benign destiny has "wired up" mankind to read the alphabet. The indisputable fact that we all have a "biological inheritance" that enables us to talk and read, to ride bicycles and play the piano, is not due to some grand teleological process, but because spoken and written languages, bicycles and pianos, were invented by and for human beings with precisely the biological equipment that we have.

4. J. Y. LETTVIN, H. R. MATURANA, W. S. MC CULLOCH, and W. H. PITTS, What the frog's eye tells the frog's brain, *Proceedings of the Institute of Radio Engineers,* New York, **47** (1959), 1940.

5. D. H. HUBEL and T. N. WIESEL, Receptive fields, binocular interaction, and functional architecture of the cat's visual cortex, *Journal of Physiology,* **160** (1962), 106–154. (Reprinted in part in Haber, listed on page 27.)

6. P. DUNN-RANKIN, The similarity of lower-case letters of the English alphabet, *Journal of Verbal Learning and Verbal Behavior,* **7** (1968), 990–995.

10

Word Identification

It is traditionally asserted that there are three theories of word recognition: *whole-word* identification, *letter-by-letter* identification, and an intermediate position involving the identification of *letter clusters,* usually "spelling patterns". In effect, these three views represent three attempts to describe the mechanism by which the skilled reader is able to identify words. They are accounts of what a reader needs to know and do in order to be able to say what a word is. One or another of the three views is apparent in practically every current approach to reading instruction.

I shall argue that these traditional theories of word recognition in their usual form have very little explanatory value; that they each leave more questions unanswered than they resolve. Nevertheless each of the theories contains a kernel of truth about reading, otherwise it could not have survived to achieve a place in the folklore of the subject. Part of what each theory has to offer is that it appears to plug a gap in one of the other theories. In the following paragraphs I shall look a little more closely at which aspects of reading each theory appears particularly competent to illuminate, and which aspects it leaves in the dark.

Criticism is a two-sided game. No theory is so prestigious nor any logic so formidable that it cannot be subjected to the scrutiny of open-minded disbelief. A demonstration that one theory is inadequate does not prove

123

that an alternative theory is better, as each of the three traditional theories exemplifies. A theory developed as an alternative to one that has not proved watertight is not necessarily any more seaworthy itself. These cautionary remarks are provided because the following critical description of the three traditional approaches will itself be succeeded by yet another alternative "model", which in turn should be exposed to the harsh light of logical analysis and empirical test. Readers encouraged to put a sharp edge on their critical faculty for the examination of the three traditional theories should not be reluctant to use it on the usurping alternative that is offered.

The *whole-word* view is based on the premise that readers do not stop to identify individual letters (or groups of letters), and to integrate this alphabetic information, for the identification of a word. The view asserts that knowledge of the alphabet and of the "sounds of letters" is irrelevant to reading (although there is frequently a failure to indicate whether this stricture applies to fluent reading alone, or to learning to read as well). One incontrovertible source of support for the whole-word view has already been alluded to—the fact that a viewer can report from a single tachistoscopic presentation either four or five random letters or a similar number of words; [1] surely if a word can be identified as easily as a letter, then it must be just as much of a unit as a letter; a word must be recognizable as a whole, rather than as a sequence of letters. Another unimpeachable piece of supporting evidence is that words may be identified when none of their component letters is clearly discriminable.[2] For example, a name may be identifiable on a distant roadside sign, or in a dim light, under conditions that would make each individual letter of that name quite illegible if it were presented separately. If words can be read when letters are illegible, how can word recognition depend on letter identification? Finally, there is a good deal of evidence that words can be identified as fast as letters.[3] It has been shown that perception is far from instantaneous, and that successively presented letters—or words—cannot be identified any faster than five or six a second.[4]

Our identification rate is limited not because we cannot speak any faster, but rather because the capacity of short-term memory seems to limit the rate of visual recognition. The limitation on our speaking rate may itself be caused, at least in part, by the short-term memory bottleneck. However, the limitation of identification rate to five or six a second applies to words as well as to letters, and if entire words can be identified as quickly as letters, how can their identification involve spelling them out letter by letter?

It is perhaps opportune to reiterate that I am talking about the skills of a fluent reader, not the process of learning to read. There is a difference between reading and learning to read that is not always respected by proponents of particular word-recognition theories. In fact it is often argued that because children somehow learn to read while being taught according to one particular instructional philosophy, it naturally follows that the theory (or slogan) behind that instructional philosophy explains reading. I should also repeat at this point that there is no suggestion that word recognition *is* reading—that once the recognition of words can be explained, there is nothing else to be said. On the contrary I shall argue that although the skilled reader may be a competent word identifier when required, he does not normally identify individual words in fluent reading.

So much for some of the arguments in support of the whole-word point of view; now we can give equal time to the counter-position that as a theory it is most inadequate. One fundamental objection is that the view is not a theory at all; it has no "explanatory power" but merely rephrases the question that it pretends to answer. If words are recognized "as wholes", how are the wholes recognized? What does the reader look for, and in what way is his prior knowledge of what a word looks like stored? It is no answer to say he has already learned what every word looks like, because that is the basic question—what exactly does the reader know if he knows what a word looks like? The qualification that words are identified "by their shapes" merely changes the name of the problem from "word identification" to "shape identification." An average reader may be able to recognize about 50,000 different words on sight; does that mean that he has pictures of 50,000 different shapes stored away, and every time he comes across a word in reading he riffs through his pack of 50,000 templates in order to find out which one it is? But in what way would he sort through this pack of 50,000 alternatives? Surely not by starting at the beginning and examining each internal representation until he finds a match. If we are looking for a book in a library, we do not start at the entrance and examine every volume until we come across the one with a title that matches the title we are looking for. Instead we make use of the fact that books are categorized and shelved in a systematic way—there are "rules" for getting us to the book we want. It would appear reasonable to suggest that word identification is also systematic, and that we make use of rules that enable us to make our decision quickly. We can usually find some explanation for any error that we make—we may misread "said" as "sail" or "send" (or even as "reported" in circumstances where the substitution would make sense), but never as "elephant" or "plug" or "predisposition". In other words, we obviously do not select a word from 50,000 alternatives, but rather from a much smaller number. An unelaborated whole-word point of view cannot account for this prior elimination of alternatives.

Besides, we have already discovered that 50,000 internal representations of shapes would be far from adequate to enable us to identify 50,000 different words. Even if we could identify *HAT* by looking up an internal representation, how could the same representation enable us to identify *hat* or *hat* or any of the many other ways in which the word may be written?

The letter-by-letter theory, which the whole-word view is supposed to demolish, itself appears to have some quite incontrovertible points in its favor. We do appear to be sensitive to individual letters in the identification of words. The whole-word point of view would suggest that if viewers were presented with the stimulus *fashixn* tachistoscopically, they would either identify "the whole word" without noticing the *x,* or else fail to recognize the word at all because there would be no "match" with an internal representation. Instead, of course, viewers typically do identify the word but report that there is something wrong with it, not necessarily reporting that there is an *x* instead of an *o,* but offering such explanations as "There's a hair lying over the end of it".[5]

A more compelling argument in favor of letter-by-letter identification is that readers are very sensitive to the *predictability* of letter sequences. Letters do not occur haphazardly in any language; in English, for example, combinations like *th, st, br,* and almost any consonant and vowel pair are more likely to occur than combinations like *tf, sr, bm, ae,* or *uo.* The knowledge that readers acquire about these differing probabilities of letter combinations is demonstrated when words containing common letter sequences are more easily identified than those with uncommon sequences (other factors not directly relevant held constant). Readers can identify sequences of letters that are *not* English words just as easily as some English words, provided the sequences are "close approximations" to English— which means that they are highly probable letter combinations. The average reader for example hardly falters when presented with sequences like *vernalit* or *mossiant* or *ricaning* [6]—yet how could these be identified "as wholes" when they have never been seen before? A letter-by-letter view might also seem to be somewhat more economical; instead of learning to recognize 50,000 words, one learns to recognize 26 letters and applies a few spelling rules.

A rather illogical argument is sometimes proposed to support the letter-by-letter view. In its most extreme form, this view seems to imply that since letters in some way spell out the sound of a word, therefore word identification *must* be accomplished by sounding out the individual letters. It would be about as compelling to suggest that we must recognize cars by reading the manufacturer's name on the front or back, simply because the name is always there to be read. Besides, there are impressive arguments that the spelling of words is not a reliable guide to their sound—this question is so complex that "phonics" will be given a chapter to itself. For the moment we are not concerned with whether knowledge of letters *can* be used to identify words, but rather whether the skilled reader normally and necessarily identifies words "that he knows" by a letter-by-letter analysis.

A number of arguments against the view that word recognition necessarily involves letter-by-letter analysis have been given in the discussion of the whole-word point of view. But in addition the letter-by-letter view must be ruled inadequate for the same reason that the whole-word view was faulted—it does not offer a satisfactory explanation of how the basic identification process takes place. The view says that words are recognized by the identification of letters, but it does not attempt to explain how letters themselves are identified.

The intermediate position—that words are identified through the recognition of clusters of letters—has the advantage of being able to account for the relatively easy identifiability of nonwords such as *vernalit*. The view is compatible with our normal experience that when a new word like *zygotic* or *Helsinfors* halts our reading temporarily we do not seem to break it down to the individual letters before trying to put together what its sound must be. But many of the arguments that favor the whole-word view over letter analysis also work against the letter-cluster view; it may be useful occasionally to work out what a word is by analysis of letters or syllables, but normal reading does not appear to proceed on this basis, in fact it would seem impossible. There is no time to "work out" what words are by synthesizing possible sound combinations. And, moreover, there still remains the question of how the clusters are themselves learned and identified.

The fact that the three traditional theories of word recognition continue to enjoy wide and uncritical acceptance obviously implies that they rest on a fairly solid foundation, despite their shortcomings. No one can conclusively prove them wrong. Each approach, however, has inadequacies that are partly met by an opposing view, which would suggest that they are not mutually exclusive, and that no one of them has any real claim to be the closest representation of the truth. In their place we need to find a theory of the reading process that will not be incompatible with any of the data, but that will also offer an explanation for inadequate aspects of the three traditional views. In short, any serious attempt to understand reading must be able to explain why it might sometimes appear that words are identified as wholes, and at other times through the identification of component letters or groups of letters.

A Feature-Analytic Alternative

There is another point of view that would appear to overcome the major weaknesses of the three traditional theories without being incompatible with any of the evidence in their favor. Such a theory proposes that words are indeed identified "as wholes", but that the manner of their identification involves precisely the same internal mechanisms as the identification of letters, and in fact makes use of the same kind of visual information.

In Chapter 9, two models for letter identification were examined, feature analysis and template matching. The traditional whole-word theory that words are identified because of the familiarity of their "shape" is essentially a template-matching model, and arguments for its inadequacy have already been presented. The remainder of the present chapter will consider the alternative—a feature-analytic model for word identification.

It may not be inappropriate to provide an advance warning that the forthcoming section will be a little longer and more complex than other parts, not so much because the processes described are complicated as because the approach is a new one and requires discussion in detail. Even so there will be considerable oversimplification, partly to reduce complexity, partly because so much is still to be learned. The intention is to provide insights, to suggest ways to understanding, but not to provide spurious "answers". It should be pointed out that the present chapter is concerned only with the *identification of individual words,* of words actually in isolation or effectively so because context is ignored. The identification of words in meaningful sequences will be considered in Chapter 13 on "Meaning".

Basically, the feature-analytic model proposes that the only difference between the manner in which letters and words are identified lies in the categories, and associated feature lists, that the perceiver employs in his analysis of featural information. If the reader's objective is to identify letters, then his analysis of the visual configuration is carried out with respect to the feature lists associated with the 26 letter categories, one for each letter of the alphabet. If his objective is to identify words, then he makes a similar analysis of features in the visual configuration, but relates this information to the feature lists associated with a very large number of word categories, the active total depending on the number of words that he is able to identify on sight. The phrase "identify on sight" will be elaborated upon in due course, and the more precise expression *immediate word identification* introduced. The implication of both expressions is that words are identified directly from featural information without the intervening identification of any of the letters that make up the word.

What are the features of words? They obviously must include the features of letters, because words are made up of letters. The arrays of marks on the printed page that can be read as words can also be distinguished as sequences of letters. The "distinctive features" of letters, those features that constitute a significant difference between one configuration and another, must therefore be distinctive features of words. For example, whatever permits the visual system to distinguish between *h* and *n* must also permit it to distinguish between *hot* and *not*. And precisely the same mechanism that distinguishes between *h* and *n* will accomplish the discrimination between *hot* and *not*. At first glance, many more discriminations and analyses of distinctive features would appear to be required to distinguish among tens of thousands of alternative words compared with only 26 alternative letters, but we shall see that the difference is very much less than we might have expected. In fact before the end of this book it will be shown that no more information—no more featural tests—may be required to identify a word in normal reading than to identify a single letter standing in isolation.

If the distinctive features of the visual configurations of letters are the same as those for the visual configurations of words, it might be expected that feature lists for letter and word categories would be similar. However, feature lists for word categories would appear to require an additional dimension to those for letters, in that the analysis of word configurations involves *the position of features within a sequence*. The following examples, imaginary and quite arbitrary, compare four feature lists—two functionally equivalent lists for the allographs *H* and *h* in the letter category "h", and two for the alternative forms *HORSE* and *horse* in the word category "horse". Each "test" represents information that could be received from an analyzer in the visual system about whether a particular feature is or is not present in the configuration being examined, and each + or − indicates whether a feature should or should not be present if the configuration is to be allocated to that particular category (see Table 3).

Table 3 Feature Lists for Letters and Words

		Letter Category "H"		Word Category "Horse"									
		H FEATURE LIST	h FEATURE LIST	HORSE FEATURE LIST *Position*					horse FEATURE LIST *Position*				
				1	2	3	4	5	1	2	3	4	5
Tests	1	+	−	+	+	−	+	−	−	+	−	−	+
	2	+	+	+	−	−	+	+	+	−	+	+	−
	3	−	−	−	+	−	+	−	−	−	+	−	+
	4	+	−	+	−	+	+	+	−	+	−	−	−
	5	−	+	−	+	+	−	−	+	+	−	+	+
	6	−	+	−	+	−	+	+	+	−	+	+	−
	7	+	+	+	−	−	−	+	+	−	−	+	+
	8	−	−	−	+	−	+	+	−	+	−	−	+
	9	−	+	−	−	+	+	−	+	−	+	−	−
	10	+	+	+	+	+	−	+	+	+	−	−	+

The number of "positions" in a word feature list indicates the number of times a particular feature could occur in the letter sequence that constitutes the word, and obviously corresponds to the number of letters. Similarly, a feature test that will be applied only once for the identification of a letter may be employed several times in the identification of a word, the maximum number corresponding to the number of letters in the word. A feature list for a word could therefore also be regarded as a set of specifications for its component letters, indicated in the previous examples where the features for the first position of *horse* are the same as those for *H* and for *h*. This congruence between "position" and "letter" lists is inevitable because distinctive features of letters are also distinctive features of words, but it does not follow that letters must be identified in order for words to be identified. The term "position" is employed rather than "letter" to avoid any implication that a word is identified by its letters, rather than by the distribution of features across its entire configuration. A number of arguments will be presented to show that the fact that feature test specifications for positions and letters are identical is irrelevant to word identification.

(It should be added that there could be a few distinctive features of words that are not features of letters—for example, the relative height of different parts of the configuration, or its length. As already noted, not enough is known of the properties either of visual stimuli or of the visual system to assert what distinctive features actually are. The present discussion is restricted to presenting the view that words can be identified without the intervening identification of letters, and does not claim to make precise statements about the actual features of letters or words.)

The feature-analytic view of *letter* identification states that because there is redundancy in the structure of letters—because there is more than enough featural information to distinguish among 26 alternatives—not all features of a letter need be discriminated in order to identify a letter. Therefore, a number of alternate "criterial sets" of features may exist within each feature list, information about the features within any criterial set being sufficient for an identification to be made. For example, Tests 1, 3, 4, 5, 7, and 8 or Tests 1, 2, 4, 5, 7, 9, or Tests 2, 3, 4, 6, 7, 9, 10 might constitute a criterial set of the *H* feature list for "h". Information about any of these combinations of features would be sufficient to eliminate all the 25 other alternative letters and permit the categorization—the identification—of the configuration as "h". Similar criterial sets would exist within the *h* feature list for the same category.

It would be expected that criterial sets also exist for word category feature lists, except that now they would cover the "second dimension", and consist of feature combinations extending across the word. Criterial sets within the feature list for *HORSE,* for example, might include Tests 3, 4, 6, and 9 for Position 1; Tests 3, 7, and 9 for Position 3; Tests 4, 6, 7, and 8 for Position 4; and Tests 4, 6, 7, and 10 for Position 5. Three significant aspects of such a criterial set of features should be noted.

First, in no position are sufficient features tested to permit identification of a letter if that letter occurred in isolation. For example, feature tests 3, 4, 5, and 9 in Position 1 would not constitute a criterial set for the identification of *H* standing alone, although they are sufficient for the first position of *HORSE* (provided certain other features are tested in other positions). The explanation, of course, is that a criterial set for *H* would have to contain sufficient information to eliminate the 25 other letters of the alphabet, while there are not that many alternatives that could occur in front of the sequence –ORSE (or that could occur even if less than a criterial set of features for a letter were identified in each of the other positions). The difference between a criterial set for the first position of *Horse* and for the letter *H* in isolation illustrates the point that the "positions" in words should not be regarded as letters; word configurations are tested for featural information that leads directly to word categories, not to intermediate letter categories. Experimental evidence is available to show that words can be identified before any of their component letters are discriminable.

Second, the illustrative criterial set of features for *HORSE* does not include any features from the second position. The omission indicates that all of that particular part of the word (the letter *O* could be blacked out and the word would still be identifiable because only one letter could fill that position. The ready identifiability of the sequence *H–RSE* is an example of the *sequential redundancy* that exists within words, permitting the fluent reader to identify words on far less visual information than may be available in their configurations.

Third, the total number of features required to identify "horse" in the particular criterial set given as an example is only 15, far less than would be required to identify the letters *H, O, R, S,* and *E* if they were presented in isolation, or in mixed up order, or to a beginning reader or foreign-language speaker who could not "read" the whole word. Again, *this economy is a consequence of sequential redundancy* within words, and it is to this topic that we shall now turn our attention.

The earlier discussion of letter identification considered how many feature tests would be required to discriminate among a single set of 26 alternatives. The answer was a theoretical "somewhere between four or five", because five binary questions permit selection from among up to 32 alternatives ($2^5 = 32$). A mathematical smattering for this kind of calculation was provided in Chapter 2, particularly note 2, page 26. It was proposed that there were a few more than five distinctive features available in every letter, but probably not more than ten or a dozen. Ten feature tests would, in fact, be sufficient to provide many alternative criterial sets for the various functionally equivalent forms of letters such as *A, a, ɑ* .

A distinctive feature, you will recall, is an element of a stimulus configuration that constitutes a "significant difference"—that enables a perceiver to eliminate some of the alternative categories to which the configuration might be allocated. In the case of letters the number of alternative categories is 26; in the case of words, just to have a figure, let us say a skilled reader must have about 50,000. (In a coda to this chapter I shall show that one figure is as good as another, give or take many thousands.)

How many feature tests would be required to discriminate sufficient significant differences among visual configurations to permit their allocation to just one of 50,000 categories? The formal information theoretical calculation shows that the answer is not so many more than for 26 letters; fifteen or sixteen binary feature tests would be enough ($2^{15} = 32,768$; $2^{16} = 65,536$), particularly if the word length could be taken into account for an initial exclusion of unlikely alternatives.

The preceding statement does not assert that tests of 15 or 16 different kinds of features need to be made—the actual set of different features need be no greater for words than for letters—but rather that 15 or 16 tests must be made in different parts of the configuration. It would not matter that some tests were repeated one or more times, provided that they are made in different positions.

Of course, many more than 15 tests could be made on most words. If we assume that there are ten distinctive features for every letter, and five or six constitute a criterial set, a five-letter word such as *horse* would contain 50 distinctive features and it might be expected that a criterial set would be 25 or 30. However, the calculations of the previous paragraph show that far fewer than 50 or even 30 feature tests are theoretically sufficient to distinguish among 50,000 alternatives, and as we shall show, there is, in fact, evidence that 15 features are sufficient for most words. If 50 features are available in a five-letter word and only 15 are required for its identification, there is a good deal of redundancy present. We have met the concept of redundancy briefly in Chapter 2 and it is now time to look at it a little more closely. While reiterating the position that words are not identified through their component letters, I can most usefully begin the consideration of sequential redundancy in words in terms of the sequences of letters that words contain.

Redundancy is information that is available from more than one source. If you see that the first letter of an English word is *T* and the second letter *H,* you do not get—or at least you do not need—as much information from the second letter as you did from the first. Knowing the first letter of a word provides information about the second. The *visual information* in the first letter enables you to discard 25 out of 26 alternatives (assuming for the sake of argument that a word is equally likely to start with any of the letters of the alphabet). The second letter also contains enough visual information, or *featural information,* to distinguish among 26 alternatives, because obviously you can distinguish it from all the other letters of the alphabet when it is standing alone. But you do not need featural information to distinguish the second letter from 26 other letters, because there are not 25 other letters that it could be. If the first letter of an English word is *T,* then there is a very high degree of probability that the second letter will be either *H, R,* or one of the vowels; the number of possible alternatives for the second letter is not 26, but less than half that number. In fact the more letters that are known of a word, the fewer alternatives there are for what each additional letter could be—and because there is much less uncertainty about each letter, less and less featural information is required to identify it.

To a very rough approximation, the actual uncertainty of letters in English words decreases by a half as every additional letter is identified. On the average there are about five bits of uncertainty for the first letter (for 26 alternatives), four for the second (for about $2^4 = 16$ possibilities), three for the third ($2^3 = 8$), two for the fourth ($2^2 = 4$), and with four letters in a sequence known, perhaps only one bit—two alternatives—for the rest of the word.[7] Since each letter contains at least five bits of visual information, whether you want it or not, there is more and more redundancy with every successive letter.

The preceding argument leads to the conclusion that even if words were identified letter by letter, one would not need the same amount of feature information to identify every letter. Remembering that one feature test gives enough information to exclude approximately half the alternatives, then five feature tests would be required for the first letter, four for the second, three for the third, two for the fourth, and perhaps one for the rest of the word—a total of 15 feature tests. As pointed out a few paragraphs ago, 15 features should in any case be enough to distinguish among $2^{15} = 32,768$ alternatives. Provided that a reader had a knowledge of the way in which letters occur in words, he would need a far smaller number of feature tests to identify a five- or six-letter word than he would need to identify five or six separate letters.

Knowledge of the way in which letters are grouped into words may be called *orthographic information.* This information, which is located within the brain of the fluent reader, is an alternative source of information to the visual or *featural information* that the reader's eyes can pick up from the page. To the extent that both of these sources of information reduce the number of alternatives that a particular letter might be, there is redundancy. Such duplication of information may be called *sequential redundancy* because its source lies in the fact that the different parts of a word are not independent; the occurrence of particular alternatives in one part of a sequence limits the range of alternatives that can occur anywhere else in the sequence.

I have been talking so far about the constraints that one letter places on the occurrence of *letters* in other parts of a word. But precisely the same argument can apply to *features*. Obviously if we can say that the occurrence of the letter *T* in the first position of a word restricts the possibilities for the second position to *H, R, A, E, I, O, U,* and *Y;* then we can also say that the occurrence of features of the letter *T* in the first position limits the possible combinations of features that can occur in the second position. In fact, we can eliminate the mention of letters and specific positions altogether and say that when certain features occur in one part of a word, there are limits to the kinds of feature combinations that can occur in other parts of the word. When the reader is implicitly aware of such limitations he is able to make use of *sequential redundancy* among features, the overlapping sources of information being the visual information that could eliminate all possible sets of alternative feature combinations and the reader's knowledge that many of the possible alternative sets do not in fact occur.

(It might be added that the sequential redundancy of English words is enormous. If all 26 letters of the alphabet could occur independently in each position of a five-letter word, there could be $26^5 = 11,881,376$ different five-letter words, compared with perhaps 20,000 that actually exist. Even if we restricted permissible letter combinations to alternate vowels and consonants there would still be over a quarter of a million possibilities.)

To recapitulate, there are two sources of information available for the identification of words: one is featural, *the visual information available to the eye, and the other is* sequential, *our knowledge of the way words are constructed. When there is an overlap between featural and sequential information—when both sources can be used to eliminate some of the same alternatives—redundancy exists. And because redundancy exists, the skilled reader can trade off between the two sources—he can make identifications on less featural information because he can make use of his knowledge of sequential constraints.*

The important point that is being made is that one does not need to identify letters in any part of a word to reduce the amount of information required to identify the entire word. Word configurations are identified by a scrutiny of their features, and the better one knows a word, the fewer features are required to identify it. Words may be identified before there is sufficient featural information in any position to permit the identification of a letter standing alone.

Here is a simple illustration of how featural redundancy might permit the identification of a two-letter word before either of the letters could be identified individually. Imagine that enough features could be discriminated in the first position of the word so that if we were looking at that part alone our alternatives would be reduced to either *a* or *e*—but we could not make a final decision between the two. Suppose also that in the second position of the word we could detect enough features to reduce the alternatives to *f* or *t,* but not to make a final choice. From the four possibilities that might be constructed, *af, at, ef, et,* only one construction would be acceptable as a word. Because word categories do not exist for the other three possibilities, the configuration would be allocated to the category "at", identified as "at" and so perceived. If there was also a word (a category) "et" in the language, then a decision could not be made, and if "et" existed but not "at", then *et* is what would be seen. That is the argument. In the following section some supporting evidence will be presented that letters are, in fact, identified sooner in words than when in isolation.

Two qualifications ought to be made regarding the preceding example. Both have been made before but bear reiterating. The first is that we do not know what the features of letters or words actually are, therefore it is not suggested that the particular *af, at, ef, et* situation might actually arise, although there are many ways of demonstrating that we often see what we think must be present rather than what is actually present. The second qualification is that it is not suggested that a reader is *aware* of his knowledge of sequential redundancy, any more than he is aware of the decision-making process that is involved in reading or any other form of perception. But I shall be giving some examples to show that the fluent reader must indeed be regarded as possessing such a knowledge of his language.

Some remarks remain to be made concerning functional equivalence for word configurations. The notion of criterial sets permits a good deal of flexibility in the operation of a feature-analytic system. With letters, for example, ability to make an identification although information about one or two features may be absent from (or even contrary to) the total specification of a feature list need not prevent the categorization of a configuration. As a result, such allographs as *A,* ⊠ *, A, A,* and such impoverished forms as /A/ and %A% might all meet the specifications of one or another of the criterial subsets of the feature list for *A,* and be allocated to the category "a". When allographs reach a particular level of featural dissimilarity, however, such as *a* and *A,* there is the additional mechanism available of setting up "functionally equivalent" feature lists for the same category. Within each such feature list a number of alternative criterial sets might exist.

Just as there may be functionally equivalent feature lists for allographs of the same letter, so alternative feature lists for functionally equivalent versions of the same word would be expected. Invented examples have been given of one feature list for *HORSE* and another for *horse*. However, it is not proposed that these two (and other) feature lists for the same word would exist completely independently, but rather that a visual configuration would be allocated to a particular category if tests of its parts satisfied positional specifications on any set of functionally equivalent feature lists. As an oversimplified example, it is not proposed that there must necessarily be a special feature list for the visual configuration *Horse,* because the first position of that configuration is congruent with the beginning of *HORSE* (and many other words) while the remainder is congruent with part of *horse* (and some other words). While tests of the configuration *Horse* will not satisfy a criterial set within the feature lists for *HORSE* or *horse* or any other word, it is only within the two functionally equivalent feature lists for the category "horse" that the configuration meets criterial set requirements at both beginning and end. In other words, a configuration may be identified if it is congruent with parts of two criterial sets of features, provided that these incomplete criterial sets are functionally equivalent for the same category, and the relevant parts of the two criterial sets are complementary rather than overlapping. Such a view would suggest that a quite unfamiliar configuration like *HoRsE* should still be identifiable through meeting the criterial requirements for Positions 1, 3, and 5 for *HORSE* and Positions 2 and 4 for *horse*—and some evidence that this is the case will be given in the next section.

It must be emphasized that we are still not talking about letters—we are not saying that *H, R* and *E* are identified from one feature list and *o* and *s* from another. It is still proposed that the identification is being made directly to the category "horse" through the various equivalent feature lists for a word and not through the unrelated feature lists of individual letters.

To summarize, the difference between letter and word identification is simply the category system that is involved—the manner in which featural information is allocated. If one is examining an array of visual information in order to make letter identification, the featural information is tested and identifications made on the basis of the feature lists for the 26 letter categories. If the purpose is to identify words the featural information is tested with respect to the feature lists for words, and there is no question of letter identification. It follows from the present argument that it should be impossible to identify a word and its component letters simultaneously, be-

cause one cannot use the same information to make two different kinds of identification. Some support for that position will be given in the following section.

The feature-analytic theory is, in effect, a "whole-word" view; it certainly does not claim that words are identified letter by letter. However, the theory does offer an explanation for how whole words are recognized, which is a considerable advance over the traditional "word shape" hypothesis. The major point, of course, is that featural information is taken from all parts of the configuration at the same time, and because of the internal redundancy in the structure the entire word may be identified before sufficient features have been discriminated to identify particular letters.

Words may be apprehended as easily as letters because like letters they involve only a single category. The span of apprehension is four or five "items", which may be either letters or words, and there is no need for letters to be identified if whole words are to be apprehended. Words may be identified as quickly as letters because few if any additional features require to be discriminated to identify a word rather than a letter. Because there is much more redundancy in words, an inability to discriminate one or two features is rarely as critical as it would be in identifying letters. Words may be identified when their individual letters are separately indistinguishable because the redundancy in words reduces the amount of featural information that must be discriminated in any letter position to less than the amount of information required to identify the particular letter in isolation.

It was pointed out earlier that words could be identified at a much faster rate than would be possible if their component letters were presented one at a time, in fact letters cannot be identified any faster than entire words —about five or six a second. The feature-analytic position, however, does not assert that words are identified "as wholes" in the sense that every part of the word is analyzed simultaneously; it makes no statement at all about whether features are discriminated and analyzed in groups (sometimes called *parallel processing*) or one at a time (*serial processing*). Whether the processing of features proceeds in parallel or serially is still an open research question; what is established is that feature processing is very much faster than categorization. The factor that limits letter-by-letter identification to six letters a minute is not necessarily that it involves serial processing, but that categorization takes a significant amount of time and short-term memory space. On the other hand, feature processing is very fast and does not involve short-term memory at all prior to categorization.

The feature-analytic view offers an explanation of how words may be identified "by their shapes" because it defines shapes in terms of features. The statement that a reader recognizes words because "he has learned what they look like" can be interpreted to mean the establishment of feature lists for word categories. The view also has an explanation for the ability of a reader to allocate such diverse configurations as *HAT, Hat, hat* to the same category that a simple "word shape" template model cannot offer.

The concept of feature lists permits an explanation of how a reader enters his store of knowledge to identify a word. In contrast to template matching, the feature model does not assume either that the reader examines all categories one at a time until he finds the one to which a configuration can be allocated, or that certain sets of alternatives are "pulled out" for special consideration before others. Either of these points of view would suggest that some words might take very much longer to identify than others, simply because they are not considered as alternatives until later. There are differences in the speed with which different words can be identified, more common words generally having a shorter "response latency", but such differences are relatively slight compared with the basic processing time for any word; a reader rarely appears to be delayed in identifying a word because he is considering that it might be something else. The feature-analytic point of view suggests there would be very little real difference in the time required to identify most words because information on all feature tests goes to every feature list, and identification occurs as soon as a criterial set is achieved in any category. Any response-time difference in favor of more common words may be attributed to their having more and smaller criterial sets; a familiar word will be identified a little bit sooner than an unfamiliar word, but not much. This possibility is congruent with one explanation for the "word-frequency effect" noted on page 25 , that more frequently used words have shorter response latencies because the perceiver establishes a lower criterion level (requires fewer features) for frequently used words. An additional possibility is that where there is an expectation that a configuration will be a particular word— perhaps because of syntactic or semantic redundancy still to be discussed —feature tests will be made in the order in which they will provide the most relevant information about the expected category.

The possibility that very small criterial sets of features may be tested when expectations about particular words are high will account for the common type of error referred to on page 125, such as misreading "said" as "sail" or "send"—or even as "reported", in which case the reader has clearly dispensed with all featural information in assigning the configuration to a category indicated by sequential information available from other sources. The latter type of "error", of course, is most likely to occur when words are being read in sentences (the topic of Chapter 13) rather than in the identification of individual words which is the primary concern of the present chapter.

The feature-analytic view is also supported by the evidence that subjects in tachistoscopic experiments may be able to identify a word and yet still be aware of an anomaly within its structure, such as *fashixn*. While anomalous information from only a small area of a configuration, especially near the middle, might be insufficient to outweigh an otherwise criterial set of tests for identification, there is no reason why analyzers should not signal an irregularity without an exact categorization of the divergent element being made. Sensitivity to structure *within* the word configuration can also account for the fact that words containing familiar sequences of letters may be identified somewhat faster than words with less familiar sequences. The fact that the feature-analytic model is sensitive to redundancy among features within the structure of a word would be expected to reveal itself in the establishment of more and smaller criterial sets for highly probable sequences of letters.

The ability of fluent readers to identify "nonword" sequences of letters such as *vernalit* and *mossiant* and *ricaning* as easily as if they were words might appear to present a complication for the feature-analytic model so far presented. As explained in the previous paragraph, there is no difficulty about applying the model to account for sensitivity to highly predictable sequences of letters in word identification; a sequentially redundant group of letters is also a sequentially redundant array of features. But the model of the feature-analytic process so far described has always terminated in one or another of a pre-established set of letter or word categories, and *vernalit* and *mossiant* appear to be readable when they are not in pre-existing individual categories.

However, new categories are quite rapidly and easily established—it would be a reasonable gamble that the "words" *vernalit* and *mossiant* will stay in your memory and sight vocabulary as long as the more "significant" terms such as "equivalence" and "redundancy" employed in this book. The fact that the identification of nonword sequences of letters may reflect their sequential probabilities is not to the detriment of the feature-analytic view, but is clearly a different question from the type of word identification discussed in the present chapter. The phenomenon will be discussed in Chapter 11 because it is most relevant to the discussion in that chapter of "mediated word identification"—the process of finding the name for a configuration for which no category exists.

A point made in the previous section was that because letter and word identification involve the same featural information, it should not be possible to identify a configuration both as a word and as a sequence of letters at the same time. The argument is that you cannot use the same material for two different functions simultaneously, any more than you can sit on your hands and scratch your head at the same time. We can see the configuration *cat* either as the letters *c, a, t* or as the word "cat", but not as both simultaneously; for that reason an experienced proofreader will try to avoid reading "words" when his task is to check spelling, sometimes by having the passage read to him letter by letter backwards to break up the word formations. Similarly, we can see the configuration *read* either as the word pronounced "reed" or as the word pronounced "red" but not as both at once; and *6oss* can be seen either as a number or a word but not as both. We cannot apply the same information to two categories simultaneously, just as we cannot use the same contour as part of two figures simultaneously—the center line of $\}$ can be seen as part of a face on the left or as part of a face on the right, but the two faces can never be seen simultaneously.

It is easily shown that the limitation in the previous cases does not lie in an inability to allocate identical configurations to two different categories —we have little difficulty in seeing *46oss 6osses* or the two faces in $\}\}$, or even *cat is cat* as "c, a, t is cat", or *read read* as if pronounced "red reed"—as in *I PICKED UP THE NOTE AND READ "READ THIS QUICKLY"*—provided that there is featural information for each of the two categories we are using. The impossibility is to use the *same* information for two purposes simultaneously.

There is one type of experiment that at first sight might appear to indicate that words are *not* identified more easily than letters, but that actually provides an additional demonstration that words are indeed processed on a featural basis with the reader making use of sequential redundancy.[8] The experimental method involves projecting letters or words at such a low intensity that there is barely any contrast with the screen upon which they are shown, and then to increase the contrast slowly, gradually making more and more visual features available until the observer is able to identify the word. Under this procedure the observer is constrained by no time or memory limitations and may choose to make either word or letter identifications with the information available at any moment. He typically identifies letters within words before he says what an entire word is, and identifies entire words before he can identify any of the letters presented in isolation. While this finding is not inconsistent with the classical evidence that words can be identified before any of their component letters *in isolation,* it does make clear that words are, in fact, not recognized all-or-none "as wholes" but by analysis of their parts. Letters may be identified before entire words if they are actually in word configurations, and the sequential redundancy that exists within the configuration may permit identification of the letters on fewer features than would be required if they were presented in isolation, that is, without any sequential redundancy to supplement the visual information. Put in another way, criterial sets of features for words need not include sufficient information in any one position for the unique identification of a letter if all sequential redundancy were removed, but when sequential redundancy is present it may facilitate the identification of one or more letters even before the word as a whole can be identified. The letter *h* requires fewer features to identify if presented in the sequence *hat* than if presented alone, even if the reader identifies the *h* before the *at*. The additional information that enables the earlier letter identification to be made in words is, of course, the redundancy that exists among features of a word. Even if the reader has not discriminated sufficient features in the second and third positions of the configuration *hat* to identify the letters *at,* he still has some featural information from those positions which, when combined with his knowledge of the redundancy within words, permits him to identify the letter in the first position on minimal information.

Recent studies with young readers have shown that the ability to make use of sequential redundancy develops very early.[9] First-grade children who had had a limited amount of reading instruction in kindergarten were shown letters in isolation and in simple three-letter words that they could normally identify easily. The children showed themselves able to identify letters in words at lower intensities than when they were presented alone. For children in fourth grade the difference between the intensity level at which letters were identified in words and the level at which the same letters were identified in isolation was equal to that of skilled adult readers, indicating that for familiar three-letter words at least, fourth-graders could make as much use of sequential featural redundancy as adults.

The same studies showed that for both adults and children, the amount of information required to identify a letter appears to be correlated with the information required to identify other letters in the word. For example, more featural information will be required to identify *s* in the word *sun* than in the word *sad* if the *un* in *sun* is harder to identify than the *ad* in *sad*. The fact that all letters within a word appear to share the same relative degree of ease or difficulty has been shown in words of up to eight letters in length.

It is obviously a gross oversimplification to talk about the relative "discriminability" of different letters of the alphabet or to assume that letters that are difficult to identify when standing alone must be difficult to perceive when in words. The "distinctive features" of letters are not a fixed and immutable set. The amount of visual information required to identify a letter has relatively little to do with the physical characteristics of the ac-

*tual stimulus but depends much more on the reader's skill and the context
in which the letter occurs. And precisely the same kind of argument applies to words.*

There is other evidence that although words are identified "as wholes",
in the sense that featural information from all parts may be taken into account in their identification, they are by no means identified on the basis of
the familiarity of their shape or contour. Examples were given earlier in
this chapter of the ease with which quite unfamiliar configurations like
rEaDiNg and *HoRsE* would be read. It has been shown experimentally
that entire passages printed in these peculiar configurations can be read
about as fast as normal text.[10] In fact if the size of the capital letters is reduced slightly so that they do not interfere with the discriminability of the
lower case letters, for example *rEaDiNg* and *HoRsE,* there is no difference
at all between the rates at which such words and normal text are read. The
result is perhaps not so surprising when we reflect upon the ease with
which practiced readers can adapt to the most distorted forms of typogra-
phy or handwriting, by making use of alternative criterial sets existing
within a single feature list or across functionally equivalent lists.

Learning To Identify Words

There are two aspects of learning to identify words which are
analogous to the two aspects of learning to identify letters outlined at the
end of the last chapter. One aspect is establishing functionally equivalent
feature lists with criterial sets of features for each category, and the other
is associating a name with a category. For letter identification it was asserted that associating the name with the category was not a problem; we
learn names for visual configurations all the time. In word identification
there may indeed be a problem in associating names with categories, not
because the reader has particular difficulty in remembering the name for a
category once he has found out what it is, but in finding out what the name
of a category is in the first place. The process of finding out the name of a
category has already been termed *mediated word identification,* to distinguish it from allocating a configuration to a category that has a name,
which I have called *immediate word identification.* The term "immediate"
is used not in the sense of instantaneous, which we know is not the case,
but to mean "not mediated", indicating that a word is identified directly
from its features.

The easiest form of mediated word identification may be—up to a point
—to ask someone what the name of a configuration is, but the commonest
method for the fluent reader is to work out the name for himself. By mak-

ing use of the unique fact that words are constructed alphabetically, the reader can to varying degrees of approximation sound out the name of a new word from the letters of the word itself. The question of mediated word identification is the topic of Chapter 12. The present chapter will conclude with notes on what must be required in learning to allocate configurations to categories through the establishment of functionally equivalent feature lists. The outline will be quite summary because the final chapters of this book will recapitulate the important but limited skill of immediate word identification within the broader context of the fluent reading process.

I shall start at the point where a beginning reader faces the problem of learning how visual configurations, which he knows should be allocated to different categories, can in fact be distinguished and appropriately identified. This problem is not the beginning of learning to read, because a child who has reached this point must already have acquired some important insights into the nature of words and the reading process generally. But the problem will serve as the basis for our summary.

It will help if we discuss specific instances. A child is about to learn to recognize his own name, *John,* which is written on a flashcard. The task confronting the child is to find out the rules for recognizing this event when it occurs again, which means that he must find out something about the configuration that will enable him to distinguish it from other configurations that he should not call "John". I shall assume that the child has passed the stage where he has discovered that a reliable distinguishing characteristic for the configuration is not the card that it is printed on, or a smudge in the corner, both of which may be reasonable cues for other types of identification but which will sooner or later prove to be inadequate for the allocation of events to word categories. I shall also assume that the child at this time is not confronted with seeing *John* in a number of different type styles. The ability to name any or all of the letters of the alphabet has no direct relevance in immediate word identification, although there will be an obvious (although by no means essential) advantage for the child if he has learned to distinguish even a few letters, because he will have begun to acquire cues about features that can be distinguishing for words.

That is the problem for the child: to discover a cue that will distinguish *John* when next he meets it. He may decide a good cue lies in the length of the word, or the two upright strokes, or the shape of the "fishhook" at the beginning. In selecting a cue that will be the basis for his recognition of the word, he will establish the first "distinctive features" that he will look for in the future when testing whether to allocate a configuration to the category "John".

Exactly what the first distinctive features will be depends on circumstances; it depends on what the child has to distinguish the configuration *John* from. Until he comes across another word that is not *John* there is no problem, he just applies his single test and calls every configuration that passes the test "John". But until he comes across another word that is not *John* there can be no learning. What brings a child to the beginning of the process of developing feature lists that will serve for *reading* is having to distinguish *John* from all the other configurations with which it is not functionally equivalent. He will only really be able to identify *John* when he has learned not to apply that name to every other word configuration that he meets. It is when the child is confronted by a configuration that should go into a different category that the soundness of his discrimination is tested, and, of course, it is soon found to be wanting. If his distinctive features were related to the length of the word, then he would respond "John" to the configuration *Fred*. If his cue was the initial fishhook, he would say "John" to *Jack* or *June* or *Jeremiah*. The more nonequivalent configurations—the more different "words"—the child is forced to discriminate among, the more he will come to select as distinctive features those that will be appropriate to the eventual task of fluent reading.

Until the child is shown what he has to distinguish John *from, he will never acquire an appropriate set of distinctive features for identifying that word.*

The preceding statement does not mean that the child has to be able to *name* every other word that he meets; not at all. All he has to do is see a representative sample of words that are not *John,* so that he can find out in what respects *John* is different. It does not matter if he cannot discriminate among all the other words (although in learning to identify *John* he will learn something about all other words); all he has to do is establish two categories: configurations that are "John" and configurations that are not "John".

The preceding statement *did* mean that teaching a child "one word at a time"—writing the word on a variety of different surfaces and occasions and insisting "This is 'John'; this is 'John' "—will not teach him how to read the word, because until this procedure is varied he will never learn how *John* may be distinguished from any other word.

The notion that a child can learn to identify a word by the repetitious presentation of just that word is a template theory—its inappropriateness is obvious as soon as we realize that there is no way in which a child can transfer a picture of what is presented to his eyes into a storehouse in his brain. He does not need to be told interminably what a word is; he has to be shown what it is *not*.

The human brain is very well adapted to the business of looking for significant differences; we do it all the time, it is the basis of our intellectual eminence. There is no need for an explanation of *why* two things are different; they merely have to be shown side by side with the information "These things are not to be treated as the same," or "This one is an *X* and that one is not," and significant differences will be sought and found. If you reflect upon it, that is the way almost all learning is done. A child is told "That is a cat"—but not given any hints about *why* it is a cat. He has to discover for himself what are the distinctive features of cats, and he does this whenever he uses the term "cat" inappropriately, for chickens or for dogs, and is told "No, that is not a cat". A child does not know how to use a name—of an object or a word—until he stops using it for objects or words that should not have that name, and the only way he can distinguish the objects or words that should have the name from those that should not is by seeing examples of both classes, and getting "feedback".

I have really reached the end of the story as far as immediate word identification is concerned. The big hurdle for a child is to find out what are the distinctive features of words. Every additional instance that a child meets that is or is not a configuration that he can categorize provides him with further information about distinctive features. As a child acquires his knowledge of the features of words, so he can construct feature lists for the different categories. He can establish a new category whenever he meets a configuration that cannot be allocated to any of the categories he already has; the feedback that tells him it cannot be allocated will help establish, and perhaps name, the new category into which he puts the configuration. (As he develops mediated word identification skills, the reader will be able to provide his own feedback for establishing new categories.) And with his growing mastery of distinctive features, it will no longer be a problem for the child if a word is presented in a variety of type styles; he will set up functionally equivalent feature sets, for example for *JOHN* and *John*. Eventually, his skills will become so well integrated that he will not have to meet functionally equivalent configurations to establish alternative feature lists; when we have reached the stage at which we can identify *interdenominational* on sight, it will not matter that we have never previously seen *INTERDENOMINATIONAL* or even *iNtErDeNoMiNaTiOnAl* for us to identify those configurations immediately.

Acquaintance with a wide variety of nonequivalent alternatives is everything. Through growing familiarity with the written form of language, the child learns not only to discriminate distinctive features, to establish feature lists, and to recognize functional equivalences, he also learns about redundancy. And by acquiring a pool of knowledge about the redundancy in words, he learns how to make identification economically, on minimal quantities of visual information; he establishes large numbers of alternative criterial sets.

It is a sobering concluding thought that just about everything that a child learns, as described in the preceding paragraph, is never explicitly taught. *Among the many positive aspects of reading instruction—providing motivation, direction, answers, feedback—we cannot include the provision of the rules by which the immediate identification of words is accomplished. We leave that part of learning to the child himself.*

A Few Words about Words

One of the inevitable consequences of examining closely a subject like reading, about which so much is taken for granted, is that it turns out to be far more complicated and less well understood than we thought it to be. An obvious first step in my discussion of word identification would have been to state clearly and precisely how many words the average fluent reader knows: this would give some useful knowledge about the dimensions of the problem. But the trouble with a simple request for a count of the words that a person knows is that the answer depends on what is meant by "word" and on what is meant by "knows", while in any case there is no way to compute a reliable answer.

Consider first the matter of deciding what we want to call a word. We have already seen (page 37) that linguists have to make an arbitrary choice about whether *cat* and *cats,* or *walk* and *walked,* should be regarded as two different words or as two forms of the same word. Dictionaries usually provide entries only for the base or root form of words, sometimes called *lexemes* or "minimally different lexical items", refusing to count as different words such variations as plurals, comparatives, adjectival forms, and various verb tenses. With written language a more simple solution might appear available—everything is a word if it has white space on either side, although it may seem a little odd to have different definitions for "word" depending on whether it is spoken or written. If we want to call *cat* and *cats,* or *walk* and *walked,* different words in writing (and certainly we would not regard them as functionally equivalent) the number of words we "know" on sight might turn out to be three or four times greater than the number of words the dictionary maker would credit us with. There would still be left the problem of words which look the same but are pronounced differently—"You should *read* the book I *read* yesterday" or "Please *permit* me to get my *permit*". Not to mention the words that sound the same but have different meanings, as in "You can *bank* on the *bank* by the river *bank*"; this again is not an insignificant matter because most of the common words of our language have multiple definitions. But while it may not seem altogether reasonable to count words as "the same" if they have quite different meanings, the alternative is also a little peculiar—why should *bank* be regarded as three (or more) words and *the* as only one?

We still need a definition of "know". With so much looseness of definition, it might be excusable to take a very rough and ready pragmatic approach and assert that a reader "knows" a word that he reads if he does not have to stop and look it up in the dictionary; if it does not hinder or delay his comprehension of the passage in which it occurs.

All this equivocation and evasion is hardly scientific, but let us move on. The problem now is to count. Obviously, it is not good enough simply to count the number of words that a person reads or hears or produces during the course of a day, for many words will be used more than once. Barely a dozen words will go by without the occurrence of very familiar words like *I* and *the* and *of;* in fact it has been estimated that a core of only fifty words accounts for over half of our spoken language. To count the number of *different* words a person produces, we shall have to look for them carefully in a torrent of very familiar words. But in how big a torrent shall we look? How can we ever be sure that we have given a person sufficient opportunity to produce all the words he knows! Without a doubt, we shall find some new words in every additional sample of a thousand that we record, but surely the law of decreasing returns would apply. After analyzing say 100,000 words from one person it would seem unlikely that he would produce many new ones. But such is not the case. Very many words with which we are quite familiar occur less than once in every million— and it may take anywhere from two months to two years for a person to produce that number of words. One very extensive analysis of nearly five million words in popular magazines [11] found over 3000 words that occurred on an average of less than once in every million, and almost all of these words would fall under our category of "known". Here is a sample of words that occurred only once in every *five million* words—earthiness, echelon, echidna, eclair, effluence, egad, egotistic—one or two may be a little unusual, but by and large they are words that we can *read*.

There is something a little eerie even to think about how we might acquire and retain familiarity with the relatively infrequent words. We meet them perhaps once a year, but it is not often we have to stop and wonder "Haven't I seen you before somewhere?"

Obviously, it is not possible to "count" how many different words a person knows, so one has to make an estimate. And many estimates have been made, varying from 20,000 to over 100,000, depending on the definitions used and assumptions made. This ends the diversion and gives an answer to the question of how many words a person might know—it is impossible to say. Instead we can make two general statements. The first is that the number of words that the fluent reader can recognize must be very

large, in the tens of thousands, and the second is that while we must respect a system that can make such a large number of distinctions, we
should not boggle incredulously. We probably have many more perceptual
categories than we have categories for words, and most of our "word" categories are established through speech before we try to organize them in reading. Every time we meet a stimulus configuration that is for any reason not
"functionally equivalent" to something we have identified before, we
establish a new category.

I can now return to my main theme, which has reached a question that
has so far been evaded. I have been saying that making—and learning to
make—the necessary discriminations to sort stimuli into functionally
equivalent categories is a complex task, but that associating a name with a
category is something we all accomplish fluently and frequently. Now the
question is how can one discover what the name of the category is so that
the association can be made.

References

Once again, the best basic sources for further information about
much of the theory and data referred to in this chapter are Neisser (listed on
page 10 and Woodworth and Schlosberg (listed on page 104).

The analysis of the "three theories of word identification" is derived from:

I. H. ANDERSON and W. F. DEARBORN, *The Psychology of Teaching Reading*
(New York: The Ronald Press Company, 1952).
but almost any book with a similar title would illustrate variants of these views.

The feature-analytic model of word identification and comprehension (to be
discussed in the following chapters) is original to the present work and will not
be found elsewhere. This model should not be accepted uncritically; it has not
so far been exposed extensively to the natural process of critical review and revision that has shaped and established more venerable theories.

Notes

1, 2, 3. The best authority for much of this work is still Cattell (listed on page
95, note 4).

4. P. A. KOLERS and M. T. KATZMAN, Naming sequentially presented letters and
words, *Language and Speech*, **9**, 2 (1966), 84–95. E. B. NEWMAN, Speed of reading
when the span of letters is restricted, *American Journal of Psychology*, **79** (1966),
272–278.

5. W. B. PILLSBURY, A study in apperception, *American Journal of Psychology*, **8**
(1897), 315–393.

6. G. A. MILLER, J. S. BRUNER, and L. POSTMAN, Familiarity of letter sequences and
tachistoscopic identification, *Journal of Genetic Psychology*, **50** (1954), 129–139.

7. This figure, of course, represents an estimate of an average computed over many readers, many words, and many letter positions. There is not a progressive decline in uncertainty from letter to letter, from left to right, in all words. An English word beginning with *q*, for example, has zero uncertainty about the next letter *u*, an uncertainty of about two bits for the four vowels that can follow the *u*, and then perhaps four bits of uncertainty for the next letter, which could be one of over a dozen alternatives. Other words have different uncertainty patterns, although in general the uncertainty of any letter goes down the more other letters in the word are known, irrespective of order. Because of constraints in the spelling patterns of English—due in part to the way words are pronounced—there is slightly more uncertainty at the beginning of a word than at the end, with slightly less in the middle (see J. S. BRUNER and D. O'DOWD, A note on the informativeness of parts of words, *Language and Speech*, **1** [1958], 98–101.).

8. F. SMITH, The use of featural dependencies across letters in the visual identification of words, *Journal of Verbal Learning and Verbal Behavior*, **8** (1969), 215–218.

9. DEBORAH LOTT and F. SMITH, Knowledge of intra-word redundancy by beginning readers, *Psychonomic Science*, in press.

10. F. SMITH, DEBORAH LOTT, and B. CRONNELL, The effect of type size and case alternation on word identification, *American Journal of Psychology*, **82**, 2 (1969), 248–253.

11. E. L. THORNDIKE and I. LORGE, *The Teacher's Word Book of 30,000 Words* (New York: Teachers College, Columbia University, 1944).

11

Three Aspects
of Features

The present chapter is in the nature of an interlude.

It would be most logical to proceed without a break from a chapter on the immediate identification of words to a chapter on the mediated identification of words. But the continuity would in any case be disrupted because a chapter on mediated word identification could not proceed very far without becoming involved in a discussion of distinctive *acoustic* features, which is a topic we have not met so far. And while elaborating on the theme of visual features and acoustic features it would be appropriate to raise the matter of distinctive *semantic* features, which will be very much a concern of Chapter 13. At this point, I shall pull together a number of threads, leaving aside for the moment the purely visual side of reading. One thread will be picked up from all the way back in Chapter 3—I shall look in a little more detail at the structure of the sounds of language and at how spoken words are identified. Another thread will be pulled forward from the chapter still to come, on Meaning, and I shall consider briefly how the sense of a spoken or written word might be determined.

To begin, it has to be explained that it is just as appropriate to talk about distinctive features of phonemes and spoken words as it is to refer to distinctive features of letters and written words. In fact if literary protocol demanded priority of reference for age and eminence, a distinctive features theory of speech perception would have had to be discussed before there was any mention of the feature-analytic model for reading. The feature model for letter identification that developed in the 1960s was inspired by a feature theory of speech perception published in the 1950s.[1] The visual theory proposed that there is no essential difference between the ways in which spoken and written language are perceived, except for the different physical source of information—the surface structure of language. In both cases a physical representation, acoustic [2] or visual, is scanned for distinctive features which are analyzed in terms of feature lists that determine a particular categorization and perceptual experience. The number of physical features requiring to be discriminated will vary inversely with other sources of information about the language (redundancy) that the perceiver is able to utilize.

Just as elements of the written or printed marks on a page are regarded as the distinctive features of letters or words, so elements smaller than a single sound are conceptualized as distinctive features of phonemes. Distinctive features of sounds are usually regarded as distinct and significant components of the process by which a phoneme is articulated, such as whether or not the sound is *voiced* (whether the vocal cords vibrate as for /b/, /d/, /g/ compared with /p/, /t/, /k/), whether the sound is *nasal* (like /m/ and /n/), its duration, and the position of the tongue. Each distinctive feature is a significant difference, and the discrimination of any one feature may eliminate many alternatives in the total number of possible sounds (the set of phonemes). Every feature cuts the set of alternatives in a different way, so that theoretically a total of only six distinctive features could be more than enough to distinguish among 46 alternative phonemes ($2^6 = 64$).

There are many analogies between the distinctive features of letters and those of phonemes. The total number of different features is presumed to be much smaller than the set of units that they differentiate (26 for letters, about 46 for sounds). The number of features suggested for phonemes is usually 12 or 13 (note again the redundancy). Phonemes can be confused in the same manner as letters, and the more likely two sounds are to be confused with each other, the more distinctive features they are assumed to share.[3] Some sounds, such as /b/ and /d/, which probably differ in only one feature, are more likely to be confused than /b/ and /t/, which differ in perhaps two, and /t/ and /v/ which may differ in three features. Obviously, spoken words may differ by only a single feature just as written words may—"ban" and "Dan", which have only a single feature's difference, should be rather more likely to be confused than "ban" and "tan", and much more likely than "tan" and "van"; experimental evidence suggests that assumptions of this kind are correct.

It is interesting to observe that the emphasis on letters in traditional reading theories is usually not accompanied by an analytic approach to speech recognition. Many people involved in the complexities of reading tend to think that the identification of spoken words is somehow more spontaneous and instantaneous and wholistic—almost as if the ears detect whole words rather than the patterned soundwaves that the brain has to analyze and interpret. Yet the perception of speech is no less complex and time consuming than that of reading; the sound that we hear is the end product of an information-processing procedure that leads to the identification (the categorization) of a sound or word prior to the perceptual experience. We do not "hear" a word and then identify it—the identification must precede the hearing, otherwise we might often just hear "noise". And we do not "hear" features of sound, any more than we see features of writing; the smallest acoustic unit that we are aware of discriminating is the phoneme and the smallest visual unit is the letter.

There is no need to belabor the analogy. The feature-analytic model for letters and written word identification has been outlined sufficiently often in previous chapters to render redundant a reiteration of all the aspects of the system in terms of phonemes and spoken words. A child beginning to learn to read may be regarded as having already established acoustic categories for words, and probably for many phonemes, with each category specified by a *feature list*. Phoneme categories would represent significant perceptual differences in the identification of spoken words, just as graphemes are significant perceptual differences for written words. The concept of functionally equivalent alternative feature lists is probably not required for spoken words, except conceivably for some aspects of bilingualism. The various physical representations of speech—different dialects, for example—would not appear to differ as radically as the alternative representations of written words.

In short, each "word category" for which a reader establishes visual feature lists may be assumed also to have an acoustic feature list to permit identification based on acoustic information. When I say that the category to which a visual configuration can be allocated may already have a name, a more precise characterization would be that a visual feature list is established for a category that already has an acoustic feature list. And just as there may be some auditory categories that do not have associated visual feature lists (spoken words and other identifiable sounds for which a reader has no visual counterparts), so there may be visual categories without acoustic feature lists (visual configurations that we can differentiate and recognize but not directly name).

The "features" on a feature list, of course, are not actual elements of sounds or visual events, but only hypothetical neurological patterns, "neural codings". A visual or acoustic feature list represents conceptually the featural information picked up by "tests" of a perceptual system to discriminate aspects of stimulus configuration. The "tests" are conducted by analyzers in the perceptual system; their precise locus is unknown. As we have seen in the chapter on the physiology of the eye, page 84, visual information is processed in a number of places between the retina and the visual area of the brain. But after the first transformation of light stimulation into neural events at the receptor surface of the eyeball, all the analysis and comparison and matching is conducted solely on different patterns of neural signals. Information from every analyzer is seen as being directed through the appropriate modality (visual, auditory) to all feature lists on which the particular analyzer is represented; in other words, every visual feature list that includes a test from a particular analyzer will be "informed" whether that test is passed in the analysis of a particular visual configuration, and the same applies for the auditory analysis of acoustic configurations. An allocation to a category is made, "identification" occurs, when the information from all analyzers reaching a certain feature list constitutes a criterial set of features for that list. All these interior analyses and allocations are made in terms of neurological messages only—there are no "sounds" or "letters" in the brain; this point will be of considerable significance in the forthcoming discussion, when I attempt to show how the various processes of mediated word identification do not involve moving from letters to sounds—although they may well involve interaction among the neural patterns representing visual features and acoustic features.

It has not been in the area of reading alone that the notion of distinctive features has been borrowed from a theory of speech perception. A theory of word meaning has been independently developed that reflects in part the approach of the generative-transformational grammarians (Chapter 3)—it attempts a description of the deep structure of language—and in part the concept of distinctive features.[4] *Meaning is the concern of a later chapter, but a brief preview will not be out of place in the present context.*

According to the arguments already presented, a word may be regarded as a cognitive category to which a set of acoustic or visual distinctive features—an acoustic or visual configuration—may be allocated; the features are irreducible elements of the physical structure of words, and a listing of their conjoint presence or absence in a particular feature list constitutes an acoustic or visual specification of a word.

According to the arguments now to be presented, a word may be regarded as a set of distinctive features of *meaning,* that is to say, lists of *semantic features* constituting specifications of the meaning of particular words.

The simplest way to explain how a single word could possibly be considered to consist of a number of smaller elements of meaning is to consider the manner in which pairs of nouns may differ. For example, we could say that the pair *man–woman* (or *man–boy* or *woman–girl*) is closer in meaning than the pair *man–girl* (or *woman–boy*) because while *man* and *woman* differ only in gender—we are obviously talking about abstract definition, not connotation—and *man–boy* differ only in age, *man–girl* differ both in gender and age. "Age" and "gender" might therefore be regarded as distinctive features of meaning for words like *man, woman, boy, girl*—they make a significant difference to their semantic interpretation.[5] There are also other semantic features of *man, woman, boy, girl* that are not distinguishing within that group because they all have them in common; however, contrast with other words will show what some of these features are. For example, the difference between *man* and *lion* has nothing to do with gender or age, but is concerned with the feature of "human", while *boy* and *lioness* differ on the features of "human", "gender", and "age". Both *humans* and *lions* share a feature "animate" in comparison with objects like *rocks* and *vacuum cleaners,* and together they all have a feature "concrete" in contrast to abstractions like *love* or *idea.*

From the preceding extremely simplified illustration it might be seen how the meanings of words could be considered as "bundles" of semantic features, just as their written and spoken forms may be represented by feature lists. Like visual and acoustic features, semantic features may also be regarded in binary "yes-or-no" terms (although this is perhaps an appropriate moment to note that there is difficulty in specifying a binary opposition of alternatives for some apparent semantic, acoustic, and perhaps even visual features). We could therefore construct partial lists of "tests" for semantic features of words similar to the visual feature lists for letters and words represented on page 129. (See Table 4.) (In the semantic case, the allocation of the + and − is obviously not arbitrary.)

There are obvious differences between semantic features and those for spoken and written words, some of which have lead to a good deal of theoretical contention. For example, the "features" of meaning are not physical attributes like marks on a page or soundwaves in the air—they are liter-

Table 4		**Semantic Feature Lists**				
Word Category:	**Man**	**Woman**	**Boy**	**Lioness**	**Rock**	**Love**
TEST			FEATURE LIST			
1 abstract	−	−	−	−	−	+
2 animate	+	+	+	+	−	
3 human	+	+	+	−		
4 male	+	−	+	−		
5 adult	+	+	−	+		

ally abstractions. However, one can no more break a semantic feature down into smaller components of meaning than one can talk of parts of visual or acoustic distinctive features. The set of semantic features must be very much larger than the round dozen visual or acoustic features that have been proposed; in fact, nobody knows how many features would be required to differentiate all the possible words in the language (and some kinds of word are very resistant to being broken down into features at all). But semantic features would appear to share another characteristic of their visual and acoustic counterparts in that a relatively small set of features will specify a very much larger set of alternatives; 20 semantic features would be sufficient to distinguish over a million shades of meaning ($2^{20} = 1,048,576$). Of course, some semantic feature tests would be completely irrelevant if other tests turned out in a particular way—there is no need to inquire whether an inanimate object is human or male. In fact, the actual manner in which semantic specifications of feature lists might be constructed and interrelated is a very complex matter.

I should not leave the distinctive feature theory of semantics without a passing reference to some of its powerful advantages, in addition to its promise of order and system among the hundreds of thousands of words in the lexicon of a language. The concept of distinctive semantic features provides a formal way to express why a sentence may be uninformative or ambiguous. "That unmarried man is a bachelor" is an uninformative (tautologous) statement because *unmarried man* and *bachelor* have exactly the same sets of distinctive features. "The plane was flown to Chicago" is ambiguous because *plane* has two alternative sets of features, one marked + for "vehicle" and − for "tool" and the other marked − for "vehicle" and + for "tool". Similarly, a sentence like "The plane took off from Chicago" can be disambiguated because the features of *plane* are congruent in only one way with semantic constraints contained in "take off" (tools do not take off). We can even see that the sentence "George Washington was the first president of the United States" is not tautologous, although this would appear to be an implication of the quite widespread view that the meaning of a word lies in the object it refers to. *George Washington* and *first president of the United States* may have the same referent (they both refer to the same person), but they do not share the same list of semantic features.

Now I can provide the promised explanation of what has been meant all along by the concept of a "category" as something to which a visual or acoustic configuration is allocated. The explanation involves a sleight of hand, because in effect it makes the concept disappear. We now have three quite independent ways in which a word category may be specified: in terms of visual features, acoustic features, or semantic features. What then is the nature of the "category" to which all these feature lists are associated? the answer is that there is no category there at all. The three different kinds of feature lists are associated with each other, and the term "category", although we shall continue to employ it for its utility, really means nothing more than the intersection of two or more feature lists.

There are considerable conceptual advantages in trying to construct an "as-if" model of reading—"as if" there existed for each word a list of semantic characteristics that can be associated directly with sets of visual or acoustic features. One advantage, which will be particularly felt in the next chapter, is that the semantic model offers a way of plugging the visual and auditory aspects of language directly into a meaning system. One characteristic of semantic features, so far not mentioned explicitly, is that they permit the establishing of relations between *different word categories. We can grasp how a statement like "John has become a father" can convey information if we think about the operation of the set of distinctive semantic features of "father" in conjunction with the set of distinctive semantic features of "John". But I have no wish in this book to argue or support a particular semantic theory—the feature framework is adopted because it is consistent with the general model of reading being developed. And I have certainly no intention to make any claim about the nature of particular semantic features, or the way in which semantic features might be theoretically interrelated. I am not even trying to say that there is a maximum of three aspects of "cognitive categories"—visual, acoustic, semantic—and no more. There are obviously all manner of complex relations in the brain. Vision involves far more than just reading, meaning involves far more than just semantics, and thinking involves far more than language. But the intention of this book—despite all indications to the contrary—is to clarify rather than complicate, and the understanding of reading is a sufficiently intricate enterprise to warrant the avoidance of technical controversy in specialist areas. We are constructing a model, and cannot avoid the rough-hewn texture of some of the building blocks.*

References

Distinctive feature theories for both speech recognition and meaning are highly complex; the sources cited in the notes below are very specialized and at this point will probably not throw much more light on the question of reading. Most introductory linguistics texts have something to say about feature (and other) theories in both phonology and semantics; one very readable example is:

J. LYONS, *Introduction to Theoretical Linguistics* (Cambridge: Cambridge University Press, 1968).

A very brief survey of some approaches to both syntax and semantics is provided by:

G. A. MILLER, Psycholinguistic approaches to the study of communication. In D. A. ARM (ed.), *Journeys in Science: Small Steps—Great Strides* (Albuquerque: The University of New Mexico Press, 1967).

The status of feature theory in semantics is particularly contentious; it is an area that is shifting rapidly and it is impossible to provide references that are written at an easily understandable level or likely to remain authoritative for long. One problem with semantic features is that the notion works fairly well for nouns but less so for verbs and adjectives. A promising alternative view is concerned with "dependency relations" among words—literally with the way words constrain each other. On this basis, the "deep structure" difference between *I was seated by the fountain* and *I was soaked by the fountain* (see page 43) lies not in any "features" of meaning inherent in *seated* and *soaked,* but rather in the different manner in which they may be employed with words like *fountain.*[6]

However word relationships are organized and acquired, the problem for the reader is still to eliminate alternatives, whether these are conceptualized in terms of features or relations (conceivably features and relations will turn out to be the same thing), and the problem for the learner is to discover the operative rules and the significant differences in the written language system. The value of competing theories about language, as far as the purpose of this book is concerned, lies not so much in the extent to which they approximate some ideal and currently unreachable truth as in their contribution to an insightful and manageable conceptual framework for reading. While the absence of definitive knowledge in many areas of science relevant to reading requires an open-minded attitude, there is no point in getting confused. The morass of literature on specialized topics should not be entered by anyone without a reliable guide and a good sense of where he wants to get to.

Notes

1. R. JAKOBSON and M. HALLE, *Fundamentals of Language* (The Hague: Mouton, 1956).
2. The distinction between the terms "acoustic" and "auditory" is often not clearly understood (partly because it is often not easy to distinguish where an acoustic event leaves off and an auditory one begins). Acoustics is specifically concerned with the transmission of sound, the physical train of events that leads to the auditory phenomenon of perceiving a particular sound. One talks about *acoustic* information and *auditory* experience—a distinction for which the closest counterpart in vision is *optical* and *visual* (or *perceptual*).
3. G. A. MILLER and PATRICIA E. NICELY, An analysis of perceptual confusions among some English consonants, *Journal of the Acoustical Society of America,* **27** (1955), 338–353. (Reprinted in Saporta, listed on page 46.)
4. J. J. KATZ and J. A. FODOR, The structure of a semantic theory, *Language,* **39** (1963), 170–210. (Reprinted in part in De Cecco, listed on page 10, and in full in

J. A. FODOR and J. J. KATZ, *The Structure of Language* [Englewood Cliffs, N.J.: Prentice-Hall, Inc., 1964], a book of readings, mostly quite specialized, that includes contributions by Halle, note 1 above.)

5. In the present passage I am temporarily contravening the convention of italicizing *written words* and placing "spoken words" or word categories in quotation marks. To avoid peppering the present chapter with quotation marks and having to find an additional way of representing semantic features, words (as category names, or dictionary entries) are *italicized* and features placed in "quotation marks". In Chapter 12, I shall revert to the earlier practice of italicizing words when their written form is indicated (while still, unfortunately, also italicizing for emphasis).

6. Some very technical papers on this topic are included in E. BACH and R. T. HARMS (eds.), *Universals of Linguistic Theory* (New York: Holt, Rinehart and Winston, Inc., 1968) (which is not recommended for anyone lacking linguistic sophistication). A readable short paper that examines very briefly alternative ways in which word meanings might be organized, primarily from the point of view of memory, is G. A. MILLER, The organization of lexical memory. In G. A. TALLAND and NANCY C. WAUGH (eds.), *The Pathology of Memory* (New York: Academic Press, Inc., 1969).

12

Phonics— and Mediated Word Identification

Consider the following statements:

Love is an abstraction; it has neither an obvious referent nor simple definition. It means different things to different people and to the same person at different times. The promise of its fulfillment is universal and unalloyed, but the disparity between the ideal and its attainment is almost invariably painful and anticlimactic.

In place of the word *love* in the previous paragraph we could substitute many vague but laudable concepts such as *truth,* or *justice,* or *education,* or *phonics.*

It is always easier to say what an abstraction is not than what it is. Let me start with what phonics is not.

Phonics is not *phonetics,* which is the scientific study of the sounds of a language, and which has nothing at all to do with writing. Skilled phoneticians can detect scores of distinct language sounds, many of which are completely indistinguishable to the average ear because they are *allophonic* (page 31)—sounds that do not constitute significant differences in the language. To say that English is not a phonetic language is to say that it has no sounds, which is not normally the speaker's intention. Phonetics is to phonics what brain surgery is to cutting-and-pasting.

Phonics is not *phonemics,* which is the study of the classes of sounds

159

that do constitute significant differences in a language. In English, as we have seen, there are about 46 phonemes.

A popular belief that phonics has something to do with fluent reading is debatable. There are a number of arguments in this book that the skilled reader is rarely concerned with the sounds of the letters—or even the sounds of the words—that he reads.

Phonics is fundamentally a teaching technique—or rather a hope underlying a teaching technique—concerned with providing clues to the sound of written words, to "letter–sound correspondences". However, no language has an alphabet that represents all of its sounds (phones), and few languages have alphabets that have any simple relation to their phonemes. English is not one of the exceptions. As we shall see, the number of rules required to provide even an approximation of spoken from written English is much greater than generally supposed, and the effectiveness of these rules is much less than generally believed. As to just how many phonic rules there are, and how efficient (or inefficient) they may be, I shall show that there is no simple answer. To reach an approximation to the answers to these questions—to have some understanding of what the possibilities and limitations of a phonic approach to reading really are, we shall examine first why the relationship between letters and sounds should be relevant to reading, and then briefly review the historical relation between the two. Finally, we shall consider what is involved in trying to teach a set of rules that will represent whatever there is in this relationship between letters and sounds.

Mediated Word Identification

Phonics, ideally, is a strategy for *mediated word identification*—a system for finding out the sound and meaning of a word that we cannot identify immediately, without asking someone else.

Chapter 10 was primarily about *immediate word identification,* which was defined as the allocation of a visual configuration to a word category directly from an analysis of its features. The normal fluent reading process is "immediate", it was argued, because there are no intermediate stages involving the allocation of parts of the configuration to other categories, such as letters, on the way to identification of a word as a whole. There was evidence that any other form of word identification had to be ruled out as a basis for fluent reading because the eye does not pick up visual information sufficiently fast to identify units smaller than words at a normal reading rate, and the limited capacity of short-term memory can not accommodate them. The process of immediate word identification was therefore seen as no different from any other form of visual perception where a configuration is identified on sight—putting a name to a letter, or a digit, a face, an automobile, an animal, a tree, with identification always proceeding directly from the visual information to the ultimate categorization. Immediate word identification can be represented by a simple diagram, as shown in Figure 4.

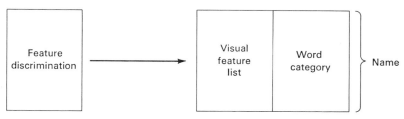

Figure   4   Immediate Word Identification

Mediated word identification is required when a visual configuration cannot be allocated to an acoustic–semantic category—perhaps, but not necessarily, because no category exists. I have already discussed (Chapter 6) how new categories might be established; the present concern is with how a category with both an acoustic and visual feature list might be formed. A trivial answer to the question—but one that is in no way inappropriate—is that the reader may ask someone else what the name is. We normally start reading words with a parent or teacher obligingly supplying names for all the configurations to be distinguished. These instructions help a child to get on with the important business of establishing feature lists for categories without having to worry about guessing what the name for the category should be. Some children get mechanical help in the form of "talking typewriters" or other devices designed to present both the visual and auditory forms of words simultaneously. Sooner or later, however, parents and teachers start to withdraw their support. The beginning reader is left to develop his own strategies for finding the name of an unfamiliar configuration. He may be given some "rules" for looking at parts of the configuration, allocating those parts first to letter (or letter combination) categories and then to sounds that have been associated with the letter categories. From the sounds of the individual letters (or letter clusters) it is either believed or hoped that the child will construct the sound of the word category to which the configuration as a whole should be allocated. This Spartan deprivation of outside help in word identification is called the "phonic approach". Many people believe the phonic approach is so efficacious, and are so persuaded that words constructed alphabetically ought to be read alphabetically, that they insist that other approaches to reading instruction are unnecessary. Some consider other teaching methods positively immoral. And there is indeed no doubt that all readers must acquire skills in the mediated identification of words. The only doubt lies in how much of a contribution "phonic rules" can make. Mediated word identification through phonics is represented in Figure 5.

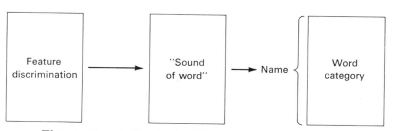

Figure   5   Mediated Word Identification: The Phonic Model

Examples of mediated visual identification—except for the obvious case of asking for or being told the name of an object—are not easy to find outside of reading because few other types of configuration provide a direct clue to their name. Some analogies are perhaps not too remote. It is often possible to discover the name of a botanical specimen, or butterfly, or postage stamp, by making an identification of its parts and checking in a catalogue for an identification of the whole. Railroad enthusiasts may count the number of wheels of a locomotive in order to identify it appropriately as a "2–6–4" or an "0–8–0". And a musician who transposes notes on the staff to effortless arpeggios probably started by interposing the name of each note between the visual discrimination and the performance. In each of these examples, you will notice, the expert eventually develops a large repertoire of distinct categories which he can identify immediately.

Words, clearly, are a special case. Their relation to their structure is neither arbitrary nor fortuitous. In some quarters any man who suggested that the spelling of the word "rough" should be revised would be regarded as a hero if he proposed *ruf* as the alternative, but not if he suggested that *rfu* or *kfpw* would be equally distinguishable. We expect the sound of words and their spelling to have a special relationship. We shall now begin to consider what this relationship is.

The Speech–Writing Relationship

The Greeks started it all. Speech appears to be such a natural biological characteristic of humans that it started spontaneously in a number of different areas of the globe and flourished so prolifically that no people in recorded history have lacked a spoken language as fully developed and structured as our own. Writing, however, still has not altogether caught on. The majority of the world's languages do not have a visual form, and many of those that do are pictographic ("picture" writing) rather than phonographic ("sound" writing).

The Greeks got the idea of representing words by symbols for their sounds from their frequent Phoenecian visitors. The Semitic script that the Phoenecians brought did not have special symbols for vowels, and it was the Greeks who tried to make the letter—sound correspondence complete. For all their insight, the Greeks did not develop their alphabetic system in the most practical manner, for example they tried to retain the original Semitic names for many of the letters, although some of the names contained sounds that the Greeks could not pronounce. However, the phonemic character of their spoken language was such that the Greeks could allocate sounds to letters on a fairly consistent, if not one-to-one, basis. And there appears to have been no argument among their educators that the phonic approach was the way to teach reading.

The Romans made a couple of advances when they adopted the Greek alphabet as a script for Latin. They renamed the letters so that their names were a closer approximation to their sound, an improvement that has not been maintained because the alphabet that English has inherited from the Romans still reflects the Latin names for letters although the sounds that many of the letters are supposed to represent are quite different from the sounds they had originally. The Romans also had the idea of introducing a space between words instead of the Greek practice of running everything together. The Greek method was not as perverse as it might seem; words in the original Greek language were regularly constructed of syllables each containing just one vowel (or diphthong), and it was not necessary to know where a word started or finished to pronounce these syllables. One of the reasons it is so useful to have the space for reading aloud in modern English—or modern Greek—is that there is not such a simple syllable rule; the pronunciation of letters in syllables is greatly influenced—among many other factors—by their position with respect to word boundaries.

The Romans made one mistake, however, which has been propagated right through to the present. Instead of merely copying the basic Greek idea and devising a special alphabetic system for Latin, they tried to adopt the Greek system directly, despite the considerable differences in the sound structure of the two languages. The match between letter and sound has progressively deteriorated as the alphabet has been patched and adapted to try to accommodate all the changes and multilingual borrowings in the history of English.

The mismatch between spoken and written English would still not be anywhere near as great as it is today had it not been for the fifteenth-century invention of movable type and the exigencies of the printer's proof-reader. Before the Gutenberg revolution, the idea that a word had a unique and immutable spelling had no currency. It was recognized that different people spoke in different ways, so what could be more natural than that their written words should reflect individual accents and idiosyncrasies? There was nothing exceptional about the fact that a man's name could be spelled in three or four quite different ways, so no one worried about variations in less personal words. After all, writing was a system for putting language into visual form, not for determining how language should sound.

Printing, however, changed that liberal attitude. A demand for standardization and conformity deprived the citizen of his freedom to write his language in any way he chose, and set up a system of spelling which, with only relatively minor changes, has persisted through the centuries. But while the spelling of the language has remained relatively steadfast and inflexible, the sound of the language has changed inexorably. We can still read the original folios of Shakespeare with a reasonable degree of comprehension, but we might have difficulty in comprehending if we could hear a contemporary recording of one of his productions. I have several times referred to the fact that language is dynamic, that one of its fundamental characteristics is change. That statement holds in all departments except spelling. The way in which words are spelled today is related to their pronunciation only through their historical antecedents, and as we saw from the way in which an alien alphabet was distorted to carry sounds for which it was never intended, those antecedents are often dubious.

The conclusion we must draw is that whatever the intentions of the Greeks, and the good will of innumerable enthusiasts and apologists through to the present day, the relationship between the sounds of words and their spelling is often complex and remote. Just how complex we shall see in the next section. Before leaving the present section, it will be convenient just to mention three important aspects of spoken language that our writing system does not even pretend to represent.

The first aspect of speech about which spelling gives no information is intonation. It is true that some cues might appear to be given by punctuation—by such elements as periods and exclamation marks and question marks—but these do not really give a guide to variations in pitch and stress. The sentence "Have you got any money?" has at least five quite different shades of meaning, depending on which word is emphasized, but neither the punctuation nor the spelling gives any information about how it should be pronounced. The initial letter *a* is pronounced quite differently in words like *acorn* and *able* compared with *about* or *adorn,* but there is no spelling clue to indicate why this is so. There is actually quite a simple rule—initial *a* is pronounced as in "acorn" only if the stress falls on the first syllable of the word. But that means that you have to know how to pronounce the word before you can say how the spelling and sound are related—our first illustration that acquiring the rules for letter–sound correspondences is easy *provided you know how the word is pronounced.* A major danger in the phonic approach to reading instruction may well be that people who *can* read do not realize how much their prior knowledge gives "rules" for letter–sound correspondences an unwarranted appearance of authority and generality.

The second aspect of speech that is not represented in writing is syntax. We have already seen that the pronunciation of words like *read* and *permit* (or *conflict* or *subject*) depend on their tense or function in a sentence. Whether we pronounce *permit* as "PERmit" or "perMIT" depends on whether we are saying it as a noun or a verb. Such syntactic cues are frequently clearly given in the spoken form of the word, but the written form gives no cue, either to the pronunciation or the syntactic role.

Finally, and perhaps surprisingly, spelling does not really attempt to represent sounds at all, but rather phonemes. Phonemes, you will recall (Chapter 3), are classes of sounds, many of them quite different physically, that are functionally equivalent in the language. The /p/ in "pin", "spin", and "nip" is actually three quite different sounds; we hear them in the same way although they are produced quite differently. So letters, if they can be said to represent sounds at all, represent the sounds we hear rather than the sounds we produce. Sometimes a single letter that we may think has only one sound is pronounced as three different *phonemes;* the *s* at the end of a plural noun or present tense verb may be pronounced /s/ as in "walks", /z/ as in "runs", or /ez/ as in "judges". Similarly the past tense *ed* may be pronounced /t/ as in "walked", /d/ as in "charged", or /ed/ as in "landed". None of these distinctions is indicated by the spelling, and they are generally disregarded in "phonic rules".

Having looked briefly at what phonics is supposed to do, and what it cannot do, I shall now examine what it can do, or rather what it might reasonably be expected to accomplish.

Rules and Exceptions

The aim of the phonic approach is to provide rules that will "predict" how a word will sound from the way it is spelled. The value of phonics would appear to depend on how many rules are, required to establish correspondences between the letters and sounds of English, or to what extent our phonemes can be predicted by the rules of phonics. But by now it is probably no surprise that any question related to language involving a simple "how many" leads to a very complicated and unsatisfactory evasion of an answer. Phonics is no exception.

Everything is wrong about the question. The first problem concerns our expectations about rules. If we expect a rule to mean a regularity that has no exceptions, then we shall have a difficult task finding any rules in phonics at all. Here is a phonic rule that would appear to have impeccable antecedents: final *e* following a single consonant indicates that the preceding vowel should be long, as in *hat* and *hate,* or *hop* and *hope.* And here is an instant exception: *axe* has a single consonant but a short /a/ (while *ache,* which has a double consonant, takes a long /a/). We have the choice of admitting that our traditional rule is not impervious to exceptions, or else we have to make a rule for the exceptions. One explanation that might be offered is that *x* is really a double consonant, *ks* (and that *ch* is really a single consonant, *k*). But then we are in the rather peculiar position of changing the notion of what constitutes a single letter simply because we have a rule that does not fit all cases. If we start to say that the definition of what constitutes a letter depends on the pronunciation of a word, how can we say that the pronunciation of a word can be predicted from its letters? Besides, what can we say about the silent *e* at the end of *have* or *love,* which is put there only because there is a convention that English words may not end with a naked *v?* Or the *e* at the end of *house,* which is to indicate that the word is not a plural?

Having made the point that phonic rules will have exceptions, the next problem is to decide what constitutes an exception. Some exceptions occur so frequently and regularly that they would appear to be rules in their own right. In fact it is quite arbitrary how anyone decides to draw the line between rules and exceptions. We have a choice of saying that the sounds of written English can be predicted by relatively few rules, although there will be quite a lot of exceptions, or by a large number of rules with relatively few exceptions. In fact, if we care to say that some rules have only one application, for example that *acht* is pronounced /ot/ as in "yacht", then we can describe English completely in terms of rules simply because we have legislated exceptions completely out of existence.

If the concept of a rule seems somewhat arbitrary, the notion of what constitutes a letter is even more idiosyncratic. It is true that in one sense there can be no doubt about what a letter is—it is one of the 26 characters in the alphabet—but any attempt to construct rules of spelling–sound correspondence is doomed from the start if we restrict our terms of reference to individual letters. To start with, there are only 26 letters to represent about 46 phonemes, so some of them at least must do double duty. We shall find, of course, that many letters stand for more than one phoneme, while many phonemes are represented by more than one letter. However, many sounds are not represented by single letters at all—*th, ch, ou, ue,* for example—so that we have to consider some combinations of letters as really representing quite distinct spelling units—rather as if *th* were a letter in its own right. It has been asserted, with the help of a computer analysis of over 20,000 words, that there are 52 "major spelling units" in English, 32 for consonants and 20 for vowels, effectively doubling the size of the "alphabet".[1]

The addition of all these extra spelling units, however, does not seem to make the structure of the English writing system very much more orderly. Some of the original letters of the alphabet are quite superfluous. There is nothing that *c* or *q* or *x* can do that could not be done by the other consonants. And many of the additional spelling units that are recognized simply duplicate the work of single letters, such as *ph* for *f,* and *dg* for *j,* and, similarly, there are compound vowels whose effect is the same as the silent final *e,* like *ea* in *meat* compared with *mete.* Some combinations have a special value only when they occur in particular parts of a word—*gh* may be pronounced as *f* (or as nothing) at the end of a word (*rough, through*) but is pronounced just like a single *g* at the beginning (*ghost* and *gold, ghastly* and *garden*). Often letters have only a relational function, sacrificing any sound of their own in order to indicate how another letter should be sounded. An obvious example is the silent *e,* another is the *u* that distinguishes the *g* in *guest* from the *g* in *gem.*

So for our basic question of phonics, what we are really asking is how many arbitrarily defined rules can account for an indeterminate number of correspondences between an indefinite set of spelling units and an uncertain number of phonemes (the total and quality of which may vary from person to person).

Some aspects of spelling are simply unpredictable, certainly to a reader with a limited knowledge of word derivations, no matter how one tries to define a spelling unit. An example of a completely unpredictable spelling to sound correspondence is *th,* which is pronounced in one way at the beginning of words like *this, than, that, those, them, then, these* but in another way at the beginning of *think, thank, thatch, thong, theme,* and so on. There is only one way to tell whether *th* should be pronounced as in /this/ or as in /think/, and that is to remember every instance. On the other hand, in many dialects there is no difference between the sounds *w* and *wh,* so that in some cases it can be the spelling that is not predictable, not the sound. (As always, you can even find exceptions to exceptions if you look for them—for example, the word *who.*)

Almost all our very common words are exceptions—*of* requires a rule of its own for the pronunciation of *f*.

The game of finding exceptions is too easy to play. I shall give only one more example to illustrate the kind of difficulty one must run into in trying to construct—or teach—reliable rules of phonic correspondence. How are the letters *ho* pronounced, when they occur at the beginning of a word? Just to start you on the way to counting all the alternatives, here are a few examples: *hot, hoot, hook, hour, honest, house, hope, honey, hoist.*

Of course, there are rules (or are some of them merely exceptions?) that can account for many of the pronunciations of ho. *But there is one very significant implication in all the examples that applies to almost all English words—in order to apply phonic rules,* words would have to be read from right to left. *The way in which the reader pronounces* ho *depends on what comes after it, and the same applies to the* p *in* ph, *the* a *in* ate, *the* k *in* knot, *the* t *in* -tion. *The exceptions are very very few, like* asp, *which is pronounced differently if preceded by a* w, *and* f, *pronounced* /v/ *only if preceded by* o. *The fact that sound "dependencies" in words run from right to left is an obvious difficulty for a beginning reader trying to sound out a word from left to right, or for a theorist who wants to maintain that words are identified on a left-to-right letter-by-letter basis.*

In summary, English is not a highly predictable language as far as its spelling and sound relationships are concerned. Just how much can be done to protect the pronunciation of a relatively small number of common words with a finite number of rules we shall see in a moment. But before we conclude the catalogue of complications and exceptions, two points should be reiterated. The first point is that phonic rules must be considered as probabilistic, as guides to the way words might be pronounced, and that there is rarely any indication of when a rule does or does not apply. In other words, it is often impossible to know for certain which phonic rules apply. The rule that specifies how to pronounce *ph* in *telephone* falls down in the face of *haphazard,* or *shepherd,* or *cuphook.* The rule for *oe* in *doe* and *woe* will not work for *shoe.* The probability of being wrong if you do not know the word at all is very high. Even if individual rules were likely to be right three times out of four, there would be nearly one chance in three of making a mistake somewhere in a word of four phonemes. The second point is that English phonics tends to look deceptively simple when you know how words are pronounced; the problem for the beginning reader trying to use phonics is not just the number of rules he must remember, but that he also has to have some knowledge of when they apply and what are the exceptions. The only way to distinguish the pronunciation of *sh* in *bishop* and *mishap,* or *th* in *father* and *fathead,* is to be able to read the entire word in the first place.

The Efficiency of Phonics

One systematic attempt has been made to construct a workable set of phonic rules for English.[2] The effort has had modest aims—to see how far one could go in establishing a set of correspondence rules for the 6092 one- and two-syllable words among 9000 different words (lexemes) in the comprehension vocabularies of six- to nine-year-old children. The words were all taken from books to which the children were normally exposed—they were the words that the children knew and ought to be able to identify if they were to be able to read the material with which they were confronted at school.

The researchers who analyzed the 6092 words found rather more than the 52 "major spelling units" to which I have already referred—in fact, they identified 69 "grapheme units" which had to be separately distinguished in their rules. A group of letters was called a "grapheme unit", just like a single letter, whenever its relationship to a sound (or sounds) could not be accounted for by any rule for single letters. Grapheme units included pairs of consonants such as *ch, th;* pairs of vowels such *ea, oy;* and letters that commonly function together, such as *ck* and *qu,* as well as double consonants like *bb* and *tt,* all of which require some separate phonic explanation. The number of grapheme units should not surprise us —the previously mentioned 52 "major units" were not intended to represent the only spelling units that could occur, but only the most frequent ones. As we shall see, there were other grapheme units in addition to the 69 that could not be accounted for in terms of general rules.

An arbitrary decision was made about what would constitute a rule—it would have to account for a spelling–sound correspondence occurring in at least ten different words. Any distinctive spelling–sound correspondence —and any grapheme unit—that did not occur in at least ten words was considered an "exception". Actually, the researchers made several exceptions among the exceptions—they wanted their rules to account for as many of their words as possible, and so they let several cases through the net when it seemed to them more appropriate to account for a grapheme unit with a rule rather than to stigmatize it as an exception.

The researchers discovered that their 6000 words involved 211 distinct spelling–sound "correspondences"—this does not mean that 211 different sounds were represented, but that the phonemes that did occur were represented by a total of 211 different spellings (obviously, some of the grapheme units were related to more than one sound). The results are summarized in Table 5. Eighty-three of the correspondences involved consonant grapheme units, and 128 involved vowel grapheme units, including no

Table 5   Spelling-sound correspondences among 6092 one- and two-syllable words in the vocabularies of nine-year-old children.

	Consonants	Primary Vowels	Secondary Vowels	Total
Spelling–sound correspondences	83	79	49	211
"Rules"	60	73	33	166
"Exceptions"	23	6	16	45
Grapheme units in rules	44	6	19	69

fewer than 79 that were associated with the six "primary" single-letter vowels, *a, e, i, o, u, y.* In other words, there was a total of 79 different ways in which the single vowels could be pronounced. Of the 211 correspondences, 45 had to be classified as exceptions, about half involving vowels and half consonants.

The exclusion of 45 correspondences as exceptions meant that a total of 661 words were not covered by the rules; over ten percent of the 6092 words had to be left aside as "exceptions".

The pronunciation of the remaining 5431 words was accounted for by a grand total of 166 rules! Sixty of these rules were concerned with the pronunciation of consonants (which are generally thought to have fairly "regular" pronunciations) and 106 with single or complex vowels.

The research that has just been described is important in a number of ways for understanding reading and the teaching of reading. Some of the conclusions that can be drawn are far-reaching in their implications. The first is very simply that phonics is complicated. Without saying anything at all about whether it is desirable to teach young children a knowledge of phonics, we now have an idea of the magnitude of the endeavor. We now know that if we really expect to give a child a mastery of phonics, then we are not talking about a dozen or so rules. We are talking about 166 rules, which will still not account for hundreds of the words that a child might expect to meet in his early reading.

It is obvious that the most that can be expected from phonics is that it will provide a *clue* to the sound (or "name") of a configuration being examined. Phonics can provide only approximations. Even if a reader did happen to know the 79 rules that are required to account for the pronunciation of the six vowels, he would still have no sure way of telling which rule applied—or even that he was not dealing with an exception. However, we should not make the situation seem more complex than it really is; it ought to be added that a reader is rarely in absolute doubt about what a word might be. Just as many letter combinations do not occur in the written language, so many sound combinations do not occur in speech. Many of the phonic rules might be excluded in particular instances because they would lead to a sound combination that is not a word. And we do not need to have all available sound cues to identify a word, any more than we need all possible visual cues to read it. There is still the possibility, however, that not all alternatives can be eliminated by phonic rules.

A more serious problem perhaps is the possibility that reliance on phonic methods will involve a reader in so much delay that his short-term memory will be overloaded and he will lose the sense of what he is reading. Particularly relevant is the possibility that a tendency to rely exclusively on the rules will create a handicap for the beginning reader whose biggest problem is to acquire speed. Use of the redundancy that exists within groups of words may be far more efficacious in identifying a particular word than dealing with the word as if it were standing in isolation.

There is still one question that has not been touched. An answer has been provided to the question of how efficient phonics might be—that a fairly complex rule system would be required to account for the pronunciation of 90 percent of quite common words, and that at best it would only operate probabilistically; there is no way of guaranteeing that a word will be correctly identified by phonics alone. The question that cannot yet be answered concerns the *effectiveness* of phonics: is the limited degree of efficiency that might be attained worth acquiring? Other factors have to be taken into account related to the *cost* of trying to learn and use a phonic system. Our working memories do not have an infinite capacity and reading is not a task that can be accomplished at too leisurely a pace. Other sources of information exist for finding out what a word in context might be, especially if the word is in the spoken vocabulary of the reader.

The Cost of "Reform"

The involved relation between the spelling of words and their sound has led to a number of suggestions for modifying the alphabet or for rationalizing the spelling system. To some extent both these ventures share the same misconceptions and difficulties. A number of contemporary linguists would deny that there is something wrong with the way most words are spelled; they argue that a good deal of information would be lost if their spelling were touched. Most of the apparent inconsistencies in spelling have some historical basis; the spelling system may be complex but it is not arbitrary—it has become what it is for quite systematic reasons. And because spelling is systematic and reflects something of the history of words, much more information is available to the reader than we normally realize. (The fact that we are not *aware* that this information is available does not mean that we do not use it; we have already seen a number of examples of the way in which we have and use a knowledge of the structure and redundancy of our language that we cannot put into words.) Spelling reform might make words a little easier to pronounce, but only at the cost of other information about the way words are related to each other, so that rationalizing words at the phonological level might make reading more difficult at syntactic and semantic levels. As just one example, consider the "silent *b*" in words like *bomb, bombing, bombed,* which would be an almost certain candidate for extinction if spelling reformers had their way. But the *b* is something more than a pointless appendage; it relates the previous words to others like *bombard, bombardier, bombardment* where the *b* is pronounced. And if you save yourself the trouble of a special rule about why *b* is silent in words like *bomb,* at another level there would be a new problem of explaining why *b* suddenly appears in words like *bombard.* Another argument in favor of the present spelling system is that it is the most competent one to handle dialect differences—a matter relevant also to those who would want to change the alphabet.

Although there is almost universal acceptance of the idea that words should be spelled in the same way by everyone, we do not all pronounce them in the same way. If the spelling of words is to be changed so that they reflect the way they are pronounced, then the question has to be asked: "pronounced by whom?" If there are to be more letters of the alphabet to indicate the various phonemes, whose set of phonemes will provide the standard? The phonic approach becomes even more complicated when it is realized that in many classrooms teacher and students do not speak the same dialect, and that both may speak a different dialect from the authorities who drew up the particular phonic rules they are trying to follow.[3] The teacher who tries to make a child see a phonic difference between the pronunciation of *caught* and *cot* will have a communication problem if this distinction is not one that the child observes in his own speech. The teacher will have even more trouble if he himself does not pronounce the two words differently, although his knowledge of the spelling of words may give him the mistaken idea that he does. Either way the teacher might well end up thinking that he is saying to the child "That word is not *cot,* it is *caught*", when the message coming across is "That word is not *cot,* it is *cot*".

The difficulty about beginning to modify the alphabet is that there is no logical point at which to stop; certainly 43 letters are not enough to account for all the possible variations in the pronunciation of words. If we reflect on the original purpose of the alphabet, to set the sounds of speech into visible form, we may wonder whether the only reform that could bring speech and spelling into closer correspondence might not be to revert to the days before printing and allow the spelling of words to vary freely. It is not difficult to find arguments in favor of maintaining one spelling for most words over large geographical areas, even though the spelling often appears far from ideal. But it is very difficult to argue that a particular alternative spelling system is preferable to any other when so many differences in speech exist.

Phonics and Features

I have asserted that a fluent reader is skilled in the process of identifying words immediately, and does not resort to mediated methods of word identification for most of the time that he is reading. It is not implied, however, that the fluent reader is not able to categorize words for which he does not have a visual feature list. Instead it will be argued that the skilled reader is so competent in identifying configurations that are new to him that he could not possibly be using conventional phonic methods.

Although there is no direct evidence available, it seems reasonable to assume that even skilled and habitual readers meet unfamiliar words all the time—sometimes words in their spoken language vocabularies that they have rarely or never seen in print, and sometimes words that are completely novel in their experience. As pointed out in the coda to the previous chapter, some quite familiar words may occur (in print as well as in speech) an *average* of only once in every five million words—which means that one might expect to read ten million words before some of these words appear. There are at least 3000 "familiar" words that occur with a frequency of less than one in a million. Even if we read at the rate of 30,000 words a day—the equivalent of a medium length novel every three days—it will take a year to read ten million words. Because of the relatively large number of words that occur very infrequently it might be expected that most days would confront us with a few words that we have probably not seen for a year or more. In addition there are probably more instances of completely unfamiliar sequences of letters occurring in our daily reading than we might expect. Apart from a proliferation of new scientific and commercial terms, we meet many "proper nouns," such as names of people or of geographical locations, that are completely novel yet do not noticeably disrupt our reading. For example, "The Moravesta Handicap at the Peddichuck Racetrack yesterday was won by the filly

Dann-Dee-Phlyer owned by Mr. Edgecomb Milliger of Spindorax Crescent, Ackleyville, South Bollington".

How does a reader succeed in reading words like those in the previous sentence, if he does not go through the "phonic" process of identifying individual letters, testing various alternative sounds for the letter combinations, and "listening" to the result in order to identify the whole? The feature-analytic model described in the earlier chapters on immediate letter and word identification can provide an account of such mediated word identification without requiring the intermediate identification of letters; in fact the model will also account for the identification of unfamiliar words without the actual or implicit production of their sounds, which is something the phonics approach—and two other theories of mediated word identification—cannot do.

One of the two additional theories was mentioned in the previous chapter—the view that words are built up from the recognition and synthesis of familiar *letter clusters;* a view supported by the easy identifiability of such nonwords as *vernalit, mossiant,* and *ricaning.* The other point of view, which might be called *identification by analogy,* is based on the notion that a word that has not previously been learned might be identified by putting together the sounds of bits of words that can be identified immediately. The examples generally given of identification by analogy tend to concern children, which means they are usually oversimplified. A child meeting *map* for the first time is supposed to be able to generate its sound by noticing that the beginning is similar to *man, mad,* and perhaps *mother* and *milkman,* while the end is similar to *cap, lap* (but hopefully not *leap* or *soap).* Logically, the identification-by-analogy position would not appear to depend on the intermediate identification of letters, or even on the fact that there is a physical separation between comparable parts of the unknown and the various known configurations. It is not difficult to see that there are parts of ▷,▢ , and ◯ that are identical and parts that differ, even though it is not possible to specify precisely where the similarities end and the differences begin. However, the identification-by-analogy view is generally fairly explicit that it is *letters* that are matched between the unidentifiable configuration and known words.

In fact, the phonic approach, the letter-cluster view, and identification by analogy all appear to have basic aspects in common—they all assume that letters or groups of letters within the visual configuration must be identified, that a sound for the entire configuration is synthesized from sounds appropriate to the identified letters, and that word identification will follow upon the production of the resultant sound.

In Chapter 10 the attempt was made to show how the feature-analytic model could account for all data about word identification that support one or another of the traditional views, in addition to filling in some of the loopholes in these theories. For the remainder of the present chapter the aim will be to show how the feature-analytic model might accomplish everything the phonic, letter-cluster, or analogy approaches to mediated word identification set out to do, without postulating a laborious procedure of letter identification and sound synthesis which a reader is obviously able to dispense with in practice.

The brief discussion of acoustic and semantic features in the previous chapter now permits a fuller account of the model for representing the word-identification processes of fluent readers. *Immediate* word identification—the major topic of Chapter 10—can occur when there is a category with *visual* and *semantic* features "back to back" with a set of *acoustic* features that will associate the word with a name. I shall give such categories a triple-barrelled label: visual–acoustic–semantic categories. When there is no visual feature list for a particular category—when there is only an acoustic–semantic category—visual word identification must be *mediated*.

A category exists whenever there is at least one feature list to specify the characteristics of configurations that should be perceived, or processed, equivalently. A feature list may therefore be conceptualized as a set of rules for deciding which configurations shall be treated as equivalent. Some feature lists are visual, some are acoustic, some are semantic, and lists may be associated in various ways. A category that consists only of a visual feature list—a *"visual* category"—will serve only to differentiate one kind of visual event from another. Such is the case when we can see that Σ is different from English letters or numbers or other symbols like @$%¢*, but when we do not have a name or a semantic interpretation (meaning) for Σ . If we have the name "sigma" but not a meaning for Σ , then we have a *visual–acoustic* category. A meaning—it means "add"— without a name indicates a *visual–semantic* category. Some cognitive categories may have only *acoustic* features, some will be *acoustic–semantic* categories (or semantic–acoustic, the order is irrelevant)—these are the words in our spoken vocabulary—and some will be *visual–acoustic– semantic*—the words in our sight-recognition reading vocabulary.

I can now detail a little more precisely the problem that faces a reader confronted by a visual configuration that he cannot identify immediately through a visual feature list. However, one immense source of assistance to the skilled reader attempting the mediated identification of a word will not be considered until the next chapter—the semantic and syntactic redundancy that exists across words in sentences. Such sequential redundancy reduces considerably the amount of visual information required to make any kind of word identification including the mediated form. The skilled reader may by chance never before have seen a coined new word like *videotape,* yet its identification would be facilitated by a context such as: "New instructional media such as closed-circuit television and videotape permit. . .". In such a sentence there is a high probability of the new word being produced by the reader even in the absence of visual information, and also a source of rapid semantic feedback to confirm or reject a mediated identification. In the present chapter we are considering the more difficult case where there is no context, and the sole initial source of information is the visual features. I shall consider the mediated identification of the word *videotape* standing in isolation.

The forthcoming discussion will be complex, but the topic is complex. The problem is not so much that reading is intrinsically complicated; in fact, all the evidence seems to be that the actual processes of reading are beautifully simple. But it is not always simple to describe an uncomplicated phenomenon. The shape of an egg is beautifully simple, but an adequate account of this simplicity for someone who had never actually seen an egg-shaped object would probably involve the calculus, structural engineering, and poetry. The description of the egg would be even more complicated if the receiver of the information had the preconception that eggs were square; one of the problems with reading is that many preconceptions are not congruent with the evidence that recent research is producing.

It may be worthwhile to reiterate briefly the objective. The aim is not to indulge in flights of fancy, nor to rephrase traditional slogans, nor to describe a neurophysiological system. The aim is to construct a model with some explanatory power and predictive value. The model will have explanatory power if it succeeds in putting together logically and comprehensively the scattered data that are relevant to the topic of reading, and it will have predictive power if it can lead to hypotheses that can be tested through the acquisition of additional data. A good amount of relevant fact has already been referred to in this book and it can be summarized in a few words: skilled readers demonstrate both immediate and mediated word identification, as well as other skills of letter identification and comprehension, and in particular (for our present concerns) they are able to identify words new in their visual experience without seeming to stop to identify individual letters or laboriously to try out alternative sounds.

The problem for our imaginary reader is that the configuration *videotape* does not constitute a criterial set on any of his visual feature lists. "Videotape", let us assume, is an acoustic–semantic category, and the reader's task is to get access to it through its acoustic feature list; therefore, I shall refer to it as the *target category.* I shall assume for the purpose of illustration that the reader does have a visual–acoustic–semantic category for "tape" but not for "video", and that in the process of building up mediated word identification skills (which will be discussed) he has established a visual–acoustic category for *deo,* but no independent category for *vi.* Thus the visual information can be allocated directly to acoustic categories for /tape/ and /deo/ but not /vi/. Acoustic features for /vi/ must be derived from visual–acoustic categories for such words as "vim", "vigor", "vinegar", "vixen" with visual feature lists whose initial portions are congruent with a configuration comprising *vi* features at its beginning. The synthesized acoustic featural information from the three parts /vi/deo/tape/ can be allocated directly to the target acoustic–semantic category "videotape" and the identification is made. The reader may if he wishes produce the sound of the word—the acoustic feature list is there—*but the sound is not necessary for the semantic interpretation.* The reader can get to the category without producing the sound.

The preceding paragraph was a condensed version of the feature-analytic model for mediated word identification diagrammed in Figure 6. I shall now go through the model again in a little more detail.

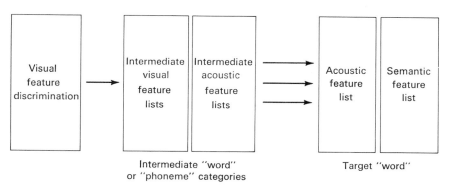

Figure 6   Mediated Word Identification—Access Routes

Intermediate Access to Target Categories

There were three "access routes" from the unfamiliar visual configuration *videotape* to the target semantic–acoustic category. Mediated word identification might be accomplished by any one or a combination of the three routes; the example was intended to illustrate all three.

The first route—for the *tape* portion of the visual configuration—might be termed *intermediate word access* because it goes directly from the visual configuration to a visual–acoustic–semantic category which provides an acoustic feature input (or more precisely, *featural information* input [4]) to the target category. If the reader had also an established visual–acoustic–semantic category "video", he could have accomplished the entire identification by *intermediate word access,* the two intermediate categories providing a joint acoustic input that could be allocated to the target category. Although the two intermediate categories would also provide semantic interpretations that might be combined (or even used to assist in identification of the target category), no semantic mediation is required because the established target category has a semantic interpretation of its own for the entire word. Observe that the intermediate *words* are not identified, nor are intermediate *sounds* produced—the intermediate categories simply provide a visual–acoustic *featural information* link between the configuration and the target category.

The second route—for the *deo* portion of the configuration—is most appropriately characterized as *intermediate nonword identification.* The term is unfortunate; partly because "nonword" is such an ungainly expression, and partly because my intention might be better served if I could use "phonic" or "letter cluster" in its place. However, the latter terms have so much additional meaning because of their more general usage, with its emphasis on "decoding to sound", that I am reluctant to use either of them without qualification at this stage. Nonword and word categories are conceptualized as similar in that they associate visual and acoustic feature lists, the only difference being that an additional semantic feature list, or set of semantic relationships, is associated with word but not with nonword categories. In more simple English, nonword categories have the same visual status for immediate identification as word categories, but they do not have meaning. Commercial enterprises often capitalize on this by taking what would appear to be a well-founded nonword, for example "vig" or "ting" or "pol", and attaching a semantic loading by making it the brand name for a cereal or deodorant. I shall explain in a moment how nonword categories would appear to become established.

Like word categories, then, nonword categories may contribute intermediate access to a nonvisual target category because they provide a ready-made visual–acoustic link. The link between the relevant part of the visual configuration (the *deo* of *videotape*) and the intermediate category is immediate because it is a direct association of visual and acoustic features in an established category; unlike the usual view of phonic associations, however, there is neither letter identification nor sound production. Intermediate nonword access is functionally exactly the same as intermediate word access in that an existing visual–acoustic category is employed to provide access to a nonvisual acoustic–semantic category. The difference is that *nonword categories* are set up precisely for the purpose of providing access for mediated word identification, while *word categories* have an immediate role in reading because of their additional semantic associations.

The third route—for the *vi* portion of the configuration—may be labeled *intermediate fragment access.* The link could be through a fragment of a word category or a fragment of a nonword category; anywhere that an appropriate visual–acoustic feature information match might be effected. The need is not to construct a "sound" for the *vi* portion of the visual configuration, but to generate a pattern of acoustic features that can be associated with the visual features. Of course, more than one pattern of acoustic features might be generated, different acoustic features would be associated with the beginning of *vine* or *visor* than with the beginning of *vim, vigor,* or *vinegar* (because they have different "pronunciations"). One could postulate different "weighting" systems that would attach different values to alternative acoustic feature patterns—perhaps the acoustic pattern that occurred most often in different categories or that could be found for the largest segment of the visual configuration would be given some kind of priority. But the most important point is that the existence of alternative acoustic patterns does not matter—unless there is more than one acoustic–semantic target category to which the alternative patterns might be allocated (for example, if there were one word /vi/deotape/ and another word /vy/deotape/). If only one of the alternative generated patterns constitutes a criterial set among the target feature lists, then an appropriate categorization can be made. The sound is produced after target category has been attained.

Similarities may now be observed between the three "access routes" linking the visual configuration with the target category and the three popular theories of mediated word identification referred to earlier: phonics, letter clusters, and identification by analogy. The first route, intermediate word access, and the third route, intermediate fragment access, together will account for the evidence that has led to theories of identification by analogy. The second route, intermediate nonword access, is a particular kind of "phonic approach"—it makes use of accumulated knowledge of visual–acoustic correspondences, but at the feature level, not in terms of "sounds". As I have shown, the production of "sounds" to match visual configurations to spoken words is at best tortuous; there is little likelihood that "phonic rules" will generate sound patterns sufficiently accurately for auditory recognition, and in any case the produced sound would have to be decomposed to acoustic features for the auditory categorization to occur. None of the routes is "letter cluster", although the second and third will account for the evidence that has led to letter-cluster hypotheses of how words are identified. But although nonword and fragment access routes both involve sequences of letters, *there is no identification of the letters as such,* any more than letters are identified in immediate word identification.

Explanation of the evidence for the easy identification of some nonword sequences like *vernalit* can now be offered quite simply. Large portions of these target sequences are parts of established feature lists. Acoustic features for the sequence can be generated through intermediate word, nonword, or fragment access, by taking advantage of the featural redundancy reflected in established criterial sets. Sequences like *vernalit* and *mossiant* are easy to identify because intermediate access routes of all three kinds are available for the construction of a single set of acoustic features to generate a verbal response (the task would not be so easy with *uobftsn*) and there is also no problem with segmentation. By contrast, the identification of a configuration like *caphet* is a catch problem—the reader might interpret it as / caffet / or / cap-het / depending on whether he dealt with the *ph* portion of the configuration by analogy to *telephone* or *cuphook,* or whether nonword access for *ph* was through just one or through two visual feature lists.

Learning Intermediate Rules

An outline has been sketched of the strategies available to a skilled reader when he comes across a visual configuration that he cannot immediately identify; now we shall start to consider what a child, a beginning reader, must do when he finds himself in the same position. It is at this point that I can develop, at least in part, the observation made in Chapter 1 that life seems particularly hard on the beginning reader. In a sense there is no easy way for a child to learn to read, just as there is no easy way to learn to swim or ride a bicycle; none of these learning experiences is as easy as actually swimming or cycling—or reading—after the skill is learned. Mediated word identification is not as easy as immediate identification, yet the beginner has to identify many more of his words by mediating methods than does the fluent reader. Identification-by-analogy methods may be easiest for mediated identification because they make use of already established visual–acoustic–semantic categories. But the child has fewer of these categories. The "phonic" approach is relatively inefficient because it involves a large number of rules that to a child must appear particularly arbitrary. Besides, the use of phonic rules is the slowest method of identifying words, and the limited information-processing and memory capacity of the visual system cannot tolerate a slow rate of reading. It is part of life's unfair return to the possessor of the least capital that the development of mediated word identification skills becomes easier only as the number of words that can be identified on sight becomes greater. Mediating identification skills improve when we need them less!

The number of *intermediate word access* routes for identification by analogy obviously increases with the number of visual—acoustic—semantic categories established. The visual—acoustic categories that provide *intermediate nonword access* are different from word categories, but there can be no doubt that their establishment is facilitated by the existence of word categories. After all, if one has to "learn" that the visual elements of *eigh* must sometimes be associated with the acoustic features of /ay/, it is a great help if one already knows that *weigh* and *eight* have the acoustic features of /way/ and /ayt/. Nonword categories must almost invariably develop from *intermediate fragment access*. If part of a word (or another nonword) feature list successfully provides access to a nonvisual category, that fragment is likely to be made into a visual—acoustic category in its own right. It would also seem likely, and in accordance with common experience, that prefixes, suffixes, inflections, and the root forms of words would, like other frequent spelling patterns, tend to become independent nonword categories. Some of these small units might also have semantic associations, depending on the knowledge of the reader and on their semantic and syntactic function. Such elements of words in fact have a technical name, *morpheme,* analogous to that for the minimal units of sound or writing, phoneme and grapheme, indicating that they might be regarded as minimal units of meaning.

Obviously, opportunities to develop intermediate fragment access routes, making use of bits of word or nonword categories, must be very infrequent until the word or nonword categories are themselves numerous. It is perhaps no wonder that the novice reader makes such a stumbling beginning; he has so little going for him.

Not only must the beginning reader develop alternative methods of word identification, he must learn to use them. In fact it is only through the use of mediated word identification skills that the nonword categories can be established. Actually to teach a child an efficient set of phonic rules as a substitute for immediate identification is, as I have shown, a logical and pedagogical impossibility—we neither have the knowledge nor the art to do it, nor has the child the capacity to learn such rules by rote.

Is phonics training useless then? On the contrary, a major objective of the present chapter has been to show that the development of mediated word identification skills, based particularly on the existence of visual—acoustic "nonword" categories, is an essential part of reading. But it has also been a major objective of the present chapter to show that phonic "rules" developed for instructional purposes are not as efficacious as we sometimes think. What the child needs is associations between visual and acoustic features, and these are not the same as "letter–sound correspondences."

It has to be remembered that there is a difference between precept and practice, between what is taught and what is learned. A child may behave as if he is following a rule provided in instruction, but that does not mean that he is using the rule. The fact that a child might distinguish *hat* from *mat* after having been told that one begins with *h* and one with *m* does not mean that he is making the distinction between the two words by looking for the *letter* they begin with. Similarly, the fact that a child may develop competent skills of mediated word identification after phonics instruction does not mean that he is making use of the "phonic rules" as such, but rather that the phonics instruction has given him enough information to establish his own categories and rules *at a featural level.*

I have at last touched upon the advantage of phonics instruction—it can provide information that a child needs to be able to establish mediated word identification skills. But such information has to be given when the child needs it; that was one of the major points made in the chapter on the acquisition of spoken language, and also in the discussion of the cognitive approach to learning.

A child learning to read is not helplessly dependent on detailed instructions; he has an active brain that will construct its own rules (which it has to do in any case) provided that information comes at the right time. And information "at the right time" involves information about whether events are functionally equivalent or not, examples of the events that should and should not fall into the same category, and feedback about whether a category decision is right or not. The human brain does not function by learning lists or rules that are presented to it; the brain learns by looking for significant differences, establishing functional equivalences, and deciding how events go together. The brain does not need to be told what to do, but it needs to know whether it is right or wrong in its decisions about what should be treated as the same, what should be treated as different, and how events should be associated. That is how a child learns to read—by drawing conclusions about similarities, differences, and associations.

The most that can be said for a phonic rule—or any other kind of precept—is that it shows where a significant difference or similarity or association lies. From that point the learner has to assimilate the information into his own structure of knowledge. Given the right learning environment he will test his new knowledge by putting it to use and seeking feedback. That, in a few words, is how a child learns any skill—by example, use, and feedback. Mediated reading skills are no exception.

The question of learning mediated reading skills will be raised again in

Chapter 14 in the broader context of reading generally, comprehension as well as word identification. Comprehension, the identification of meaning in groups of words, is the topic of the next chapter, which will show that the issue of phonics is not as critical as the present chapter might have made it appear. The fact that words are arranged in meaningful sentences can take a large part of the burden of learning new information off the beginning reader.

References

A fascinating book on the development of writing, although it underrates the significance of non-Western systems, is:

J. GELB, *A Study of Writing* (Chicago: University of Chicago Press, 1963).

As an example of the manner in which useful information is often to be found in sources that on the surface seem most unlikely, there are brief and readable recapitulations of theories about the origins of speech and writing (largely from a noncognitive point of view) in:

K. U. SMITH and MARGARET F. SMITH, *Cybernetic Principles of Learning and Educational Design* (New York: Holt, Rinehart and Winston, Inc., 1966), Chapter 3.

A brief summary of the development of alphabetic writing is also provided at the beginning of:

M. M. MATHEWS, *Teaching to Read: Historically Considered* (Chicago: University of Chicago Press, 1966).

Mathews goes on to discuss the manner in which "learning to read became difficult" because spelling changes did not keep pace with changes in the sound of language. His scholarly and lucid review of the changing fashions in reading instruction leads him inexorably to the conclusion that there is only one "natural" way to learn reading—"to learn letters and the sounds for which they stand" (page 208).

Another book that takes a scholarly and informative course to a rather narrow conception of reading instruction is:

C. C. FRIES, *Linguistics and Reading* (New York: Holt, Rinehart and Winston, Inc., 1962).

There are, of course, many books on phonics; I cannot recommend any of them as supplementary sources for the approach taken in the present chapter. I would prefer to suggest that anyone wanting to go into the subject further should critically reread any book with which he is familiar. Two questions should be asked in the light of the present chapter: What does the author really expect phonics to accomplish for a child? How is his proposed system likely to work out for the child in terms of cost (effort involved) and return (words identified)?

For the basic data underlying my analysis of the effectiveness of phonics I am indebted to ongoing work by a number of researchers in two centers: the

University of Wisconsin Research and Development Center for Cognitive Learning, Madison, Wisconsin and the Southwest Regional Laboratory for Educational Research and Development, Inglewood, California. Neither group has yet published any definitive findings in easily accessible form. Some specific citations are given below.

Notes

1. R. L. VENEZKY, English ortholography: its graphical structure and its relation to sound, *Reading Research Quarterly,* 2 (1967), 75–106. See also RUTH H. WEIR and R. L. VENEZKY. *The Psycholinguistic Nature of the Reading Process* in Goodman (listed on page 10).

2. BETTY BERDIANSKY, B. CRONNELL, and J. KOEHLER, *Spelling–Sound Relations and Primary Form–Class Descriptions for Speech-Comprehension Vocabularies of 6–9 Year-Olds.* Southwest Regional Laboratory for Educational Research and Development, Technical Report, no. 15, 1969.

3. W. LABOV (listed on page 46).

4. I do not want to suggest that feature lists themselves generate features. Visual (and acoustic) features are properties of the stimulus that are discriminated by analyzers in the visual (or auditory) system. These analyzers provide "featural information" to the feature lists of the appropriate modality categories. The statement that intermediate visual–acoustic categories may provide an *acoustic input* to acoustic–semantic target categories to permit mediated identification of a visual configuration is a shorthand method of saying that featural information from visual analyzers may be transformed into an acoustic specification that can be directed to acoustic feature lists.

13

The Identification of Meaning

The topic of the present chapter is comprehension and meaning, and I shall try to avoid making it incomprehensible by skirting the question of what *meaning* and *comprehension* "really are". Different people use these words in different ways—and quite properly use them differently in different contexts. The attempt to find a single definition for all the various and idiosyncratic aspects of meaning is a rock on which many theoretical vessels have foundered.

The nautical analogy is appropriate because in broaching the question of meaning we are delving into the deep structure of language. Meaning is at a level of language where words do not belong. Words, you will recall from Chapter 3, are part of the surface structure of language, the physical representation, whether they are written or spoken. Meaning is part of the deep structure, the semantic, cognitive level. And you may recall that between the surface level and the deep level of language there is no one-to-one correspondence. Meaning may always resist mere words.

Can you feel the pull of the tide? At this point we could be swept out of the depths of the present discussion, into eddying metaphysical speculation. I shall move back into the shallows, abandon the marine metaphor, and define how we shall use our terms.

I shall define comprehension—or the extraction of meaning from text —as the reduction of uncertainty.

This is precisely the same definition that I gave for "information" on page 16, although now hopefully the statement may not seem at first glance quite so empty. Because by now the expression "reduction of uncertainty" must have a familiar ring. I have used it with respect to both letters and words.

The acquisition of letter information—the reduction of uncertainty about *letters*—occurs when a reader is able to eliminate some or all of the alternatives that a particular visual configuration of a letter might be. Identification takes place when the configuration can be allocated to just one of the 26 alternative letter categories.

The acquisition of word information—the reduction of uncertainty about *words*—occurs when a reader is able to eliminate some or all of the alternatives that a particular visual configuration of a word might be. Identification takes place when the configuration can be allocated to just one of the indefinite number of alternative word categories.

And the acquisition of information about meaning—or *comprehension,* the reduction of uncertainty about *meaning*—may be considered to occur when a reader is able to eliminate some or all of the alternative meanings that a particular visual configuration might convey. The present chapter is entitled "The Identification of Meaning" because comprehension can be regarded as taking place when the visual configuration, the written phrase or sentence or passage, can be allocated to one of an unknown number of alternative cognitive structures, or meanings.

The use of the term "identification of meaning" is appropriate, if unusual, because the comprehension of a passage of written language can be regarded not just as a process similar to that of word identification, but as essentially the same.

The visual "input" for comprehension is exactly the same as the raw material of letter or word identification, the distinctive features of visual configurations. And I shall try to show that meanings can be extracted *immediately* from the visual configuration, without the intermediate identification of words, just as words may be identified without the prior identification of letters. Just as there is an alternative *mediated* method of identifying words, however, there can also be considered to be a *mediated* process of identifying meanings. As with mediated word identification, the indirect method of comprehension is more complex than the immediate method, and presents a greater risk of overloading short-term memory and the limited-capacity visual system.

A comparison of immediate and mediated meaning identification is one of the objectives of the present chapter, which will also examine evidence that the fluent reader does identify meaning immediately—and, indeed, that there is no other way to read fluently. I shall also present examples of the way in which redundancy in syntax and meaning may be used in fluent reading, and discuss the development and use of both immediate and mediated meaning identification skills. First, however, let us look a little more closely at what it means to say that comprehension is the reduction of uncertainty about meaning—the allocation of a visual configuration to one of an unknown number of alternative cognitive categories or structures.

The Structure of Knowledge

Of course, when I refer to "the structure of knowledge" or "cognitive categories" I am talking about abstractions, not about actual physical organization within the neural architecture of the brain. There are no filing cabinets in the brain, no pigeonholes to accommodate categories, any more than there are actual "feature lists" available for inspection. In fact, when I talk about cognitive categories I am really talking about our perceptions, which are the output of mental activity, rather than a working part of the mental activity itself. Categories are postulated in the cognitive model for the same reason that feature lists and analyzers are postulated —they are theoretical constructs that have an explanatory and predictive power with respect to the data with which we are concerned, the observable processes of reading.

Having made the inevitable qualifications, let us take off the top of an imaginary skull, push aside all the squishy network of living thinking matter that stands between us and our understanding of the literal processes of thought, and examine the model being constructed in its place.

It was proposed in Chapter 6 that all perception might be regarded as a process of decision-making based on significant differences detected in the environment. The actual nature of the significant differences is not determined by the physical events themselves, but by the perceiver's rules for distinguishing those events that he wishes to treat as functionally equivalent from those that he wishes to treat as different. Events to be treated as equivalent will be allocated to the same cognitive category, which is specified by the rules that are represented in its feature lists. In other words, the perceiver brings a highly structured knowledge of the world into every perceptual situation. Rather than saying that he discovers order and regularities that are properties of the environment, it is more appropriate to say that the perceiver imposes his own organization upon the information that reaches his receptor systems. The organization of his knowledge of the world lies in the structure of his cognitive categories and the manner in which they are related—in the way the perceiver *partitions* his knowledge of the world.

We shall examine a very simple part of the model of the cognitive organization—a part of the structure within the category "human" and the manner in which partitioned areas are related through their respective semantic feature lists. We shall be concerned with only two of the ways in which this structure can be "partitioned"—on the basis of gender (male or not-male) and on the basis of age (adult or not-adult), as shown in Figure 7. By comparison of the cognitive structure and associated feature lists in the figure, I shall show what it means to say that feature lists specify the types of events and meanings that are allocated to each cognitive category. Because I shall be talking about both events and meanings, it will be convenient to have a single neutral term for both: I shall use the word "instances".

(a) Partial partitioning of structure of
     category "human"

"Male" (+) Gender partition "Female" (−)	"Man" "Woman"	"Boy" "Girl"

	(+) "Adult" Age partition	(−) "Child"

(b) Partial feature lists for eight categories

Category: test	Human	Male	Female	Adult	Child	Man	Woman	Boy	Girl
Human	+	+	+	+	+	+	+	+	+
Male		+	−			+	−	+	−
Adult				+	−	+	+	−	−

Figure   7   Relation of Cognitive Structure and Feature Lists

I have not yet explained what is meant by a *partition* in a cognitive category. Let us first regard a partition as a rule that divides the set of instances that could be allocated to a category into two subsets. When a particular rule is used, the instances allocated to the partitioned category are no longer functionally equivalent but are divided into two smaller categories. For example, establishment of a partition concerning "age" within the category of "human" subdivides all the instances that could be functionally equivalent in that category into two groups. If the partition is not used—if we are considering just the category "human"—then age is not a significant difference, and all humans are functionally equivalent as far as category allocation is concerned. But when the category "human" is partitioned, when the specifying rule regarding age is applied, two categories are established. These two categories may be given names, such as "adult" and "child," by associating them with acoustic and visual feature lists.

Figure 7 shows the category "human" subdivided by two partitions: one for "age", which I have just discussed, and one for "gender", which operates in exactly the same way. Together the two partitions can serve to divide the functionally equivalent set of instances in the category "human" into four mutually nonequivalent categories: adult male, adult female, nonadult male, and nonadult female. And each of these smaller categories, of course, can be associated with a name: *man, woman, boy, girl.*

Each partition reduces uncertainty within the category that it subdivides. Obviously, we know more about a particular human—the number of alternative instances is less—if we know on which side of the age partition he should be allocated, or on which side of the gender partition. The more partitions there are, the less uncertainty there is in the organization of one's knowledge of the world. And the more partitions that can be taken into account in allocating a stimulus event to a category, the more uncertainty is reduced.

There should be no problem about explaining what constitutes a partition in our cognitive structure, because a partition is not a new concept to be added to the model already developed in earlier chapters of this book. *A partition is simply the operational effect of a distinctive feature test.* Every distinctive feature, every significant difference that the perceiver can distinguish, can function as a partition, or, rather, can allocate an instance to one category or another.

As indicated in Figure 7 the feature test for "male" will allocate instances within the class of "human" to either the "male" or "not-male" side of the cognitive partition, depending on whether they are marked + or − for the feature. Similarly the "age" test will bifurcate the alternatives into adult or not-adult. And together the two tests will determine to which

of four subordinate categories—*man, woman, boy, girl*—an instance
might be allocated. The feature lists for all the categories are marked +
for the feature "human" because the superordinate category "human" is itself marked by that feature, and partitioned categories must carry all the
features of the higher-level structures.

Semantic features are in one critical way different from visual or acoustic features—they do not have immediate physical referents. We cannot
look directly for the feature "human" or "male" or "adult" in the external
world, but instead have to look for visual features that have been associated with semantic feature lists. Visual, acoustic, and other sensory feature lists must exist for stimulus configurations that can be allocated to
cognitive categories, otherwise the category allocations could not take
place. As stated in Chapter 11, we do not know enough about the exact
nature of visual or acoustic systems to be able to say with precision what
are the features that the analyzers in the perceptual systems look for. But
since we can visually distinguish males from females, or adults from children, it is a reasonable assumption that the visual system, under the direction of the brain, has identified distinctive features that it scans for in visual configurations.

Although semantic features lack the aspect of direct external reference
that distinguishes them from visual and acoustic features, they have one
additional aspect that makes them especially significant in our present
discussion. *The presence or absence (or irrelevance) of particular semantic
features in the multitude of cognitive categories determines how these categories are related.*

I said at the beginning of this chapter (and in Chapter 6) that our
knowledge of the world is represented cognitively in the structure of categories and the manner in which they are interrelated. But, in fact, the concept of partitioning based on semantic features accounts both for the establishment of categories and the relations among them. The partitions of age
and gender within the category of "human" not only determine that there
are the eight subcategories of male, female, adult, child, man, woman, boy,
girl, but also determine how these eight subcategories are related to each
other. The relation of *boy* to *female,* for example, is that they are on opposite sides of the partition "gender", and that *boy* is restricted to one side
of the "age" partition while *female* is on both. The partitions do more
than establish relations within a small group of subcategories; they relate
any instance within a particular subset of partitions with all the other categories in the perceiver's cognitive structure.

The amount of information gained by such a complex relationship cannot be overestimated. Allocation of a stimulus configuration into the category "boy", for example, does more than distinguish it from *man* or from
female. By virtue of being placed in the category "human", the instance is

associated with semantic features of all humans and of higher-order categories, such as "primate" and "mammal" and "vertebrate" and "animate" and "organic"—however far the accumulated knowledge structure of the perceiver has been differentiated. The instance is also associated with a lack of all the distinguishing attributes of nonhuman primates, nonprimate mammals, nonmammalian vertebrates, and so forth.

It is perhaps becoming clear what the "meaning" of a category might be —meaning is not simply the "semantic feature list" that I described a couple of chapters ago, but rather it is the way in which the specification of semantic features—or relationships for a particular category—relates that category to all other categories in the cognitive system. Identifying a person, or a letter, or a word, does far more than just pin a label on a stimulus event; the identification locates the event in the entire structure of knowledge of the perceiver.

It may now be a little clearer what was meant by the earlier statements that all perception may be regarded as the reduction of uncertainty. We do not perceive anything unless we can allocate it to one or another of our cognitive categories, and as soon as we can allocate it to a category, we have reduced our uncertainty about the event because we have eliminated all those categories that fall outside the partitions of the category into which the event is placed. The actual amount of uncertainty reduced depends on the initial degree of uncertainty, the number of alternatives that are eliminated. Each distinctive feature of the configuration that we can discriminate reduces uncertainty, because it permits placing the event on one side or the other of a particular partition.

Sometimes the partitioned categories have names—this is the case where the partitions specify a category that forms a distinctive perceptual set, such as *man, woman, boy, girl,* or the letters of the alphabet. Such "named" categories must always have associated semantic feature lists. But sometimes the partitions are not named, in fact, they do not form a part of our semantic structure at all. Such is the case for the distinctive features of sounds, or for those elements of visual configurations that constitute distinctive features for letters or words or for meanings. We do not have names for these visual features, any more than we have semantic features associated with them (they have no meaning for us), but nevertheless they may be regarded as partitioning uncertainty because they reduce the number of alternatives that the letter or word or meaning might be.

Language and Uncertainty

One function of language is to reduce uncertainty in listeners or readers—which is the same as saying that language provides information. Uncertainty reduction is not the sole function of language—speakers and writers may use language for a number of other social or personal reasons—but the communicative aspect is the concern of this book. The comprehension of communicative language by the listener or reader means that his structure of knowledge about the world is in some way reorganized; partitions are moved. The statement "Your friend John has become a father", for example, may be regarded as rearranging the location of the category "John" with respect to the partition that subdivides all men on the basis of fatherhood, while at the same time adjusting the contents of the category "fathers" to include John. As pointed out earlier, the actual "moving" of the partitions may be regarded simply as a modification of a feature list; "John" now becomes marked $+$ rather than $-$ for the semantic feature of "father" and a search for all semantic feature lists marked positively for "father" will produce the list for "John".

Cognitive structure may be reorganized more drastically by some instances of information than others. Very little readjustment is likely to take place following reception of the information that Queen Elizabeth I of England died in 1603 or that ownership of the latest model Thunderclap convertible is highly correlated with social advancement and sexual allure. On the other hand, quite a dramatic realignment of one's internal representation of the world might follow a simple statement such as "you're fired", or documented evidence that a retired Arizona chicken farmer had written nineteen outstanding novels under the personal direction of Dickens, Tolstoy, and Twain through the auspices of the Venusian Ministry of Intergalactic Culture. (It might be noted in passing that the more cognitive restructuring a piece of information is likely to necessitate, the less likely we are to believe it; we have a great personal investment in the way we organize our knowledge of the world.) Some information is treated in quite a peripheral way, being kept apart from the store of knowledge upon which we base decisions concerning our activity. We are not likely to refuse to venture onto the streets because we learn that the Penguin has escaped from Batman's clutches.

The actual processes and effects of language are too complex and obscure to delay us at this point; I shall stay with our more general definition that comprehension is the reduction of uncertainty through the elimination of alternatives by the allocation of a statement to a particular cognitive structure. The idea of defining reading comprehension in this pragmatic fashion is not original, in fact it is the method by which comprehension is normally assessed in the classroom. We test whether a child has grasped the meaning of a passage by asking questions and seeing whether his answer excludes all the alternatives that are incompatible with the sense of the passage. If the statement presented for comprehension is that Queen

Elizabeth died in 1603, we do not expect a reader asked for the year of her death to respond "1815" or "1794" or "1602". The number of alternative responses that the reader might make would be reduced to just one if the passage were comprehended. Any comprehension-testing question can be regarded as a test of whether the reader will reject alternative responses that he might produce if he has not comprehended the meaning of the passage.

The ability to select among alternatives within a passage is frequently made the basis of a test that can measure both the comprehensibility of a passage or the comprehension of a reader.[1] Consider half a dozen passages of text, each with every sixth word eliminated, for example:

a moth's ears are located————the sides of the rear————part of its thorax and————directed outward and backward into————constriction that separates the thorax————the abdomen. Each ear is————externally visible as a small————, and within the cavity is————transparent eardrum.

Suppose we present the six passages of this kind to ten readers, and ask them to fill in as many of the spaces as they can, scoring as a correct response every guess that coincides with the word that was removed from a particular position. One way of interpreting a high score for a particular space would be that there were very few alternative words that could be fitted into that position—the uncertainty is low. And the only reason that uncertainty is low at that position must be that most of the alternative words that could fill the space have been eliminated by information acquired from other parts of the passage—from the words that have not been removed. Passages that get a relatively larger number of missing words correctly guessed may be regarded as more easily comprehended than those whose spaces are more in doubt; this type of score is sometimes interpreted as a measure of the "intelligibility" or "readability" of a passage. On the other hand, a reader who succeeds in filling in correctly a relatively large number of the spaces in all passages might be regarded as a person who has acquired more information from reading the words that are present.

The previous example illustrates another aspect of meaning in sentences. Meaning is not something that suddenly appears when we have read or listened to the end of a sequence of words. Instead information is available at every point to reduce the number of alternatives remaining for those parts of the sequence that have not yet been encountered. As we shall see, this sequential information may in part be viewed as syntactic—the space in "The young ———— wrote the prizewinning song" can only be filled by a noun, because verbs, prepositions, and other alternatives are eliminated by grammatical relations among the observable elements of the sentence. But the sequential information is also semantic; we know that such nouns as "rock", "octogenarian", "heifer", "tablecloth", must also be excluded by the sense of the other words. This sequential aspect of the meaning of a sentence, or semantic redundancy, is one to which we shall turn our attention in due course. It might be noted that this kind of information does not run solely from left to right in a sentence. While the adjective "young" may exclude some of the alternatives that could be substituted in the space that follows it, other alternatives are eliminated by the words that are given at the end of the sentence.

One final point about language that should be made clear is that the meaning of a sentence cannot logically be organized in the same linear manner as its surface representation. When we say that "Your dog is chasing my cat" has the same meaning as "My cat is being chased by your dog", we are clearly referring to a meaning that is independent of the particular ordering of elements in the surface structure of the sentence. The speaker's motivation in selecting one or another of the alternative sentence forms will depend upon where he particularly wants to draw the listener's attention—to the activity of the dog or to the plight of the cat. But the result of comprehending either sentence would be the same as far as the structure of the listener's knowledge about his dog and the speaker's cat is concerned.

While the surface structure of English is organized linearly, meaning cannot be discussed in terms of order. Words are elements of the surface structure, of the physical representation, not of meaning. The meaning of a sentence is something global, a "state of mind", an instantaneous set of relationships established in the cognitive organization, and not something strung out over time. The purpose of the sentence-producing grammatical device is to convert a "thought" that simply exists, with no spatial or temporal organization, into a sequence of words. Or, to go in the reverse direction, grammar translates a sequence of words into a simultaneous cognitive whole. The listener or reader uses grammar to comprehend the relationships that exist among the serially ordered elements of the sentence, to alter the organization of his cognitive structure.

So far in this chapter I have tried—without being too technical or dogmatic or specific—to provide an explanation of what is meant by the statement "Comprehension is the reduction of uncertainty". I have adopted the pragmatic and operational point of view that for the purpose of understanding the general processes of reading, comprehension—the identification of meaning in a passage—may be regarded as a process that results in the elimination of alternatives. Further illustrations of the way in which apprehension of the "sense" of a passage tends to reduce the number of alternative responses that a reader might make will be given in the following sections. It will also be shown that the rate of reading aloud is also a reasonable indicator of the extent to which a reader can comprehend a passage. Because of the channel limitations of the visual information-processing and short-term memory systems, only a limited amount of visual information can be processed within a given period of time. The less a reader depends on visual information, the more he is able to overcome the limitations of the visual system and read fast. And a reader depends less on visual information when he can make use of information from other sources, notably an understanding of what the passage is about.

The model of comprehension that will be presented is a feature-analytic model—it is proposed that a fluent reader is able to identify meanings directly from the visual features without the mediation of word identification, provided he is able to make use of the syntactic and semantic redundancy that exists within sequences of words. I shall begin the discussion of this aspect of reading by considering some of the arguments that we can (and, in fact, must) go directly from the visual configuration to comprehension of the meaning of a passage.

Reading for Meaning

The question can be posed as a simple opposition of alternatives: either the fluent reader identifies individual words in order to obtain the meaning of a passage, or he acquires knowledge about the meaning of the passage in order to identify individual words. The alternatives are put into this contrastive form because in some ways it is a little difficult to demonstrate the major thesis that the identification of individual words is completely irrelevant to reading for meaning. While it is not difficult to show that moderately competent readers read too fast to identify every word, methods of measuring comprehension are not sufficiently precise to show whether they, in fact, extract all the meaning they might acquire if they were to identify every word individually. Besides, fluent readers generally *can* say something specific about the words in a passage that they have scanned, so that it is obviously incorrect to assert that they have not read any words. The argument is not that the fluent reader is unaware of any of the words in a passage that he has read, but only that he extracts meaning from a sequence of words before identifying any particular ones. I am saying that comprehension of meaning normally precedes word identification.

We shall consider first the case of *reading aloud,* where we know that every word has to be identified at some time. What is the evidence for asserting that the skilled reader identifies the meaning of a sequence of words before he actually articulates any of them?

One piece of evidence is related to the "eye–voice span".[2] It is a well-documented fact that the skilled reader's eye usually runs four or five words ahead of his voice when he is reading aloud. A demonstration of this phenomenon can easily be arranged—simply switch off the lights while a person is reading aloud, and note how many words he is able to continue uttering in the dark. Obviously, the visual information for words uttered in the dark has been acquired while the lights are on.

It is interesting that the eye–voice span of a skilled reader is about the capacity of short-term memory, four or five words. It is also noteworthy that the contents of the eye–voice span are not simply the next four or five words on the page; instead the span tends to extend to a phrase boundary, to a significant point in the structure of the sentence. If the phrase that the reader happens to be reading ends three words after the light goes out, he will probably only be able to recite those three words in the dark, but if the phrase ends just one or two words later and the following phrase extends to no more than six words from the point at which illumination is removed, then the eye–voice span may well extend to six words. In other words, the size of the eye–voice span is not so much determined by the number of words as by the structure of the passage being read.

There are several good reasons why the skilled reader should want to keep his voice four or five words behind his eye, all relevant to the assertion that meaning is processed before words are identified. We have already seen that the pronunciation of many words—for example, *read* and *permit*—depends upon the function of the word in the sentence. And the function of a word in a sentence depends just as much on what has still to come as on what has gone before. This "right-to-left" dependency is particularly noticeable with respect to pronunciation. In the sentences "We gave her dog biscuits because the poor animal was hungry" and "We gave her dog biscuits because she said animals were fed better than humans", the pronunciation of the first six words (and especially "dog biscuits") is determined entirely by what comes after.

The capacity of the eye–voice span varies with the "meaningfulness" of the configuration. We have seen (Chapter 7) that a skilled reader is able to identify in a single brief visual exposure four or five letters, a couple of unrelated words, or four or five words in a short sentence. The difference between the unrelated words and those in a sentence cannot be attributed to memory limitations—short-term memory is able to hold four or five unrelated words without difficulty—so the ease of perceiving the words must be related to the way in which they are organized into a sentence. But how can the reader make use of the fact that words are organized into a sentence unless he reads the sequence through to the end before identifying individual words?

A related phenomenon—to which I shall refer again—concerns a frequent kind of "error" that both fluent readers and children make in reading aloud.[3] If they err in reading a passage containing the words *He said that I should . . .* they are far more likely to say "He told me that I should . . ." rather than something like "He sent that I should . . . ", although *sent* is far more likely to be a visual confusion for *said* than *told me*. The explanation of this common phenomenon must be that the reader is attending to the meaning of the passage, not the identity of individual words, so that his errors are semantic rather than visual confusions. And if he makes an error on the word *said,* he is obviously looking ahead at what is to come, although he cannot be identifying *words* or he would not make substitution errors at all. Speakers who have their talks written in advance know how frequently they diverge from the literal text without straying significantly from the meaning.

News readers and public speakers like to glance through their script shortly before they begin to read it. They are obviously not trying to memorize the words, but instead checking on the meaning of the material, knowing that this is one of the greatest aids to a smooth and accurate presentation. Proofreaders, on the other hand, are painfully handicapped if they are aware of the meaning of a passage they are correcting, because attention to meaning is almost inevitably accompanied by the overlooking of errors in individual words. The only safeguard against proofreading oversights is to read the words—or to have them read—in a monotone, preferably not faster than one a second, so that the burden on short-term memory makes their semantic relations barely comprehensible.

The tendency of readers to be faithful to the meaning of a passage rather than to its actual words is dramatically demonstrated in a type of experiment that has been conducted to test the language processes of bilinguals.[4] The experiment involves asking bilinguals to read passages of text in which words in two languages are all mixed up together, although they make reasonable sense. An example of the kind of material used would be *un homme and his frère walked towards la porte. . . .* Not only are readers who can understand French and English separately able to read such a passage with no apparent additional difficulty, they are often unaware when the transition from one language to the other takes place. In fact, they will sometimes substitute a translation for a printed word; they will say "the door" when the printed text gives *la porte.*

Words do not actually have to be organized into "sensible sentences" for them to be read as easily as normal text. As long as a passage is a fairly close approximation to English over sequences of four or five words, it can be read fairly fluently.[5] (The limit of four or five words is again indicative of the involvement of short-term memory.) "Close approximations" to English are constructed by a team of individuals in the following way. The first person writes four words that could occur together at the start of a sentence, such as *As long as the.* The second person is shown the last three words, *long as the,* and asked to supply a fourth which could follow the other three; he might add *road* to make his sequence *long as the road.* The next person is again shown only the last three words, *as the road,* and might add *winds.* Every person in the chain is shown the last three words of the sequence and asked to add another one. Eventually, they produce a sequence like *As long as the road winds left through the door went slam on his fingers were cold to touch but not take five* . . . which may not make very much sense, but is certainly closer to English than the same sequence backwards: *five take not but touch to cold were fingers his on slam went door the through left winds road the as long as.* It may be helpful to try two tests on the preceding pair of sentences: to see how fast you or a friend can read them, and to see how many of the word sequences you can recall after one reading. In both cases the first sentence, the closer approximation to English, will probably prove the easier, again supporting the view that you do not simply read "word by word", but rather by taking into account whatever relations can be established between words that have gone before *and words that are still to come.* However, there is a limit on how much structure can be used if every word is being read—it does not matter much what happens more than three or four words ahead, probably because a total of four or five words will fill short-term memory. But it should be noted that the same limit of four or five words of connected sense would not apply if the passage were being read silently for meaning rather than aloud for words. The only reason that the four- or five-word limit applies for word identification is that the reader is forced to stock up his short-term memory with individual words; if he were able to fill his memory with meanings, he might well be responsive to dependences extending over a dozen words or more.

The theory of the transformational linguists supports the view that the fluent reader has to read directly for meaning, because words represent only the surface level of language. We have only to think of the difficulty we have in trying to read a relatively unfamiliar foreign language, even with the aid of a dictionary, to see that understanding a sentence is much more than putting individual word meanings together. Most words in isolation have so many alternative meanings that it is impossible to work out their meaning one word at a time. How many changes of direction would you have in comprehending the sequence *I know a bank where the wild thyme grows* if you were given the words one at a time, from left to right?

A particularly compelling illustration of the manner in which we read for meaning rather than to identify words can be found in the way that sentences are remembered. It is, of course, very rare that sentences of seven or eight words or more, or sentences heard more than a few minutes previously, can be repeated word for word correctly. But the errors of recall that are made are usually related to specific words, or to the syntactic structure of the sentence, rather than to the meaning of the sentence as a whole.[6] Can you remember either of the sentences given earlier that referred to dog biscuits? What have you forgotten, their wording or their meaning? Often we may mistakenly feel quite convinced that we remember a passage word for word, only to discover that the original was quite different. We remember only the deep structure, the "meaning", and our knowledge of the way language is organized "reconstructs" the rest. This phenomenon of "filling in" the surface structure is similar to the manner in which the processes of perception and memory fill in our blanks about nonlinguistic aspects of the world, as described in Chapter 6.

Oddly enough, we can read and remember sheer nonsense much more easily when it is embedded in a meaningful framework.[7] Nonsense syllables like *tul, zeg, niv* are much easier to remember if organized into the "statement" the *tul zegged the niv,* even though there are more elements in the second sequence than the first. Three unrelated letters are more easily retained in the setting *That man's initials are R. M. W.* than if we are simply told to remember "R–M–W". In each of these cases, nonsense material appears to be more easily retained when it is in a framework that requires processing at the deep structure level of language.

In addition to presenting evidence that attention to meaning precedes the identification of words in fluent reading, one can also argue that fluent reading could not be accomplished in any other way. We have seen in Chapter 8 that physiological constraints related to the speed at which visual information can be processed appear to limit the rate of fixations in reading to about three or four a second, and that a reader of "college-level" skill requires an average of about eight or nine fixations to identify ten words. There might be a tendency to conclude therefore that one word or a little more is identified in every fixation—that the reader is reading one word at a time. However, such a conclusion would appear to be in conflict with the evidence of the eye–voice span and span-of-apprehension experiments indicating that four or five words can be held in the visual system at any one moment; these experiments suggest that in normal reading the skilled reader must look more than once at every word. So on the one hand we have evidence suggesting that a person reading aloud produces an average of only one word for every fixation, while on the other hand there is evidence that four or five words may be contained within a single fixation. The resolution of the apparent paradox must be that the reader is actually looking in the area of every word more than once and that he sees each word (in a slightly different context as the fixations change position) three or four times. Such a hypothesis is, of course, entirely in line with the evidence from the "approximation to English" studies that the reader is sensitive to sequential structure over segments of three or four words, but no further. The hypothesis is also in accord with the eye–voice span evidence that the word being uttered when visual information is removed can be followed by the identification of three or four more words. To put the matter in another way, every time the reader actually makes an identification of a word in normal reading, he has had that word in three or four successive fixations and had the opportunity to examine its visual relationship to the three or four preceding words and the three or four that come after it.

An overlapping-fixation strategy of reading would appear to have three advantages: it enables the reader to make maximum use of the limited span of apprehension, he can use sequential redundancy in both directions, and it also helps him to overcome the additional physiological constraint that items can only be transferred from short-term to long-term memory at the rate of one every three or four seconds. The most efficient strategy would obviously be to transform the visual information from four or five words into larger meaning units at the deep structure level before committing them to long-term storage. If this strategy is followed, the reader will be much more successful in reading for sense, even though he may not be able to recall the exact words.

The use of redundancy to "fill in the empty spaces" in visual information and permit the extraction of meaning when many individual words are missing is particularly apparent when we consider silent reading. *With a moderate degree of skill, the adult reader is able to read silently much faster than he can read aloud, although no one would suggest that he gets less information from the page if he does not vocalize every word. It is true that there is a tendency to "subvocalize"—to read every word "silently"—when a passage is difficult. But one cannot conclude that subvocalization or reading aloud is required to make a difficult passage easier. Even if every word is articulated, there is still the problem of working out what it means; the meaning of language is no more given directly in its sound than it is available in the surface structure of writing. The explanation for subvocalization is more likely to be that reading a difficult passage automatically reduces reading speed, and we have a habit of articulating individual words when we read at a speed slow enough for individual words to be enunciated, especially when we happen to be loading our short-term memory with individual words rather than higher-order "meanings".*

The Use of Redundancy

Several examples have already been given of the way in which the use of redundancy—the elimination of alternatives by information from nonvisual sources—facilitates reading. While the facilitatory effect of redundancy has frequently been remarked upon, the explanation for the advantage is not usually given, at least not further than the fact that the presence of redundancy reduces the load on short-term memory by permitting the organization of elements into "higher-order units", into words rather than letters, or meanings rather than words.

But it is unnecessary to suggest, and a little difficult to explain, that the organization of letters into words or words into meanings takes place in short-term memory itself. A far more economical explanation would be that redundancy facilitates reading by making far less visual information necessary in the first place. It is not that we put letters into short-term memory and make use of redundancy to code them into words, but rather that we read words with far less visual information than we would require for all the individual letters. Similarly, when we read for meaning we do not actually put the words into short-term memory, but instead use the visual information directly for comprehension.

Knowledge of redundancy constitutes a readily available, internalized source of information that reduces the amount of visual information required to read. Or to put it more precisely, discrimination of exactly the same number of distinctive features will permit identification of a much larger area of redundant text. More letters or words can be identified from the same number of features if the reader is able to use prior knowledge of both featural and orthographic redundancy. And more meaning can be extracted, and greater comprehension can be gained, from the same number of visual features if *syntactic* and *semantic* sequential redundancy can be applied.

A single illustration will show how the two forms of sequential redundancy among words permit word identification on minimal visual information. First, as a kind of pretest, I shall ask whether you can identify the following "word", or any of the letters in it ⌐ˡ⌐ˡⁱ⌐⌐ . Now we can proceed with the illustration.[8]

I have already explained the nature of syntactic redundancy, the fact that a sentence like *After dinner let's all go to the* ———— is almost certain to end with a noun rather than a verb or adjective or preposition, a piece of grammatical information that reduces considerably the number of alternatives that the word in the final position might be. In addition I have said that there are semantic constraints that go even further in reducing the number of alternatives. In fact, it can be shown that just one word has a much higher probability of being put into the blank position in the sentence than any other—the word "theater". You can discover experimentally that "theater" is the most probable word for that context by canvassing your friends—you will probably find that the proverbial four-out-of-five think "theater" is the most appropriate way of concluding the sentence. "Theater", however, is not the most probable word in all contexts; at the end of a sequence such as *It was agreed that he would meet me at the* —————, the word "station" has a very much higher probability of occurring than "theater" and a number of other words.

We have now established a couple of pieces of semantic information and shall use them to test empirically our hypothesis that semantic redundancy results in the reduction in the number of visual features required to identify a word. We shall flash each of the two words tachistoscopically onto a screen, and ask groups of people to try to identify them. For one group we shall flash the word "theater" after they have been told the other words of the first sentence, and the word "station" after they have been given the words of the second sentence. For the other group we shall reverse the order, flashing "station" after the first sentence and "theater" after the second. You will notice, of course, that both words are equally feasible in each context—there is nothing wrong with going to the station after dinner or arranging to meet at the theater, it is just that these combinations are not so probable. Our experimental assumption is that if more people manage to identify a word from a brief exposure on one occasion than on another, then they must be identifying it on less visual information on the first occasion; they are making use of other sources of information.

The result of the experiment probably comes as no surprise at this point. A much greater proportion of viewers is able to recognize the word "theater" from a brief flash if it follows the first sentence than if it follows the second. And more people identify the word "theater" after the second sentence than after the first. It must be noted that the viewers are not guessing, they are making use of visual information, because they do not respond "theater" when *station* is presented. But the amount of information required to identify either word depends on the sequence of words that it follows, on the semantic redundancy.

This experiment is more than just an example of the way in which redundancy exists in language and can be made use of. It helps to underline the fact that there is not a fixed amount of visual information required to identify a word, but rather that the amount of featural information needed depends on how much information is available elsewhere.

To nail down the point, let us see once more if you can identify the elements printed in our pretest ⌒ˡ⌒ˡⁱ⌒⌒ . You probably can now. If you can't, then you will have no difficulty in the context "There was a happy reunion at the ⌒ˡ⌒ˡⁱ⌒⌒".

Of course, the preceding demonstration shows only that less featural information is required to identify a word if information is available from other words; it does not prove that no other words need to be identified for semantic redundancy to be employed. There is, however, a growing body of evidence to suggest that meaningful sequences of words can indeed be identified when there is insufficient featural information to identify any of the individual words in isolation, or in an unmeaningful sequence, just as letters can be identified in words in circumstances under which none of the letters can be identified in isolation.

But perhaps the most compelling piece of evidence that redundancy can be used to avoid the identification of *any* words is the fact that fluent readers can extract meaning from passages at a rate that would absolutely preclude word identification. Many people can follow the meaning of a novel or newspaper article at the rate of a thousand words a minute, which is four times faster than their probable speed if they were identifying every word. There is a prevalent misconception that the explanation for this kind of fast reading must be that the reader identifies one word in every four, and that this gives him sufficient information at least to get the gist of what he is reading. But it is very easy to demonstrate that one word in four will not contribute very much towards the intelligibility of a passage. Here is every fourth word from a randomly selected newsmagazine film review: "Many - - - been - - - face - - - business - - - sour - - - If - - - to. . .". The passage is even less easy to comprehend if the words provided are selected in groups, with correspondingly larger gaps between them. It is somewhat easier to comprehend what a passage is about if every fourth *letter* is provided rather than every fourth word, and, of course, my argument is that reading at a thousand words a minute is possible only if the omissions occur at the *featural* level, where redundancy is greatest. It has been argued that even in words in isolation, probably well over half of the available distinctive features are redundant (Chapter 10). But this redundancy can be used only if the remaining information is available from all parts of the configuration; the skilled reader may require to see only a fraction of the features available in a word, but not if these features are all concentrated in a single letter.

The fluent reader who scans at a thousand words a minute or more is less likely to be able to report what actual words in the passage were than the reader who plods through at only a tenth of the speed. But the fluent reader will be able to tell you much more about the meaning.

Our final piece of evidence that a fluent reader does not depend on individual words will be provided by the record of eye movements of a very fast reader as she read at the rate of only a dozen fixations for every two facing pages of text, an average of about two pages every three or four seconds or about 10,000 words a minute.[9] Obviously, such a reader is placing her fixations on the pages in positions where they give her optimum information—but this is not in the order that any word-identification model would predict. She reads *down* the left-hand page, making three or four fixations along the center line of the text, then *across* to the bottom of the right-hand page, three or four fixations *up* the center of the right-hand page, and then one sweep *back* to the left, ready to turn to the next pair of pages. Of what utility would it be to identify just a single word or two in each of these fixations, half of which would be characterized conventionally as "regressions" because they go against the linear progression of the text? What the speed reader is doing, of course, is getting a cognitive picture of an entire page in about one second. She does not pick up a photographic representation of the page, because that would be quite useless; it would still have to be read. Instead she snapshots the "meaning" of the entire page. Such a reader can comprehend an entire page from the same number of features that a normally skilled reader might require to read barely a tenth of the words. The reason that she can afford to ignore convention in ordering her fixations in the opposite direction to the sequence of words is that at her rate of reading—a page in less than two seconds—information from the first fixation on the pages is still available while the last fixation is being made. We have seen that all readers appear to be limited to carrying not more than four fixation loads of information in their short-term memory at any one time; any additional information is either lost or has to go into long-term memory at the very much slower processing rate. At the speed reader's rate of progress, she would be able to submit only one item of information to long-term memory every page, but since her information about that page is very much more condensed than that of normal readers, she would be able to pack much more of its meaning into a single memorization.

The Featural Model of Meaning Identification

I have asserted at some length that immediate identification of meaning is the process by which a fluent reader normally reads for comprehension; I have argued that immediate meaning identification is both an actual and necessary fact. But I have not specified in detail how it is accomplished.

And it is not possible to specify how comprehension is accomplished, at least not in the kind of neurophysiological detail that would explain any of the actual processes and connections and changes of state within the brain. It would be presumptuous to try to do so, and in any case largely beyond the present state of the art in several sciences. As far as the brain is concerned, I was just as abstract and indefinite in the discussion of letter and word identification. But there is an additional reason why any consideration of comprehension will be less precise than theories of letter and word recognition, and that is that we cannot specify what the alternatives are. For letters we know how many alternatives exist, 26. For words we cannot put a number to the set of alternatives, but there is a certain intuitive ease about establishing a "category" for a word, and even for relating word categories to each other through semantic features. But meaning is elusive. It melts at the touch of words. A sentence meaning is not a category, it is a state; it is a relation among several categories. How many meanings there might be, how many possible relations among categories, evades us. There is a tendency to think of the number of possible meanings as enormous, even infinite, but perhaps the total is not quite so astronomical. It is true that when one considers the number of cognitive categories there might be, and the number of ways even sets of three or four categories might be combined, then the number of possibilities defies the imagination. But there can be a huge difference between the number of combinations that logically could occur and the number that actually do. The number of different words that could be produced by combining four or five phonemes, or four or five graphemes, is also enormous—over 40 million. But the number of those possible words that actually occurs is well over a thousand times smaller. Perhaps there are fewer meanings than there are words, because many word combinations have the same meaning; it is a possibility. There may be an infinite number of ways of saying *The dog chase the cat, The cat was chased by the dog, Rover pursued Kitty,* and so forth, but these variations have just one meaning. We do not know, and may never know, the number of possible meanings but we can still construct a model of reading. At least to a very high level of agreement, we can discover whether two sentences have "the same meaning" or are different. By posing a question in terms of alternatives, we can discover whether a reader's uncertainty reduction is consistent with the interpretation of the majority.

In other words, the question of meaning has to be handled pragmatically. As more than one authority has observed, the ultimate solution to the question of how reading is accomplished will provide an explanation for human thought. We cannot use words to describe meanings, but we can use words to describe models, and it is only at the level of the model that we can attempt to integrate comprehension with other aspects of reading.

In Figure 8 the two alternatives are presented, mediated and immediate meaning identification.

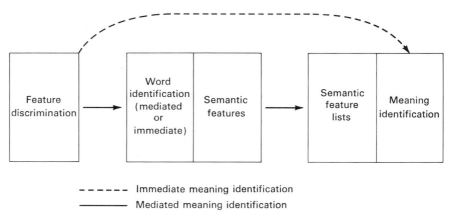

- - - - - - Immediate meaning identification
——————— Mediated meaning identification

Figure 8   Immediate and Mediated Meaning Identification

Mediated meaning identification is the lower route, by which one gets to comprehension through the identification of individual words. To keep the figure uncomplicated I have not elaborated on the manner in which words are identified. Either immediate or mediated word identification is possible on the way to mediated meaning identification, and however complex comprehension must be if it has to be mediated through words, it will be very much more complicated if the words themselves have to be identified on the basis of individual letters. Yet there are many works on reading that seem to assume that there is *no alternative* explanation of reading except that letters are identified, letters make words, and words make sentences.

I am not asserting that mediated meaning identification is not possible, or even that it is not done. Quite the reverse. Every reader probably has to depend on mediated comprehension some of the time, and beginning readers, unfortunately, very often rely on it most of the time. I am merely asserting that immediate meaning identification is preferred.

Consider what is involved in the mediated identification of meaning. First, words have to be identified, and this is no casual matter. We spent an entire chapter examining the complexities involved in putting a name to a word. Even if the name could be applied immediately, without going through the identification of letters, the identification of word after isolated word would require an average of about two or three fixations, half of short-term memory capacity and the best part of a second, for every word in the sentence.

Any objection that perhaps isolated words might be identified two or three at a time is a red herring. If words "identified in groups" are processed quite independently—as "unrelated words"—then the problem has not been changed; each word still takes up just as much processing time and space because just as much visual information is required to identify it. But if two words identified together require less visual information than the two words taken independently, then this is no longer mediated identification. If the presence of two words together facilitates the identification of each, then the reader must be making use of semantic constraints, of meaning, before identifying the individual words.

"Reading for meaning" entails making use of information simultaneously at both the surface and deep structure of language—using elements of both visual and semantic information. Because the fluent reader operates simultaneously at the surface and deep structure level—discriminating visual features and using his knowledge of grammar to associate them with the developing semantic interpretation—he is able to read with a minimum of visual information.

Even when all the individual words of a sentence are identified, in this relatively slow and cumbersome manner, the reader is a long way from having the meaning of a sentence. There is another widespread misconception that spoken words have a kind of magical character; that their meaning is apparent the moment they are uttered. Therefore, all one has to do to acquire the meaning of written words is to convert them into vocal or subvocal speech. But spoken words in their physical manifestation are just as far removed from meaning as the marks on a printed page. Meaning is not in the surface structure of language, either spoken or written; meaning in each case has to be constructed by exactly the same grammatical and semantic processes. "Converting" a written message into verbal form does not itself provide the meaning, it merely interposes an additional stage in the process of comprehension.

The additional stage of word identification involved in mediated comprehension is a snag, a hindrance, not a help to comprehension. It is an oversimplification to assume that one can identify and interpret isolated words in reading at the same rate that one can produce words in speech. It is true that a skilled reader is able to read aloud as fast as he can talk, but it is not difficult to show that such a reader must be using meaning as an aid to producing his words. It is just not possible for most readers to produce isolated words, unrelated by meaning, at the same rate that they can read meaningful text. To prove this, just try to read the following passage of backwards text, in which most of the meaning is lost; you will find you read with much less speed and accuracy.[10]

Accomplished is it how detail in specified not have we but. Fact necessary and actual an both is identification meaning immediate that argued have we. Comprehension for reads normally reader fluent a which by process the is meaning of identification immediate that length some at asserted have we.

Unrelated words cannot be read at the same rate as meaningful text, and it is very difficult indeed to extract meaning from words that are read slowly. Unless we can get four or five words at a time into short-term memory, we cannot acquire meaning in a form that we can get into long-term memory. It is not necessary to show that a poor reader has trouble comprehending a passage if he gets the words at the rate of only one a second—even a skilled reader has the same trouble if the words are presented to him, visually or acoustically, one at a time at this slow speed. This again is easily tested; try having monotone words read to yourself at the steady rate of one a second. Your only hope of comprehending will be to keep rehearsing words subvocally in short-term memory so that they can be dealt with in groups of four or five, an impossible task if one is busily engaged at the same time in trying to identify the next word.

Mediated word identification, then, is one way to read for meaning; it is a feasible method, but not the best, because it is indirect. I suggest that mediated word identification is used by any reader, fluent or beginner, only when he has to, and he has to when he finds the passage difficult, when immediate comprehension is not possible. Before I discuss the conditions under which immediate comprehension is not possible, I shall say a little more about what immediate comprehension is.

Immediate meaning identification is very simply represented in the diagram of the model; Figure 8 depicts it as a route running directly from the visual feature discrimination to comprehension. For the reasons given at the beginning of this section, I cannot offer a very satisfying explanation of how immmediate comprehension is accomplished, although I can argue vigorously that it is accomplished, and suggest the circumstances in which the skill is acquired. In very broad brush strokes I can describe the process: the distinctive features that are available to distinguish one visual configuration from another can be used to eliminate cognitive alternatives —not alternative words, but alternative meanings.

I cannot elaborate upon the relation between visual features and meaning for two reasons. First, I cannot describe the features any more than I could during our discussion of letter and word identification—not enough is known about the visual system. But it can be said that the distinctive visual features must be the same for all three kinds of identification—

a feature that will serve to distinguish between two alternative meanings must at least be sufficient to distinguish between two alternative letters. The second reason that I cannot more adequately describe the relation of distinctive features to meaning is that we cannot get any more of a purchase on the notion of "meaning". But since—at least in terms of the model—a meaning is conceptualized as a particular relation among a number of categories (or, alternatively, among a number of lists of semantic features), we may postulate that a specification of visual features that is associated with a particular semantic feature list can be associated directly with a meaning. And I have already argued that direct associations between sets of visual and semantic features can be established easily, both in reading and in visual perception generally.

What are the circumstances in which the skill of immediate meaning identification is acquired? I shall go into this question in a little more detail in the next chapter, but for the moment I can sum up the answer in a single word, "experience" (or to use a slightly more traditional term, "practice"). Learning to read is akin to any other skill; there are perhaps some specialized exercises that one can undertake to iron out particular difficulties, but there is no substitute for engaging in the activity itself. Reading involves looking for significant differences in the visual configuration to eliminate alternatives, and knowledge can be acquired of what differences are significant only through experience. This knowledge cannot be taught, it has to be acquired; the major contributions that the teacher can make are to provide information, feedback, and encouragement.

When is immediate comprehension not possible? Obviously, when the reader's experience has not previously provided him with the opportunity to select among two or more alternative semantic interpretations on the basis of visual featural information. If a reader cannot find a distinctive pattern of visual features that will permit him to select between alternative meanings, then his only available strategy is to turn the situation into words and try to resolve his uncertainty verbally. And since the beginning reader lacks the fluent reader's experience, he will be forced to rely more on words to provide significant differences. In the same way a fluent reader will have to fall back on mediated comprehension when he is confronted with "difficult" material with which he has not had much experience. We learn the distinctive visual features of meaning in the same way that we learn the distinctive visual features of words, letters, faces, and furniture. We look for the significant differences that enable us to establish classes within which all events, or meanings, will be treated as functionally equivalent.

It is sometimes argued that the analogy between what I call immediate word identification and immediate meaning identification is specious; that while there is a reasonable case for asserting that visual configurations may be associated through learning with verbal labels, a "meaning" is far too much of an abstraction to become associated with actual sets of visual features.[11] But there are many objections to this objection. True, the notion of "meaning" is an abstraction, but only to the theorist, who is forced through lack of knowledge to define meaning in an abstract way. In the brain itself a "meaning" must be just as much of an actual physical event as the uttering of the sound that is a visual configuration's "label". The objection oversimplifies the processes of word identification and of speech comprehension; unless some unique way can be shown in which sounds and meaning are related, there is no point in asserting that visual events and meaning cannot be directly related. It is moreover a misapprehension to assume that particular semantic features must previously have been associated *directly* with visual events if an immediate semantic interpretation is to be possible. A falling object, a runaway vehicle, a broken piece of glass may all be interpreted as "dangerous" although never seen in a threatening context before. And it takes no longer to identify (categorize) an object as "dangerous" than it does to identify it simply as a brick, truck, or piece of glass.

References

There are many books on meaning and comprehension, by philosophers, psychologists, linguists, and educators in a variety of disciplines, but none of them is written along the lines of the present chapter. Some of the references cited at the end of Chapters 3 and 6 would be closest. One psychologist has performed several relevant experiments and drawn general conclusions similar to my own, although we differ on some points of detail. His approach, with which I concur, is succinctly stated in the title of the following paper:

P. A. KOLERS, Reading is only incidentally visual. In K. S. GOODMAN and J. T. FLEMING (eds.), *Psycholinguistics and the Teaching of Reading* (Newark, Delaware: International Reading Association, 1969).

Informative summary papers by Kolers also appear in the volumes edited by Goodman, and by Levin and Williams, listed on page 10.

Notes

1. This is the "cloze" technique—for example, W. L. TAYLOR, "Cloze" readability scores as indices of individual differences in comprehension and aptitude, *Journal of Applied Psychology,* **41** (1957), 19–26.

2. H. LEVIN and E. A. TURNER, Sentence structure and the eye–voice span, *Project Literacy Reports* (Ithaca, N.Y.: Cornell University), **7** (1966), 79–87. J. J. GEYER,

Perceptual systems in reading: the prediction of a temporal eye–voice span. In HELEN K. SMITH (ed.), *Perception and Reading* (Newark, Delaware: International Reading Association, 1968).

3. K. S. GOODMAN, Analysis of oral reading miscues: applied psycholinguistics, *Reading Research Quarterly*, **5** (1969). ROSE-MARIE WEBER, The study of oral reading errors, a survey of the literature. *Reading Research Quarterly*, **4,** 1 (1968), 96–119.

4. P. A. KOLERS, cited above.

5. G. A. MILLER, J. S. BRUNER, and L. POSTMAN (listed on page 148, note 6).

6. J. MEHLER and G. A. MILLER, Retroactive interference in the recall of simple sentences, *British Journal of Psychology*, **55** (1964), 295–301.

7. W. EPSTEIN, The influence of syntactical structure on learning, *American Journal of Psychology*, **74** (1961), 80–85. W. EPSTEIN, A further study of the influence of syntactical structure on learning, *American Journal of Psychology*, **75** (1962), 121–126.

8. The illustration is based on J. MORTON, The effects of context on the visual duration threshold for words, *British Journal of Psychology*, **55,** 2 (1964), 165–180. See also E. TULVING and CECILLE GOLD, Stimulus information and contextual information as determinants of tachistoscopic recognition of words, *Journal of Experimental Psychology*, **66** (1963), 319–327 (reprinted in Haber, listed on page 27).

9. E. LLEWELLYN-THOMAS, Eye movements in speed reading. In *Speak Reading: Practices and Procedures*, 10 (Newark, Delaware: University of Delaware Reading Study Center, 1962).

10. P. A. KOLERS, cited above.

11. U. NEISSER (listed on page 10), 134–137.

14

Reading— and Learning To Read

This book was started upon the assumption that few insights could be gained into the process of learning to read until there was some understanding of the fluent reading process itself. So far we have been concerned mainly with fluent reading, although occasional references to the learner have been made. Now we are in a better position to look at the skill of fluent reading from the point of view of the child beginning reading instruction, and to see what justification there is for two initial assertions—that a distinction must be made between fluent reading and learning to read, and that reading is really a very difficult task for the beginner until he has achieved a certain degree of fluency.

Two ways of summarizing the model of skilled reading suggest themselves. One is simply to refer the reader back to the first chapter, which was entitled "Understanding Reading" and which presented in preview form the model of fluent reading that was going to be developed. The implicit objectives for the rest of the book were to make the contents of Chapter 1 meaningful and convincing. The alternative way of summarizing the model is to present an overview that integrates the major points made in Chapters 9–13.

In view of the importance that has been attached to redundancy in this book, both alternatives will be adopted. In the following section I shall construct a "working model" of a fluent reader. But I also invite readers to reread Chapter 1 either now or at the end of the following section, for an alternative description of the model.

Fluent Reading

I shall make a "task analysis" of fluent reading, and then explain my earlier definition of a fluent reader—as a person who is able to make optimal use of all the redundancy available in a passage of text.

The reader's objective is to extract information from the written text, to reduce uncertainty. The purpose of reading is defined in these general terms because on different occasions a reader may require information to identify letters, or to identify words, or to "comprehend"—to identify meaning. For each of these "aspects" of reading the visual information that the reader acquires may be regarded as reducing uncertainty; the information available from the text may be used to eliminate alternatives among 26 letters, among an indefinite number of possible words, or among an even more indefinite number of alternative meanings, or semantic interpretations.

The three aspects of reading in which a reader may engage—the reduction of letter, word, or meaning uncertainty—are quite independent. By "independent" I mean that a reader may apply visual information to any one of the three aspects of uncertainty reduction without the prior reduction of uncertainty in any other aspect. For example, he may reduce his word uncertainty without making any decisions about letters, or he may reduce his meaning uncertainty without making any prior decisions about words. I have termed this "direct" reduction of uncertainty as *immediate* word or meaning identification, in contrast to various indirect ways of reducing uncertainty which I called *mediated* identification. For example, words may be identified through the prior identification and synthesis of individual letters, and comprehension accomplished by the identification and integration of word information. But none of the mediated routes to uncertainty reduction is as efficient as immediate identification of meanings or words.

Although the three aspects of reading are independent, in the sense that none of the three kinds of uncertainty reduction necessarily has to precede any other, they cannot be conducted simultaneously. One cannot read to reduce both letter uncertainty and word uncertainty at the same time, or word and meaning uncertainty simultaneously. Any attempt to identify individual letters while "reading for words", or to identify words when the aim is comprehension, must inevitably result in delay and disruption of both identification processes.

The three aspects of identification are mutually disruptive because they all involve using the same visual information for different purposes. One can no more try to identify a visual configuration as letters and a word, or as words and meaning, than one can simultaneously see both aspects of an ambiguous figure such as the vase (or the two faces) in or of a "reversible figure" such as ▢ .

In short, from the same visual information, the distinctive features of written language, a fluent reader can reduce uncertainty in three different ways: by identifying letters, words, or meanings. Figure 9 presents the alternatives diagrammatically. Any two visual configurations (samples of written text) to which a reader would allocate different semantic interpretations must necessarily differ by at least one distinctive feature that would permit the differentiation of at least one word and at least one letter. As a minimal example, the featural difference that permits the allocation of different semantic interpretations to *The horse fell down* and *The house fell down* will also permit the differentiation of the word *horse* and *house* and of the letters *u* and *r*. This is not to argue, however, that differentiation of a letter or differentiation of a word is required before differentiation of the two sentences can be accomplished. As indicated in Figure 9, the fluent reader can go directly from discrimination of the distinctive features to the reduction of whatever aspect of uncertainty he desires.

The reduction of uncertainty for letters or words can be accomplished directly from visual "tests" for the discrimination of features. The results of the feature tests are carried to visual feature lists that specify alternative letter or word categories. Allocation of a configuration to a category occurs when the results of featural tests meet the specifications of a visual feature list.

A letter category may be regarded as the association of visual and acoustic feature lists, the acoustic features specifying the category's "name" and the visual features its possible configurations. A letter category may also have semantic aspects, for example, when a letter represents a particular object or value, such as *X*, but that is not relevant to our discussion. A letter category may be specified by more than one visual feature list, in order that allographs of the same letter, such as *A, a, α* may be allocated to the same category. The availability of alternative feature lists to specify the same category allows visual configurations that are different in features but not in function to be allocated to the same category.

A word category, for written language, may be regarded as an association of visual, acoustic, and semantic feature lists. More than one semantic feature list may be associated with a set of functionally equivalent visual feature lists, but the alternative semantic sets would not be functionally

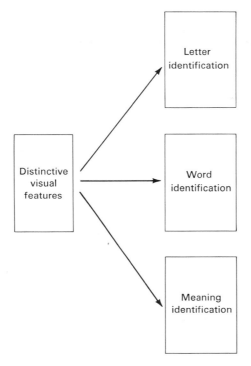

Figure 9 Three Aspects of Uncertainty-Reduction in Reading

equivalent. Rather they would represent alternative semantic "readings" for a visual category that has a variety of interpretations, such as *bank* (river or commercial).

Exactly the same visual analytic process accomplishes identification of a letter or identification of a word; the only difference is the set of alternative categories to which the featural information is directed. The difference lies in the nature of the reader's uncertainty, not in the information that he acquires. The analyzers of the visual system examine the distinctive features of the visual configuration and transmit + or − information for the presence or absence of a feature to all the feature lists to which the output of that analyzer is relevant in the area of the reader's uncertainty. When the featural information acquired by the visual analyzer tests is identical with a featural list for a relevant category, then an "identification" will be made, relating the visual input to the acoustic and semantic features of the category.

The allocation of featural information to word categories is somewhat more complex than its allocation to letter categories because letter feature lists have only "one dimension"—a given feature either is or is not present on the list. For words, however, there may be as many tests for each feature as there are letters in the word, and the allocation of featural test information to feature lists must take into account the position of each feature in the configuration. However, such feature tests may be conducted simultaneously ("in parallel") on different parts of the visual configuration.

There are no individual categories of "meaning"; instead a meaning is regarded as a particular reorganization or partitioning of cognitive structure that may involve two or more categories (two or more sets of semantic features). The identification of meaning may, however, be accomplished directly from the results of visual analyzer tests by the reorganization of cognitive structure based on the semantic associations of patterns of visual features, and on the rules of syntax. The rules of syntax determine how the particular visual–semantic associations should be interpreted for a cognitive reorganization. Although we normally regard *words* as having semantic interpretations, in the model the semantic aspects are associated with the *feature patterns* of words, in view of the evidence that word identification is not necessary for the acquisition of meaning. Similarly, our usual conception that rules of syntax must be applied to words has to be modified in the light of the evidence that at the cognitive processing level, syntax involves feature patterns.

The allocation of visual information to visual feature lists permits the elimination of alternatives; this is the process by which uncertainty is reduced. The discrimination of the presence of a single distinctive visual feature, for example, permits the elimination of all those letter or word or semantic categories that are not marked + for that feature. But while a single distinctive feature may be sufficient to eliminate many letter or word alternatives, reduction of meaning uncertainty cannot take place without the additional application of rules of syntax. As pointed out in Chapter 3, the rules of syntax relate the surface structure of language to its meaning. Syntax is the bridge between visual and semantic features to be discussed more fully in the following pages.

All the functional aspects of the visual information-processing system in reading are established through experience, specifically by the reader looking for significant differences or functional equivalence in visual configurations to reduce letter, word, or meaning uncertainty. If two configurations have to be allocated to different cognitive categories, then the perceiver has to find some differences in them that are "significant". The determination of what features are distinctive, the construction of feature lists, and the establishment of categories all go together. On the basis of continued experience in seeing significant differences, the reader builds up feature lists that serve to define the categories visually and to specify which configurations can be allocated to them. "Feedback" information that two configurations should be allocated to the same category, even though they differ on one or more distinctive visual features, provides the impetus to establish alternative, functionally equivalent feature lists for the relevant category.

A visual feature is not distinctive unless it is marked + on at least one feature list and − on another. The result of an analyzer test that indicates the presence of that feature in a visual configuration eliminates as alternative identifications all those categories or semantic interpretations that do not have that feature marked + on the appropriate position in their associated visual feature lists. Similarly, a negative test result for the feature excludes all alternatives except those where feature lists are appropriately marked −.

Whenever immediate word or meaning identification is not possible because a visual feature list does not exist to specify the appropriate word category or semantic interpretation, *mediated identification* has to take place. Mediated identification involves not only the prior allocation of the visual configuration to intermediate categories, it also requires the application of a quite different set of rules. For example, mediated *word* identification requires not only the allocation of featural information from the visual configuration to letter or other intermediate categories, but also spelling or "phonic" or "analogy" rules to integrate the information from the identified segments into words. As we saw in Chapter 12, such rules are both complex and approximate, and dependence on their use places a severe burden on the information-processing capacity of the reader.

In the case of mediated *meaning* identification, the reader must allocate the visual information to individual *word* categories, and then use the acoustic or semantic features of these words to try to generate an appropriate meaning identification. Mediated meaning identification in reading is particularly unproductive, because it involves the reader in what in effect is mediated comprehension for spoken language, although the least complex route for speech comprehension is the extraction of meaning from a sequence of sounds before segmentation of the sequence into individual words. Both in listening and reading for meaning, identification of individual words merely gets in the way. Therefore, the mediated identification of meaning in reading may be doubly disruptive.

Mediated meaning identification is particularly undesirable in reading because it slows the reading process and overloads the visual information-processing and memory system. The visual system is capable of processing only a limited amount of visual information in every fixation, and requires a quarter of a second or more to process the information that goes into "sensory store" from a single fixation. The exact amount of featural information that the visual system can process from a single glance is difficult to specify, but it is sufficient to identify only four or five unrelated letters of the alphabet. From the sensory store of a single glance a reader can also identify a couple of short unrelated words, which indicates that the amount of visual information required to identify two unrelated words is equivalent to the amount of information needed to identify four or five letters. Since each of the words may consist of more than four letters, obviously half the featural information in a word is redundant, a conclusion that has been supported on a number of other empirical or theoretical grounds. Twice as many words may be identified in a single fixation if they enjoy some syntactic and semantic cohesion, if they are a meaningful sequence of words, than if they are unrelated to each other. Put another way, the immediate identification of a fragment of English text requires less than half the visual information needed to identify the same words individually, and less than a quarter of the visual information that would be required to identify all the letters if they occurred in isolation. No more visual information may be required to identify a word in text than to identify a letter in isolation.

There is, therefore, a limitation on the rate at which information can be processed from sensory store—namely, the number of features required to identify four or five unrelated letters three or four times every second. The "output" from a single fixation may be four or five letters, two unrelated words or four or five words in a meaningful sequence. There is the additional limitation that not very much more than one element may be fed into long-term memory every three or four seconds. Each "element", however, may be a letter or a word, or a "meaning". While waiting to get from sensory store to long-term memory, items have to be held in short-term memory, which also has a very limited capacity. It appears that all items in short-term memory have to be constantly "rehearsed", otherwise they are rapidly lost, and no more than five or six items can be rehearsed at any one time.

It is clearly to the advantage of the reader, therefore, to be able to "group" his information into larger and larger units, to combine letters into words, or words into "meanings". However, it is not actually the case that combination into larger units takes place in sensory store. Instead the nature of the information available from sensory store—whether letters, words, or meaning—is determined by the basis upon which the reader first acquires visual information. If the reader examines the visual configuration to reduce letter uncertainty, then he has letters in his sensory store. He can get a maximum of about five letters for every fixation, and has to fill his short-term memory with these letters while he tries to put them into long-term memory or to organize them into word or meaning units. If, however, he examines the text for words, he may pick up two in a single fixation and he will be able to hold the contents of two or three fixations in short-term memory while he processes them further. And if the reader examines the visual image for meaning, he may be able to pick up four or five words that he can dispatch far more easily into long-term memory (because the very process of using semantic cues in acquiring the visual information accomplishes some of the integration required to get the sequence into long-term memory as a single semantic unit of meaning).

Obviously, the severe restrictions of the visual information-processing system and memory can be overcome only if the reader uses immediate identification procedures as often as possible. Whenever mediated identification is employed, twice as many features are required to identify a given group of words or meaning, and more elements have to be held for longer periods in short-term memory. In addition, the various rules for integrating letters into words or words into meaning also take up some of the limited processing time and space. And as a result much information will be lost before it is even processed; this is why it is almost impossible to read a passage for meaning the first time if the processing is not immediate.

Immediate identification would be of little value in reading were it not for the redundancy that exists in language. There would be far less advantage in reading to identify words rather than integrating individual letters if as many features were required to identify a word as to identify all its letters in isolation. But as we have seen, perhaps only half the visual information is required to identify a five-letter word as to identify five letters in isolation. And a similar economy of visual information results if the words can be read in a meaningful sequence. In other words, the structure of written English is highly redundant, a fact that the fluent reader can turn to his advantage to overcome the limitations of the visual processing system.

Redundancy occurs at a number of levels. There is *featural redundancy* in individual letters—we can often identify a letter on less than the full amount of visual information that is available. Therefore, not all the feature tests in feature lists for letter categories require to be fulfilled for an identification to be made, and alternative "criterial subsets" of feature tests may be established within a feature list, each subset constituting an alternative specification for the relevant category. The same featural redundancy occurs in words, and by extension in meanings. Obviously, the more knowledge a reader has of the featural redundancy of his language, the more alternative criterial subsets he can establish within his feature lists, and the less visual information he will require to identify letters, or words, or meanings. He can only acquire this knowledge through experience.

There is also considerable redundancy within the structure of *words* because letters, or rather patterns of features, tend to occur only in certain combinations. Therefore, a word is identifiable on only half the visual information required to identify its component letters in isolation. If the reader is aware of this redundancy—if he acquires the knowledge that certain patterns of features just do not occur together in English words—then he can construct criterial subsets within the feature lists specifying word categories, and identify words on much less visual information. Once again this knowledge of the relative probabilities of particular feature combinations in English words—their *orthographic redundancy*—can be acquired only through experience in reading. Featural information in words is most useful when it is spread out across the entire configuration—it is far more informative to be able to see half of each letter in a word than all the letters in only half the word. Therefore the criterial subsets in the feature lists for words may permit word identification to occur even in conditions where there is not sufficient visual information for the identification of any of the letters in isolation.

Finally, the fluent reader is able to make use of the redundancy that exists *across* sequences of words. He knows (implicitly) that for various syntactic and semantic reasons, many combinations of visual feature patterns are not possible in the language. We could translate the previous statement into more usual terminology by saying that the reader knows that certain combinations of *words* cannot occur in the language, but that is not getting to the heart of the matter. If certain words cannot occur, then certain featural patterns cannot occur, and it is far more efficient to use redundancy at the feature level than at the word level, because word identification is not necessary for the identification of meaning. Again, the ability to use syntactic and semantic redundancy is acquired only through practice—by discovering the minimum number of significant differences required to distinguish among alternative identifications and interpretations.

We can return now to the definition of a fluent reader as a person who can make optimal use of all the redundancy in a piece of text.

It can be shown that fluent readers make use of all the different aspects of redundancy because they require less visual information to identify letters in words than letters in isolation, and less visual information to identify words in meaningful sequences than in unrelated sequences of words. It can also be shown that fluent readers are capable of immediate word and meaning identification. Immediate word and meaning identification are not possible unless the reader is able to make use of orthographic, syntactic, and semantic redundancy.

It can be shown that the fluent reader does and must make use of redundancy because he is able to overcome the channel capacity limitations of the visual system. A reader who had to get enough visual information to identify every letter, or even every word, would not be able to read a passage for sense; the limitations of his own memory systems would defeat him. A fluent reader provides much more information to reduce uncertainty from his own store of knowledge about redundancy in the language than he acquires from the text. More alternatives are eliminated by what he knows about the nature of language than by the actual visual information that he gets from the page.

To conclude this section I must reiterate that it is not asserted that the skilled reader cannot identify words or meaning by mediated reading methods—which are the methods by which it is generally believed reading is accomplished. Mediated reading is required to support immediate identification whenever the reader meets material that goes beyond his previous experience. But the skilled reader uses mediated reading techniques as little as possible, and the fact that he does so requires no elaborate explanation. Immediate comprehension is synonymous with facile and interesting reading. But mediated reading is hard work. The rate of progress is slower, there is a greater burden on memory, and the rewards, in terms of comprehension, are less. If we cannot read with immediate comprehension, we soon feel tired and bored.

Fluent and Beginning Reading: The Difference

The more difficulty a reader has with reading, the more he relies on the visual information; this statement applies to both the fluent reader and the beginner. In each case, the cause of the difficulty is inability to make full use of syntactic and semantic redundancy, of nonvisual sources of information.

This difference between fluent and beginning reading may be epitomized in the manner in which the reader makes use of syntax, the bridge between surface structure and meaning. The fluent reader can be regarded as crossing this bridge from the meaning side, merely sampling the visual information to confirm his expectations. In other words, analysis of meaning at the deep structure level leads to the analysis of the surface visual structure. Syntax is a tool that the fluent reader uses to predict what the surface representation should be, and he needs only a minimum of visual cues to provide a confirmation of that prediction—provided he is able to make use of redundancy accurately.

The beginning reader, however, spends most of his time crossing the bridge of syntax in the opposite direction. Rather than predict surface structure from meaning, which requires only a minimum of visual information, he must deduce meaning from surface structure. Crossing the bridge in this direction requires a maximum of visual information. Since there is no prediction of what surface structure will be, the novice reader is forced to analyze all the constituents of the surface representation in order to be able to apply his syntactic skills. As we have seen, this is a slow and laborious process that is almost certain to result in a loss of comprehension. Attempting to identify all the constituent words of the visual representation, one at a time without any prediction, may create such a memory overload that it will in fact be impossible to apply the rules of syntax.

The "decoding" that the skilled reader performs is not to transform visual symbols into sound, which is the widely held conventional view of what reading is about, but to transform the visual representation of language into meaning. That decoding is effected through syntax, as outlined in Chapter 3. The role of syntax to "mediate" between visual (or acoustic) surface structure and meaning is precisely the function that generative-transformational grammarians attribute to it. The view that the fluent reader crosses the bridge from deep to surface levels is also particularly compatible with the view of many theorists about how spoken language is understood. They propose that the *listener* predicts and produces the surface structure, in order to generate both the phonemes and the "silent spaces", which we saw in Chapter 3 are not directly represented in the actual sound waves.

The diagrams in this book, Figure 9 for example, have for simplicity not indicated where syntax is located. Since the function of syntax is to mediate between surface structure and meaning, however, its placement is obvious; syntax must be the process by which visual information is allocated to meaning identification. Syntax is the arrow between visual information and meaning identification (and between word identification and meaning identification) in Figure 9.

We do not need syntax to identify individual words; in fact, there can be no syntax when words are identified independently of each other. But the identification of words in this manner will not lead to comprehension; whether meaning is identified immediately from the visual configuration or is mediated through the identification of words, syntax has to intervene. For oral reading, word identification must, in fact, be mediated by meaning identification, because that is the only way in which information about the appropriate intonation pattern, largely unmarked in the visual surface structure, can be deduced.

Obviously, a case could be made for making the arrows in Figure 9 two-way, especially between the visual information and meaning identification. The task of the novice reader is to learn to go from deep structure to the surface, to predict from meaning to the visual configuration. But prediction in any venture is possible only when there is a good deal of ex-

perience and prior knowledge. The process by which experience and knowledge are acquired in reading is the next topic to be considered.

Learning To Read

We shall look at three aspects of the process of learning to read: at the relevant skills and knowledge that a child has already acquired before he begins to learn to read, at the additional skills and knowledge that he requires in order to be able to read, and at the available means—and difficulties—of acquiring the additional skills and knowledge.

Two things are perhaps surprising about the skills and knowledge that a child brings with him when he is about to learn to read: the sheer quantity and complexity of his ability, and the small credit that he is usually given. To start with, he has a rich and fully functioning knowledge of the spoken aspects of his language. The awkward phrase "spoken aspects of language" is used—just once—instead of the more usual "spoken language" to avoid helping to perpetuate the notion that there are two distinct languages, spoken and written. Speech and writing are both aspects of the same language; it is only at the surface level that differences occur, and it is generally quite an unfounded assumption that reading instruction must involve teaching children about language.

Not only do the vast majority of children have a firm grasp of language by the time they get to school; more impressive, perhaps, is the manner in which they have acquired this skill. As we saw in Chapter 4, a child acquires his mastery of the complex processes of language in a very few years, with minimal formal instruction, in spite of the well-meaning but usually misconceived intervention of adults, and at an age often regarded as the most distractable and the least intellectual. We examined briefly the manner in which the child must acquire his spoken language skills—by his making assumptions about what are the relevant elements and relations of his language, looking for significant differences in the physical representation of speech, establishing his own grammatical and semantic categories and rules, and testing his hypotheses on a trial-and-error basis, learning through feedback whether a rule applies or not. We shall see in due course that this extreme learning proficiency is most important for learning how to read. A child may in some circumstances require to be motivated to learn, but he does not need to be taught how.

These complex learning skills—"discovery" skills might be a better term if it had not been so sullied in educational contexts—are manifested in more than just the young child's linguistic ability. During the first half-dozen years of his life, a child develops a complexly differentiated and integrated cognitive structure, his internalized representation of the world. To be sure his thinking in many respects is unsophisticated. His notions of cause and effect, of necessary and contingent relations, of permanence and transience, probability and proportion may diverge from those of adults; he obviously thinks and talks "like a child". But his *processes* of thought and perception are the same as an adult's—he establishes cognitive categories within which all instances are treated as functionally equivalent; he establishes specifications (feature lists) for the distinguishing characteristics of objects and events and concepts; he integrates visual, acoustic, and other sensory information with semantic attributes; and he continually develops and refines his store of knowledge by testing its implications and relations. In particular the child learns in the same way as an adult—by making a response, and thereby getting feedback about whether the supposition upon which the response was founded is appropriate (restated in everyday, but misleading, parlance, the child finds out whether his response is right or wrong).

We might usefully recall an observation that was made about the language of very young children. The words that children speak in the first two or three years of life may not sound very much like adult words, and their grammar is considerably different. But children do not use words randomly; they are systematic, they use rules. And the rules children use are not rules that adults have taught them; children do not speak a miniature or inferior version of adult language. Instead, the language of young children is a rich and fully articulated system with a logic and consistency of its own, which a child gradually shapes to correspond more and more to the language spoken around him. Precisely the same statements might be made about child thought.

A child coming to reading instruction has had considerable experience with all the cognitive skills involved in learning to read. He "knows" how to look for the significant differences between objects, to establish equivalence categories, to create and associate internalized "feature lists", to make use of redundancy, and to accumulate new information by "testing hypotheses", trying out possible rules and getting feedback. The visual and auditory acuity of most children is perfectly adquate for the discriminations that they have to make in reading; if there is a defect, it will manifest itself in other, nonreading contexts. A child who can pick up a pin has acquired the visual acuity to identify distinctive features of letters as well as an adult; in fact, even better, because for most of us acuity starts going downhill from the age of four. What the child does *not* know is *where* to look for the distinctive features of letters; he knows how to look, but not what to look for.

This raises the question of what additional knowledge a child requires in order to be able to read. Part of the answer has already been given; he needs to learn what are the distinctive features of written language and their relations to letters and words and meanings. He needs to know what makes and what does not make a difference in reading. Some of these differences and similarities he can perhaps be shown in a very general way, like the white space between words and between lines, the correspondence between spoken and written aspects of the same word or meaning, or the fact that while a 1949 Thunderclap convertible is still a 1949 Thunderclap convertible whether it goes from left to right or right to left, *was* is not the same as *saw*.

We might observe at this point that the "error" of reading words backwards can occur only if the child is applying mediated word identification, constructing the word through the intermediate route of identifying letters. But for fluent readers who have a feature list for the entire word configuration, such an error cannot occur. A fluent reader, in fact, has relatively little difficulty in reading a "backwards" word if it is a mirror image ƨuoᴚ *rather than* esuoh*—or upside down,* ǝsnoɥ*. In both the mirror image and upside down words, of course, all the featural relations are preserved.*

Many of the significant differences of written language, however, a child cannot be shown; he has to discover them for himself. Nobody knows enough about the distinctive features of print, for example, to give a child the knowledge that he really needs in order to be able to distinguish letters or words. Instead the teacher must make sure that the child gets the information he needs to discover features—and establish feature lists—for himself.

The argument that a child must discover features for himself applies also to the way in which visual and acoustic and semantic category associations must be learned. All the teacher can do is provide the raw material, the written word and its "name". The child also has to discover for himself what are the sources of redundancy in written language; as we have seen, this knowledge is vital if he is to overcome the limitations of his visual information-processing system. In one sense, of course, the teacher does "know" what these critical rules of featural and orthographic and semantic redundancy are; otherwise, he could not be a fluent reader himself. But this special information about redundancy is not accessible to our awareness, we acquire and use it quite unconsciously, with the unfortunate result that not only can we not pass it on verbally, but we often fail to realize how important it is. And therefore a child may not get the opportunity to acquire a knowledge of redundancy by the only route that is open to him—by experience in reading.

Finally, a child has to learn to read fast. There may be occasions when he is required by the difficulty of the text or the exigencies of the teaching situation to read slowly, letter by letter, word by word, but he has to learn that *fluent* reading is relatively *fast* reading, perhaps not much less than 200 words a minute. The reason that reading has to be fast we now know. The processing of visual information is not instantaneous but takes a significant amount of time, *during which losses always occur.* Information is very quickly lost in reading, especially if it is not condensed into "meaningful" form and put into long-term memory. A child who has to read letter by letter, or even word by word, has very little chance of comprehending. So while it is true that a child needs the intermediate skills of mediated word and meaning identification, he should not have to rely on them. It is not necessary that he learn them all before he gets on with the major objective of immediate comprehension, because it is only when the larger part of reading can be accomplished immediately that the reader can afford to stop and use, or learn, mediated reading skills.

Obviously, the same argument applies to "phonics". The actual, as opposed to the traditional, objective of phonic training is to establish in the child the visual–acoustic categories that will enable him to mediate the identification of words that he cannot identify on sight. But to a large extent the child has to learn these phonic rules for himself, and he will only acquire them through experience in reading. Yet reading will prove impossible, he will never get enough opportunity to acquire the information he needs, if he is not able to read *fluently,* immediately, without pausing to identify every word.

We are now at the heart of the question of how a child actually does, and must, learn to read. What are the sources of information available to him, what are the difficulties, and what is the role of the teacher? First, let us consider one by one the elements of reading.

A child has to discover the distinctive features of written material, the significant differences by which alternative letters, words, and meanings can be differentiated. And the only way he can get this information is to be shown what the alternatives are. Consider the problem of distinguishing one letter from another. If a child is shown just the letter *H,* and told its name, he gets practically no information at all. What is it about *H* that gives it that name—its size, the cross bar, the way it is leaning, the color of the ink on the paper? The child will use whatever cue he can. But suppose he is shown two alternatives, *H* and *F;* now at least he can see a difference. *H* has one cross bar and *F* has two, so he has a "distinctive feature" for *H.* But then what happens when he meets *A?* And how will this property that helps him to distinguish *H* from *F* enable him to see that *B* and *R* are different? A child needs *examples* and *contrasts.* He literally needs to be told only one bit of information—that these things should be considered the same, and those things considered different. The child a verbal label, saying *This letter is "H" and that letter is "A"* may be highly useful for communication purposes, but it is not directly relevant to the process of visual discrimination, to learning how to categorize some things as the same and some different. The child needs evidence, not instructions.

It is necessary at this point to clarify the relation between "learning the alphabet" and learning to read. There is an empirically well-founded correlation between the ability of children to identify letters and their ability to learn words, leading some theorists to believe that learning letters is a necessary first step for learning to identify words, and even that word identification must depend on letter-recognition skills. It is one of the basic aspects of my analysis of reading, of course, that the distinctive features of letters are *the distinctive features of words, and also the distinctive features of meaning. Anything that will distinguish two letters is capable of distinguishing two words or two meanings. But that does not entail that learning the alphabet must precede learning words or comprehension. Quite the reverse; since the features of letters and words are the same, one might just as well learn what the features are from words as from letters. Certainly it will be easier to read if one learns some words first (as most children do). Redundancy is a great help in all aspects of reading, and the most redundant way to learn what visual features are distinctive in reading may be to look for them at the letter, word, and meaning levels, rather than at one of those levels only.*

In addition to discovering what distinctive features are, a child has to establish his "categories" for letter and word identification, as well as establish all the visual–semantic associations required for comprehension. The type of information that the child requires to establish categories and associations is exactly the same as that which he needs to discover distinctive features; he needs to know what the alternatives are and which configurations should or should not be treated as the same. If told that two letters, or two words, or two meanings, are the "same", he puts them in the same category; he decides that none of the differences between the members of each pair is significant. He establishes rules and lists for functional equivalences. But if told that two letters, words, or meanings are not the same, he must use two categories, one for each member of this pair. And if he cannot fit either member into any existing category, he will put it into a new one. He will also associate the new category with a "name", if that is given. And if he gets the information that a configuration which he could not identify should go into a category that already has a "name", he will establish a visual feature list for that category to permit future allocations.

The child has to learn how the rules of syntax are related to the written aspect of language, together with the relation of visual configurations and semantic interpretations. All this can come about only if the child is given examples, if he is shown what is the same and what is different. He has to be given the raw material so that he can develop the rules for himself. He can only look for the "regularities" that are the basis of all cognitive activity if he is exposed to a large enough sample of "evidence".

And, once again, a child needs to build up reading speed. He needs as much help and encouragement as possible to develop fluent reading, because the discovery of rules is made enormously more difficult if the reading rate is slow. A child may be able to learn to distinguish letters at a plodding one-at-a-time pace, but to learn to read for meaning, and to have an opportunity to acquire knowledge about redundancy, he has to keep moving ahead of losses in sensory store and short-term memory. Learning to read is a bootstrap operation.

The Teacher's Role

The preceding analysis may leave the impression that there is nothing a teacher can usefully do but provide a pat on the back and keep plenty of reading material around. Of course, the learning situation is nothing like that. Apart from all-important motivational and managerial functions, the teacher's contribution can be summed up in one word— *information.* A child has to be shown the type of material from which he must reduce uncertainty; he must be told where the uncertainty lies. He must be told what the task is. A child has to be given the information as to whether two configurations are the same or different; the knowledge that they are different in effect establishes the uncertainty, "How do I distinguish one from the other?" A child has to be told the "names" that are conventionally associated with letters, and should not be left too much to work out for himself the names of words by phonic methods. Once again, an overdependence on mediated reading places an almost intolerable burden on the visual information-processing system. Similarly, a child has to be given examples where differences in meaning lie, so that he can establish the necessary visual and semantic relationships.

But all this information is useless if a child tries to remember a simple listing of associations, a set of "instances". What the child has to do is induce *rules,* to predict a regularity on the basis of information received on one occasion, and try it out to see if the rule is valid on another occasion. And this is perhaps the most critical aspect of the teacher's role as a supplier of information, to *provide feedback;* to say "right" or "wrong".

Feedback is the most important kind of information that a child can receive in any learning situation for this reason; it supplies him with just the right kind of information at the precise moment that he needs it. It may be just fortuitous that a child learns to identify a letter or word or meaning at the time his teacher gives him formal instruction on that point. Some happy coincidence between the child's implicit "question" and the teacher's information must occur. The "implicit question" lies in the child's uncertainty. Unless he is, in effect, presenting himself with the question "Which of these alternatives must this configuration eliminate?" then his teacher's information is irrelevant to the child.

A child looks for feedback when he tries out one of his rules, when he "predicts" which of a number of alternative responses he should make. Feedback then is information that is right to the point.

Feedback should be given all the time. Every response a child makes, every identification of a letter or word or meaning, should be given the feedback of whether it is right or wrong. But these terms "right" and "wrong" should not be interpreted in a negative or punitive sense. The question a child is asking when he makes any response is "Does the rule that I have just used apply?" And if he is reading for meaning, he may not be in need of feedback that a particular word is "wrong".

Of course, a child does not need to be given positive feedback overtly all the time—he does not need the teacher to say "right" after every word. But he has to get the message, one way or another, that what he has just done *works,* that his prediction is confirmed. Silent approval is just as informative as a round of applause. And being told that he is "wrong" is just as informative for the child as being told that he is "right", provided there is no emotional overloading. If he does not know whether a word is "race" or "rice", it makes no difference informationally whether he says "race" and gets the feedback "wrong" or says "rice" and gets the feedback "right". Unless there is a price for making "mistakes".

Here is the crunch. A child cannot get feedback unless he "asks for it" —he needs to make a response that he knows may *or may not* be "correct". If he makes a response that he already knows *is* correct, there can be no informative feedback. Only a hazarded response when the rule employed might equally well apply or not apply can be rewarded with useful information. But a child will not hazard such responses if the cost is too high.

We saw in the section on signal detection theory (page 23) that no one can be right all the time. And that to be right a lot of the time, you have to be prepared to be wrong occasionally. We have seen a number of times in recent chapters that you cannot read for meaning unless you read relatively fast, which means that you do not necessarily read word for word.

You may read a word in error occasionally. And now we see that there can be no learning unless rules are tested, with the possibility that incorrect identifications will frequently occur. The implication of all these statements is so obvious it needs no underlining; fluent reading, and learning to read fluently, require a willingness to "make mistakes". And the extent to which a child is prepared to risk mistakes is directly related to the tolerance of the teacher in accepting them.

I have noted on several occasions that the model of the reading process developed in this book is not a conventional one. Readers are not usually regarded as "predicting" their way through a passage of text, eliminating some alternatives in advance on the basis of their knowledge of the redundancy of language, and acquiring just enough visual information to eliminate the alternatives remaining. It is also unconventional to suggest that most of the information required by beginning readers is not information that teachers can give them directly.

But nothing that I have said should start a classroom revolution. There is no suggestion that teachers of reading should throw away their instructional procedures, or their years of experience, and start all over again. As I said in the Preface, no theoretical analysis of the reading process can dictate an instructional method; pedagogy always has to be tested in the classroom. But the type of theoretical analysis outlined in this book will provide insights about why many teaching methods work, and why on occasion all may fail. A clearer understanding of what the skilled reader can do, and of what the beginning reader is trying to do, is far more important for the reading teacher than any revision of instructional materials.

References

The circle is closed. For further reading see the comments and suggestions contained in the References to Chapter 1, starting on page 9.

Indexes

Name Index

233

234 *Name Index*

Name Index

Subject Index